The Textile Industry in India

The Textile Industry in India
Changing Trends and Employment Challenges

BINDU OBEROI

OXFORD
UNIVERSITY PRESS

OXFORD
UNIVERSITY PRESS

Oxford University Press is a department of the University of Oxford.
It furthers the University's objective of excellence in research, scholarship,
and education by publishing worldwide. Oxford is a registered trademark of
Oxford University Press in the UK and in certain other countries

Published in India by
Oxford University Press
YMCA Library Building, 1 Jai Singh Road, New Delhi 110 001, India

ISBN-13: 978-0-19-946935-2
ISBN-10: 0-19-946935-0

Typeset in Adobe Garamond Pro 11/13
by Tranistics Data Technologies, New Delhi 110 044
Printed in India by Replika Press Pvt. Ltd

Contents

Tables and Figures

Tables

Figures

Acknowledgements

This book is largely based on my doctoral dissertation in economics written for Jawaharlal Nehru University (JNU), New Delhi, which was completed in July 2011. The study was carried out under the supervision of Professor C.P. Chandrasekhar. I would like to sincerely thank him for his guidance and mentorship throughout the study that contributed to this book. During this period, I recall having numerous intellectually stimulating conversations with him that increased my interest in the textile industry and helped in improving my understanding of the Indian economy. I am also grateful to D. Narasimha Reddy and Surajit Mazumdar for their valuable suggestions and extensive comments on various chapters.

I would also like to pay my sincere gratitude to M.R. Murthy for his encouraging words and useful comments. I would like to express my gratitude to two anonymous reviewers whose comments were helpful in bringing about improvements in this book.

While writing this book, I have also reproduced my pre-published works. Parts of Chapters 1 and 2 were published in an article, 'Determinants of Demand for the Indian Textile Industry', in *Economic and Political Weekly*.[1] Parts of Chapters 4 and 5 were published in 'Structural Change, Technology and Employment in the Indian Textile Industry: 1980–2010' in *Arthaniti*,[2] and in 'Casualisation of Employment in the Indian Textile Industry' in

---

[1] 'Determinants of Demand for the Indian Textile Industry', *Economic and Political Weekly*, XLVIII(3): 62–70, January 2013.

[2] 'Structural Change, Technology and Employment in the Indian Textile Industry: 1980–2010', *Arthaniti* (New Series), 2012, Vol. XI (Nos 1–2), published by the Department of Economics, University of Calcutta in February 2015, reprinted by permission of *Arthaniti* (ISSN: 0976-7479 Print version), available at http://www.econcaluniv.ac.in/arthaniweb/arthaniti.html (last accessed on 6 October 2016).

Labour and Development.[3] I am thankful to the editors of these journals for their permission to reproduce these works.

I would like to thank all my teachers who have taught me at Navayug School, Hansraj College, and Delhi School of Economics (DSE); I owe them a great debt of gratitude. In writing this book, I have also drawn heavily from the resources available in the libraries at JNU, Institute of Economic Growth, National Council of Applied Economic Research, DSE, Confederation of Indian Textile Industry, and Ministry of Statistics and Programme Implementation. I express my gratitude to the staff of these libraries for their kind help.

I completed the bulk of my work on a study leave granted by the management of Indraprastha College for Women. I am thankful to the Principal, late Aruna Sitesh, for the same. My heartfelt thanks to our current college principal, Babli Moitra Saraf, for her constant support during this endeavour. I am grateful to my friends and colleagues at Indraprastha College for Women for encouraging me to undertake this study. I am also grateful to my friends, Neha, Kusum, and Suman, for their support throughout this period.

I was deeply touched by the enthusiasm of my late father-in-law towards my study. I would not have been able to complete this work without the support of my mother-in-law. My parents, especially my father, have always been a source of inspiration in my life. I thank Hema, Manoj, Alka, Suresh, Kanchan, and Rajesh for their moral support. Special thanks to Suman and Sunil for their support during the critical stages of this study.

It is difficult for me to acknowledge what my son Karmanya and my daughter Neeti have had to bear in the course of my work on this manuscript. I thank them for their patience. And finally, a special thanks to my husband Gagan, who helped me in learning various computer programmes. His moral support, throughout the course of my work, cannot be acknowledged in a few lines.

I take full responsibility for all the lacunae and errors that remain.

---

[3] 'Casualisation of Employment in the Indian Textile Industry', *Labour and Development*, 21(2), December 2014, published by V.V. Giri National Labour Institute, NOIDA, India.

Abbreviations

ASF	Acrylic Staple Fibre
ASFI	Association of Synthetic Fibre Industry
ASI	Annual Survey of Industries
ASY	Acrylic Staple Yarn
ATC	Agreement on Textile and Clothing
ATIRA	Ahmedabad Textile Industry's Research Association
BICP	Bureau of Industrial Costs and Prices
BoP	Balance of Payments
BRPL	Bongaigaon Refinery & Petrochemicals Limited
CIF	Cost, Insurance, and Freight
CITI	Confederation of Indian Textile Industry
CMIE	Centre for Monitoring Indian Economy
CPI	Consumer Price Index
CPI-AL	Consumer Price Index Numbers for Agricultural Labourers
CPI-IW	Consumer Price Index Numbers for Industrial Workers
CPI-UNME	Consumer Price Index for Urban Non-manual Employees
CSO	Central Statistical Office
CVD	Countervailing Duty
DGCIS	Directorate General of Commercial Intelligence and Statistics
DME	Directory Manufacturing Establishment
DMT	Dimethyl Terephthalate
DRC	Domestic Resource Cost
EGP	Expert Group on Petrochemicals
EOU	Export-oriented Unit
ERP	Effective Rate of Protection
EU	European Union

g	gram/s
GATT	General Agreement on Trade and Tariff
GDP	Gross Domestic Product
GNP	Gross National Product
GoI	Government of India
GVA	Gross Value Added
ha	hectare
HOK	Hours of Workers required to produce 100 Kilogram of Yarn
ICMF	Indian Cotton Mill Federation
IMF	International Monetary Fund
IOCL	Indian Oil Corporation Limited
IPCL	Indian Petrochemicals Corporation Limited
ITMF	International Textile Manufacturers Federation
JNU	Jawaharlal Nehru University
K	Potassium
kg	kilogram/s
LES	Linear Expenditure System
LPG	Liquefied Petroleum Gas
LTA	Long-term Agreement
m	metre/s
MEG	Monoethylene Glycol
MFA	Multi-fibre Agreement
MHRD	Ministry of Human Resource Development
MMF	Man-made Fibre/Filament
MoU	Memoranda of Understanding
MPCE	Monthly Per Capita Consumer Expenditure
MPCP	Monthly Per Capita Consumer Purchases
MRP	Mixed Reference Period
NAAS	National Academy of Agricultural Sciences
N	Nitrogen
NAS	National Accounts Statistics
NCAER	National Council of Applied Economic Research
NCEUS	National Commission for Enterprises in the Unorganized Sector
NDE	Non-directory Establishment
NIC	National Industrial Classification
NOCIL	National Organic Chemical Industries Limited

NSF	Nylon Staple Fibre
NSS	National Sample Survey
NSSO	National Sample Survey Office
NTP	New Textile Policy
OAE	Own Account Enterprise
OECD	Organisation for Economic Co-operation and Development
OGL	Open General Licence
OMI	Overall Modernisation Index
P	Phosphorous
PDS	Public Distribution System
PFY	Polyester Filament Yarn
PS	Principal Status
PSF	Polyester Staple Fibre
PTA	Purified Terephthalic Acid
QR	Quantitative Restriction
RBI	Reserve Bank of India
RIL	Reliance Industries Limited
SDP	State Domestic Product
SITRA	South India Textile Research Association
sq. m	square metre/s
SS	Subsidiary Status
T&C	Textiles and Clothing
TEXPROCIL	Cotton Textiles Export Promotion Council
tpa	tons per annum
TUFS	Technology Upgradation Fund Scheme
UAE	United Arab Emirates
UNCTAD	United Nations Conference on Trade and Development
URP	Uniform Reference Period
WPI	Wholesale Price Index
WTO	World Trade Organization

Introduction

India is the world's second largest producer of textiles and apparel after China (Confederation of Indian Textile Industry [CITI], Annual Report 2014). Currently, the textile and clothing (T&C) industry contributes about 2 per cent to India's gross domestic product (GDP) and 14 per cent to industrial production.[1] The industry provides a source of livelihood to 4.2 million citizens.[2] It is the fifth largest employer in the country.[3] Exports of textiles and clothing industry account for about 11 per cent of country's total exports of goods.[4]

The textile industry in India experienced a recession[5] from the mid-1960s to the 1980s when the demand for textile products

---

[1] Calculated for the year 2012–13, based on figures from Central Statistical Organisation (2014).

[2] Includes usual status employment (PS + SS; PS refers to principal status and SS refers to subsidiary status) engaged in preparation and spinning of cotton and man-made fibres (MMF) (including blended), weaving of cotton and man-made textiles (including blended), manufacture of knitted and crocheted fabrics and articles , and manufacture of textile garments and clothing accessories. For National Industrial Classification (NIC) codes used and other details, refer to Chapter 5, 'The Employment Fall Out'. The figure increases to 14.13 million if spinning, weaving, and finishing of textiles using all types of fibres, manufacture of other textiles, manufacture of wearing apparel, dressing and dyeing of fur, and manufacture of leather and fur products, using codes 171, 172, 173, 181, and 182, are included following NIC 2004. This has been computed from unit-level data from National Sample Survey (NSS) 66th round for the year 2009–10.

[3] After agriculture, construction, retail trade (*excluding motor vehicles and motor cycles, repair of personal and household goods*), and land transport. Computed based on usual status employment (PS + SS) figures from NSSO (2011).

[4] Available at www.txcindia.gov.in (last accessed on 5 September 2015).

[5] For deceleration from the mid-1960s to the mid-1970s, refer Chandrasekhar (1984). For stagnation during 1973–86, refer Goswami (1990).

almost stagnated. However, a significant increase in the per capita consumption of textiles, along with a substantial increase in exports of textiles, reversed this trend after the early 1990s. Total cloth output, which was growing at a rate of 2.71 per cent per annum during 1975–89, registered an increased rate of growth of 4.46 per cent per annum during the period 1990–91 to 2013–14.[6] This acceleration in the rate of growth since 1990–91 was not specific to textiles. A similar trend was observed in several other industries like steel, automobiles, pharmaceuticals, transport equipment, and metal products. However, the revival of the textile industry is considered important mainly for two reasons. First, the textile industry is labour intensive. It employs substantial numbers of unskilled or semi-skilled labourers, and it is the fourth largest source of employment after agriculture. Second, the exports of the industry, which were insignificant before the mid-1980s, grew substantially thereafter. It was expected that the growth of output and exports of the textile industry would lead to an increase in employment in its more labour-intensive segments and the industry would regain its position as a major foreign exchange earner.

However, the experience of the economy since the 1990s suggested that while the exports of textile products grew substantially as expected, there was hardly any growth in the number of workers employed by this industry. Further, there were changes in the structure of employment since the 1990s, which pointed to an increase in casualisation of employment in the industry. This unsatisfactory performance of the textile industry on the employment front during the period of its revival was of particular concern as the 1990s was a decade of jobless growth. The fast growth of the economy was associated with falling employment elasticity of production and growing unemployment. At the all-India level, there was a significant decline of usual status employment elasticity (measured as the ratio between the growth of employment and growth of output) from 0.42 during 1983 to 1993–94 to 0.15 during 1993–94 to 1999–2000 (Bhattacharya and Sakthievel 2004). Weekly status and

[6] Average annual compound rate of growth calculated using data from the Office of the Textile Commissioner, published in *Handbook of Statistics on Textile Industry* (CITI 2008), up to 2005–06 and txcindia.gov.in (last accessed on 15 February 2016) for later years.

daily status employment also showed deceleration in growth. The employment elasticity of output in the primary sector declined considerably to almost zero in the later period. Although there was a spurt in industrial growth in the post-reform period at the all-India level, the employment elasticity in the secondary sector declined from 0.46 for the period 1983 to 1993–94 to 0.20 during 1993–94 to 1999–2000. It decelerated in the tertiary sector as well. Overall, though the employment scenario in the Indian economy improved from 1999–2000 to 2004–05, it deteriorated again from 2004–05 to 2009–10. In addition to this, the income inequalities also worsened during this period. The Gini ratio in the rural areas, which declined from 30.4 per cent in 1983 to 28.6 per cent in 1993–94, increased to 30.5 per cent in 2004–05. The Gini ratio in the urban areas, which rose from 33.9 per cent in 1983 to 34.41 per cent in 1993–94, continued to rise and reached 37.6 per cent in 2004–05 (Himanshu 2007). It increased more steeply in urban India than in rural India during 2004–05 to 2009–10 (Himanshu and Sen 2014).

In this context of widening income inequalities and increasing concern for rising unemployment, the present book examines the growth of the labour-intensive textile industry during the period after 1980. The period since 1980 also corresponds to the period that witnessed considerable changes in the domestic and global textile industry. On the domestic front, liberalisation in terms of reductions in customs duties and excise duties started during the 1980s and got intensified during the 1990s. The New Textile Policy (NTP) (1985) marked the beginning of a period of rapid restructuring of the industry via the removal of restrictions on capacity expansion, flexibility of fibre use, and easy import of polyester fibre. Industrial licensing, which had restricted the growth of the Indian textile industry, was abolished in July 1991. The protection for the industry producing textile machinery was withdrawn after the 1980s by reducing customs duties on the import of machinery. The protection for the synthetic fibre and filament yarn industry also declined considerably due to tariff reductions on a wide range of commodities. More recently, the industry had been relying on Technology Upgradation Fund Scheme (TUFS), introduced in April 1999, for their investment plan in view of 5 per cent compensation available under the scheme. Overall, the period since the 1980s was marked by a policy regime that was quite different from the one which characterised the period up to the 1970s. These policy changes facilitated the growth of India's textile industry that was driven by increase in home demand and exports.

In addition to this, the global textile industry also experienced important changes during the period when the Multi-fibre Agreement (MFA) (1984) was phased out in steps through the implementation of the Agreement on Textile and Clothing (ATC) (1995). It led to dismantling of the quota regime which exempted the trade in textiles and garments from the discipline of the General Agreement on Trade and Tariff (GATT). It may be argued that the fast growth of India's exports of T&C from the mid-1990s onwards was the result of the changing world scenario with the ATC replacing the MFA. However, the book shows that such change, at best, can be seen as only indirectly helping by building expectations and keeping the morale of the industry high, leading to capacity expansion and modernisation during a period when domestic demand had started rising and the competition was expected to increase after the expiry of the ATC. The book suggests that a combination of depreciation of the rupee, global market developments, and availability of cheaper inputs allowed India to acquire a larger share in world markets leading to an expansion of exports.

The present volume examines the process of growth of India's textile industry in this broad context. The key objectives are to analyse the process of growth, identify the factors that have contributed to that growth, and to explore possible explanations for its unsatisfactory performance on the employment front. Three aspects of the revival of the Indian textile industry that are central to the analysis are:

1. the increase in home demand for and exports of textile products;
2. the changes in the underlying structure of the industry, involving inter-fibre and inter-sectoral shifts;
3. the unsatisfactory performance of the industry on the employment front.

The book relates these aspects of the industry's performance to the context and character of its development. The key argument made is that although the Indian textile industry performed well in terms of production and exports, there were changes in the underlying structure of the industry due to which the growth of output did not lead to the expected growth of employment and the quality of employment also deteriorated.

Further, the general perception is that the growth of the textile industry was primarily driven by the expansion in exports of textile products. However, as this book shows, though the exports of textile products did grow substantially since the early 1990s, the growth of the industry continued to be driven mainly by domestic demand. The domestic demand continued to account for approximately 70 per cent of the total value of output of the industry since the mid-1990s. The proportion increased after the crisis in the developed economies adversely affected the demand for India's exports. It increased to about 82 per cent during the year 2010–11.[7]

In order to understand the main argument of the study, it is important to first have an overview of India's textile industry as a whole, which is broadly classified into two categories, the organised mill sector and the unorganised or decentralised sector. The mills in the organised sector may be spinning mills or composite mills. While spinning mills are engaged in the spinning of yarn, composite mills carry out spinning, weaving, and processing activities. The decentralised sector comprises power looms, handlooms, hosiery, khadi, and garment sectors. While spinning process is dominant in the organised mill sector, weaving, stitching, and dyeing mainly take place in the unorganised sector. The unorganised khadi and handloom sectors are the oldest in the country, while the organised sector is barely around 187 years old.

The production of fabric involves fibre cleaning, spinning, processing, dyeing, and knitting (hosiery) or weaving. The fabric thus produced is either domestically consumed or exported. While the hosiery fabric is produced in the unorganised hosiery sector, the woven fabric is produced either in the organised mills or in the unorganised power loom and handloom sectors. The type of fabric produced also depends on the composition of fibre/filament, that is, natural or man-made fibre/filament (MMF). Natural fibres are cotton, wool, and silk. The MMFs include polyester, viscose, acrylics, and other miscellaneous fibres/filaments produced through chemical processing.

---

[7] This came down to about 70 per cent during 2012–13.

Yarn production from these fibres/filaments can be classified into spun yarn and filament yarn. Spun yarn is the yarn produced by spinning various fibres. The filament yarn is the product of the chemical industry and can be used for weaving directly without resorting to spinning. Spun yarn production predominantly takes place on cotton spun system in the organised sector in India. The yarn production in the wool and silk spinning system mainly takes place in the unorganised sector. Cotton, polyester, viscose, acrylics, etc. are the fibres spun on cotton spinning system. The yarn spun from these fibres can be 100 per cent cotton, 100 per cent polyester, 100 per cent viscose, 100 per cent acrylic, or blended yarn produced from the mixture of various fibres in different proportions.

A brief overview points to various difficulties involved in the task of analysing changes in the structure and employment of India's textile industry, which has heterogeneous components like spinning, weaving, and garment making. The task poses serious challenges as these components, in turn, are spread over organised and unorganised sectors with varying forms of organisation ranging from household, shed, to the mills. Nevertheless, this book attempts to provide a comprehensive analysis of the textile industry in India over more than three decades, beginning with the 1980s. The main argument of the manuscript is developed in five chapters.

Chapter 1 presents a critical analysis of the reasons for the increase in demand and the resulting revival of the Indian textile industry. The chapter focuses on examining whether the determinants of textile demand advanced in previous studies to explain the deceleration in the growth of the industry continue to play an important role in explaining the growth in demand for textiles after the early 1990s. It is argued that while incomes and prices of textiles continue to play an important role in explaining changes in demand, the prices of foodgrains no longer constrain the demand for textiles and clothing, except for the recent years. Further, it is argued that the growth in demand for the industry was led by the rich and the middle income groups.

The core argument in Chapter 2 is that the stimulus for the substantial shift from demand for and, therefore, the output of cotton towards synthetic and blended textiles was provided by the changes in the relative price of cotton in comparison to synthetic fibres and filament yarns. While the prices of synthetic fibres declined substantially during the 1990s due to reductions in customs duties on the intermediates and raw materials for synthetic fibres, the price of cotton continued to remain high because of a deep agrarian crisis caused by the movement of international cotton prices and a decline in public investment in agriculture.

Chapter 3 provides an analysis of the growth in exports of the Indian textile industry. Besides presenting a detailed analysis of the reasons that have led to the growth of exports, it also examines the changing nature of the exports of the industry and their underlying implications. The argument stressed here is that though there is substantial increase in its exports, the proportion of exports in the value of output of T&C has remained almost stagnant since the mid-1990s, with the notable exception of the year 2010–11 when it declined significantly after the crisis in the developed economies. The industry continues to be driven mainly by domestic demand.

Chapter 4 discusses the influences of supply-side and features of the growth of the textile industry. It presents an analysis of the important structural changes that have occurred during the course of the revival. The key argument is that the substantial growth in internal and external demand and the associated changes in the nature of demand have led to inter-fibre and inter-sectoral shifts in production, characterised by the faster growth of synthetic textiles and the decline of composite mills and handlooms. The growth of demand has resulted in substantial capacity expansion and modernisation in the spinning sector. Further, these demand-side changes have led to the growth of the sector producing ready-made garments, which have replaced tailor-made goods.

Chapter 5 presents an analysis of the trends with respect to employment in the textile industry. The analysis suggests that employment has continued to decline during the period of the revival. In addition, the quality of employment has also deteriorated. Though employment has increased in the garment sector, the overall performance of the industry remains unsatisfactory. The core argument is that technological progress and modernisation in the spinning sector have led to an increase in productivity, but have adversely affected employment. Further, while power looms and hosiery units are affected favourably by changes on the demand side and have grown fast, composite mills and handlooms have declined. The failure of composite mills to compete with the fabric produced in power looms and hosiery units in the decentralised sector has led to the decline of composite mills. Though the handlooms were always at a disadvantage in comparison with power looms and mills due to lower productivity, they were the largest source of employment within the textile industry. The demand for and, therefore, the production and employment in handlooms was increasing up to the late 1980s. However, it has been argued that there were changes after the late 1980s, which aggravated the problem of low productivity faced by handlooms and led to a period of intensified decline of handlooms. These changes included a massive shift in consumer demand towards synthetics and blended textiles, changing consumer demand towards knitted and crocheted textiles, and a substantial increase in the export of cotton yarn. Collectively, these shifts have favoured the growth of power looms, which produced almost the entire synthetic cloth. However, the rise of power looms and the fall of handlooms resulted in a decline in employment since the power looms generate less employment for a given increase in output.

The quality of employment in the textile industry has also deteriorated. There was increasing informalisation of the formal spinning sector. Weaving sector was characterised by a shift from self-employment to wage employment as handlooms declined and power looms and hosiery units flourished during this period. The key outcomes of these changes were a decline in the share of regular employment and an increase in the casualisation of employment in the textile industry. Overall, the performance of the industry on the employment front remained unsatisfactory in terms of both numbers and quality.

The concluding chapter summarises the discussion by linking all the chapters.

Finally, a point about the empirical basis of this book: for the analysis of the various aspects of growth of textile industry, the book relies on evidences from the Office of the Textile Commissioner, the Textiles Committee, the CITI, the National Sample Surveys (NSSs) on consumer expenditure, employment–unemployment, and unorganised manufacturing sector, the Office of the Economic Advisor, the Association of Synthetic Fibre Industries (ASFI), the Directorate General of Commercial Intelligence and Statistics (DGCIS), the Annual Survey of Industries (ASI), the National Accounts Statistics (NAS), and various textile research associations, including the Ahmedabad Textile Industry's Research Association (ATIRA) and the South India Textile Research Association (SITRA).

It is difficult to get comparable estimates for such a long period from such a wide variety of sources for a number of reasons. The conversion factors used in the estimation of cloth output by the Office of the Textile Commissioner changed during the early 1990s. There are no dependable data on different segments of the industry like handlooms, power looms, and mills, or in terms of organised or unorganised components. The National Industrial Classification (NIC) (1970) was revised four times during the period. The inter-sectoral analysis of the employment scenario based on NSS employment–unemployment surveys is not permitted after 1993–94 due to change in NIC, where focus has shifted from the sector of manufacturing to the process of manufacturing. As a result, the evidence used in different chapters is uneven in quality and strength. The data may not appear sufficient in quantity in the absence of annual figures on various important variables. This is mainly because in order to ensure the comparability of data, the book relies on the quinquennial rounds of the NSS, which are based on larger samples. In the absence of comparable data over time from a single source, the book has relied on multiple data sources. The analysis of exports of the industry is mainly based on the data from the DGCIS. But, the DGCIS data on the exports of fabrics and made-ups is problematic due to a change in units from square metres (sq. m) to kilograms (kg) during 1996–97 to 2002–03. Therefore, for the analysis of exports of fabric during this period, the book has also relied on data from the Cotton Textiles Export Promotion Council (TEXPROCIL). Due to these reasons, the available data are insufficient to allow any econometric estimation, which requires comparable information on important variables for a sufficiently long period of time.

The framework of the analysis undertaken in the book is one which tries to extract the story of historical movement from the data that it draws from a variety of sources, circumventing the mechanical empirical work. By allowing an analysis of changes in an industry, like textiles with heterogeneous components spread across organised and unorganised sectors, with varying degrees of technology and forms of organisation, this framework permits the study to go much further than would otherwise have been possible. The trends that emerge from the analysis of this type of data throw light on various aspects of growth of the industry and are crucial for an overall understanding of that process of growth. Therefore, notwithstanding the difficulties posed by the nature of the available data, the book attempts to develop an argument based on these trends.

1

Trends in Domestic Demand and Their Implications

The textile industry in India experienced a recession with demand stagnating or decelerating during the period stretching from the mid-1960s to the 1980s. The trend has reversed itself since the early 1990s, after which the per capita consumption of textiles increased significantly. The increase in per capita consumption has been sustained by increases in the consumption of synthetic and blended textiles. The increase in home demand represented by the reversal of the recessionary trend triggered a revival of the Indian textile industry, which had remained under the grip of stagnation for long.

There are two sources of data available to study the demand for textiles: the Market Research Wing of the Textiles Committee and the Office of the Textile Commissioner. According to the data collected by the Market Research Wing of the Textiles Committee, the estimated per capita household purchase of textiles increased from 14.01 metres (m) in 1990–91 to 25.01 m in 2011–12[1] (Figure 1.1). The data suggest that the per capita consumption was almost stagnant, fluctuating between 13 m and 16 m until 1994–95, after which it registered a sharp increase.

[1] Textiles include fabric, made-ups, ready-made garments, dress material, dhoti, saree, and chaddar. Figures are computed based on calendar year figures.

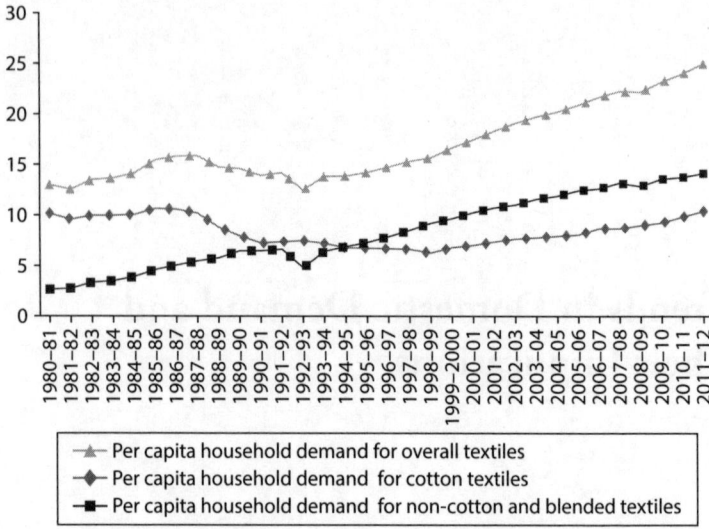

Figure 1.1   Per Capita Household Demand for Textiles (m)
Sources: Textiles Committee, published in *Consumer Purchase of Textiles*, Part 2 (various years) up to 1999–2000; *National Households Surveys* (various years) for 2000–01 to 2005–06; and www.txcindia.gov.in (last accessed on 5 September 2015) for recent years.

In contrast to this evidence, the data available from the Textile Commissioner's office suggest that while the per capita availability of cloth[2] increased from 17.3 sq. m in 1980–81 (Figure 1.2) to 43.96 sq. m in 2010–11, much of the increase took place earlier, during the period from 1992–93 to 1997–98. The per capita availability was

[2] For arriving at per capita availability of cloth, production of fabrics in the decentralised sector was estimated based on revised conversion factors by the Textile Commissioner's office. Per capita availability of cloth equals to production plus actual imports minus actual exports of cloth. The figures are not adjusted for stocks of cloth (as they are reported in metres), but the data indicate that the annual stocks of cloth (calculated as the average of the highest and lowest monthly figures), which were as high as 310 million m in 1985, declined thereafter and varied between 116 and 196 million m during the 1990s. They declined further to 84 million m by 2002–03.

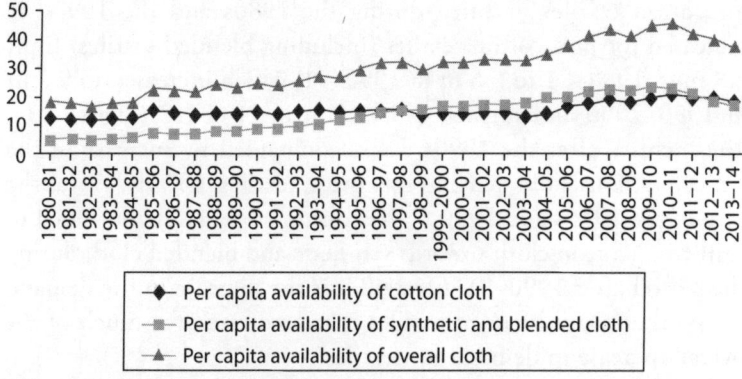

Figure 1.2 Per Capita Availability of Cloth (sq. m)
Sources: Office of the Textile Commissioner (1996) for figures up to 1984–85; CITI, *Handbook of Statistics on Textile Industry* (2008) for 1985–86 to 2005–06; and www. txcindia.gov.in (last accessed on 5 September 2015) for later years.

almost stagnant since then until 2004–05, when it started increasing again. It reached its peak in 2010–11, before declining in recent years. The difference in the two data sources seems to be arising because one is a query-based estimate from the consumption side and the other is a record-based estimate from the production side.

An interesting feature of the movement in per capita availability is that the increase in apparent consumption has been dominated by synthetic textiles. The data from the Textile Commissioner's office indicate that the per capita availability of cotton cloth (Figure 1.2) remained almost stagnant around 12 sq. m till 1984–85 and between 14 sq. m and 16 sq. m from 1985–86 to 2004–05. The entire increase in the aggregate per capita consumption was on account of synthetic and blended cloth, the per capita availability of which increased from 6.18 sq. m to 19.43 sq. m during the period. After 2004–05, the per capita availability of cotton cloth also started rising. The per capita availability of synthetic and blended cloth, however, has declined after 2009–10, leading to a decline in the per capita availability of cloth in the recent period.

A similar shift in the fibre-wise composition of demand is reflected in the data from the Market Research Wing of the Textiles Committee as well. While the per capita household demand for cotton textiles declined during the 1980s and the 1990s, it increased for non-cotton textiles (including blended textiles) from 2.8 m in 1980–81 to 6.6 m in 1990–91, which increased to 9.7 m in 1999–2000 and further to 14.24 m in 2011–12 (Figure 1.1). The increase after the 1990s was accompanied by increase in the per capita household demand for cotton textiles. Clearly, as was the case in the 1970s and 1980s,[3] the consumer demand continued to shift from cotton cloth towards synthetic and blended cloth during the period after 1990–91. Overall, it is the increase in the demand for synthetic and blended textiles that accounted for much of the overall increase in demand for textiles.

In what follows, an attempt is made to analyse the reasons for this increase in demand and the resulting revival of the Indian textile industry. The focus, here, is on examining whether the determinants of textile demand identified by previous studies aiming to explain the deceleration in the industry are important in the more recent context. The intention is to assess whether movements in the variables that explained the deceleration in demand for textiles since the mid-1960s continue to play an important role in explaining the growth in textile demand since the early 1990s. The analysis is limited to the period since 1980–81, as the Indian textile industry has experienced major changes with respect to demand, output, exports, etc. during this period. The analysis relies on the per capita availability data on demand for textiles from the Textile Commissioner's office.[4] It also draws on the income-wise, fibre-wise, and variety-wise estimates of demand for textiles available from the Textiles Committee.

Increasing Incomes

The period after 1990 has witnessed India's transition to a new, higher growth trajectory, with GDP increasing at about 6 per cent

[3] For this period, refer Chandrasekhar (1984), Goswami (1990), and Murty and Sukumari (1991).

[4] Since the per capita household demand data from Textiles Committee broadly reflect similar trends, the choice of data source does not affect the analysis. The corresponding figures using per capita household purchase data for demand are provided in Appendix A (Figures A.1 to A.4).

and per capita product at 3.5 per cent per annum. The rates appear to be quite impressive when compared with the old 'Hindu rate of growth'[5] of national income of around 3.5 per cent per annum. The acceleration in income growth seems to have had its impact on the growth of textile industry. Total cloth output, which was growing at the rate of 2.71 per cent per annum during 1975–89, registered a much higher rate of growth of 4.46 per cent per annum during the period 1990–91 to 2013–14.[6] This acceleration in the rate of growth since 1990–91 is not specific to textiles but is also observed in several other industries like steel, automobiles, pharmaceuticals, transport equipment, metal products, basic metals, and repair services. A number of other industries like chemicals, food products, and other manufacturing have continued to experience high growth during the period.

Growth in the Indian textile industry during this period has largely been driven by final consumption demand, since the industry has not faced severe constraints on account of raw materials and other factors of production and since the household sector is the largest buyer of textile products. Therefore, increasing demand, and hence production, in this industry during the period needs to be seen as resulting from the growing incomes of the households.

The trends in per capita demand for textiles appear to follow the trends in the rate of growth of real per capita income, with much of the increase taking place in the period from 1992–93 to 1997–98, and then from 2003–04 to 2007–08 (Figure 1.3). During the intervening period, from 1997–98 to 2003–04, when the growth rate of real per capita income was fluctuating, though remaining positive and reasonably high, its relation with the rate of increase in per capita

[5] In the first 30 years of planning, the trend rate of growth of national income was 3.5 per cent. Eminent economist Raj Krishna called this slow but steady economic growth—the Hindu rate of growth. Per capita income increased at the trend rate of 1.3 per cent during this period.

[6] Average annual compound rate of growth calculated using data from the Office of the Textile Commissioner, published in *Handbook of Statistics on Textile Industry* (CITI 2008), up to 2005–06 and txcindia.gov.in (last accessed on 5 September 2015) for later years.

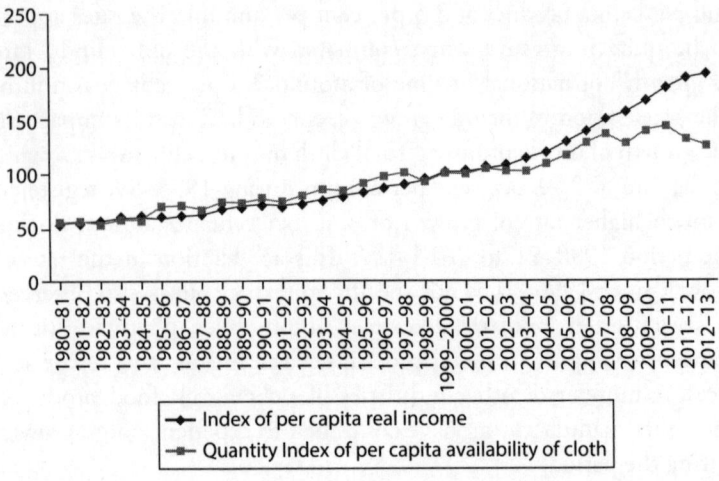

Figure 1.3 Indices of Per Capita Availability of Cloth and Real Per Capita Income with Base Year 1999–2000

Sources: Computed based on figures from Central Statistical Organisation (2014) for index for real per capita income; Office of the Textile Commissioner's (1996) for figures up to 1984–85 and CITI, *Handbook of Statistics on Textile Industry* (2008) for 1985–86 to 2005–06; and www.txcindia.gov.in (last accessed on 5 September 2015) for recent years, for index of per capita availability of cloth.

demand for textiles was far less robust. Later, when rate of growth of real per capita income decelerated after a sharp recovery from the global financial crisis and two successive years of robust growth, the per capita demand for textiles started falling. Overall, this suggests that there were other factors besides the rate of growth of per capita income that affected the increase in demand for textiles since the early 1990s. These additional factors need to be explored to clearly explain the growth in demand for textiles.

The National Sample Survey Organisation (NSSO) collects data on consumer expenditure in the country. Quantitative data on household incomes are not collected in NSS household surveys because of the difficulties of getting reliable information on incomes through direct enquiry. However, the data on monthly per capita consumer expenditure (MPCE), collected through the NSS consumer expenditure surveys are considered to be reliable indicators of the standards of living of households. Data from household consumer expenditure surveys are available both quinquennially from what are referred to as large sample surveys and annually from what are referred to as thin or small sample surveys.

For analysing the trends in the pattern of consumer expenditure, the present study relies on the official estimates obtained from the 38th round (1983), the 50th round (1993–94), and the 61st round (2004–05) of the NSS. All three are quinquennial rounds and provide estimates based on a uniform 30-days reference period for all items (uniform reference period or URP) and are therefore fully comparable.[7] The availability of comparable information from these three rounds allows us to examine trends in the pattern of consumer expenditure during the periods 1983 to 1993–94 (period 1) and 1993–94 to 2004–05 (period 2). This will highlight the changes that have occurred across the two periods, when there was a revival of demand in a number of industries. These changes in the pattern of consumer expenditure over time may also explain the increase in home demand for textile products during period 2. The choice of time periods has been motivated by the desire to study consumer behaviour over a fairly long time. It also enables us to avoid complexities that could arise by including the results of the controversial 55th round of the NSS, which departed from the earlier practice with respect to the choice of reference period and produced estimates with mixed reference period (MRP).[8]

A feature which is common to all the three rounds is that the value of monthly consumption of clothing per person and its share in total consumer expenditure increases as we move up the expenditure classes, both for the urban and the rural areas (Tables 1.1 and 1.2).

---

[7] Mixed reference period (MRP) estimates are also published for the 61st round.

[8] The official estimates before the 55th round were based on the data using uniform 30-days reference period (URP) for all items. The quinquennial survey of the 55th round corresponding to July 1999 to June 2000 period, however, departed from the earlier practice. No URP estimates are available from the 55th round since this used only a 365-day recall for five low frequency items, including clothing, footwear, durable goods, education, and institutional medicine. For food and intoxicants, estimates are obtained for both seven days and 30 days.

Table 1.1 Value (Rs) and Percentage of Consumer Expenditure on Clothing during 1983, 1993–94, and 2004–05 (Urban)

Expenditure class	Value of MPCE on clothing 1983	% of MPCE on clothing 1983	Value of MPCE on clothing 1993–94	% of MPCE on clothing 1993–94	Value of MPCE on clothing 2004–05	% of MPCE on clothing 2004–05
1	0.11	0.50	0.80	0.60	3.44	1.23
2	0.13	0.36	1.60	0.91	5.50	1.49
3	0.38	0.83	2.70	1.28	11.23	2.54
4	0.40	0.72	3.80	1.54	14.31	2.68
5	0.82	1.26	6.10	2.13	15.20	2.43
6	1.38	1.78	7.80	2.35	24.73	3.39
7	2.33	2.52	11.90	3.13	30.19	3.52
8	3.57	3.19	17.50	3.91	38.13	3.76
9	5.83	4.25	26.00	4.78	47.98	3.91
10	10.92	6.35	41.20	5.90	73.84	4.63
11	18.85	8.47	63.10	6.83	99.03	4.59
12	26.56	9.73	131.50	8.00	225.00	5.31
13	63.25	13.99				
All Classes	12.52	7.63	21.40	4.67	42.09	4.00

Source: Computed based on figures from NSSO (1986, 1996, and 2006).

Table 1.2 Value (Rs) and Percentage of Consumer Expenditure on Clothing during 1983, 1993–94, and 2004–05 (Rural)

Expenditure class	Value of MPCE on clothing 1983	% of MPCE on clothing 1983	Value of MPCE on clothing 1993–94	% of MPCE on clothing 1993–94	Value of MPCE on clothing 2004–05	% of MPCE on clothing 2004–05
1	0.31	1.25	0.90	0.90	2.37	1.19
2	0.41	1.14	1.40	1.07	3.76	1.48
3	0.70	1.54	2.20	1.44	5.70	1.92
4	1.22	2.21	2.90	1.63	8.05	2.35
5	1.80	2.76	4.20	2.10	10.73	2.77
6	2.77	3.58	5.90	2.66	13.48	3.12
7	4.32	4.68	7.60	3.05	17.52	3.64
8	6.99	6.26	10.70	3.80	21.85	4.02
9	11.58	8.48	16.10	4.96	29.07	4.61
10	18.70	10.93	27.70	6.95	44.53	5.75
11	32.71	14.77	47.20	9.43	63.39	6.34
12	50.03	18.39	98.50	11.29	136.43	6.97
13	78.42	17.93				
All classes	9.66	8.59	15.10	5.37	25.33	4.53

Source: Computed based on figures from NSSO (1986, 1996, and 2006).

Note: There were 13 expenditure classes in NSS consumer expenditure survey, 38th round conducted in 1983. For the 50th and the 61th rounds conducted in 1993–94 and 2004–05, 12 expenditure classes were drawn up. The class limits were chosen so that each class (excepting the top two classes and the bottom two) approximately contained an estimated 10 per cent of population (rural or urban), while the remaining two classes each contained an estimated 5 per cent of the population.

Higher aggregate expenditure levels are associated with higher expenditure on textiles and clothing (T&C). Also, the average value of consumption of clothing per person for all the rounds is found to be lower for the rural sector, though it formed a larger proportion of their total consumer expenditure compared to the urban sector. This seems to be associated with lesser diversification of aggregate consumption in the rural areas, as compared to the urban areas, because of the need to focus on the consumption of necessities.

To analyse the responsiveness of demand for clothing to changes in expenditure, the expenditure elasticity of demand for clothing is calculated as the ratio of the percentage increase in per capita consumption of clothing to the percentage increase in monthly per capita expenditure. For the ith expenditure class, expenditure elasticity of demand for clothing is calculated as the ratio of the percentage increase in value of monthly per capita consumption of clothing, or $100 * (V_{i+1}-V_i)/V_i$, to the percentage increase in monthly per capita expenditure, or $100 * (E_{i+1} - E_i)/E_i$, where V_i is the value of monthly per capita consumption of clothing of the ith class and E_i is the monthly per capita expenditure of ith class.

For the year 1983, the expenditure elasticity of demand for clothing in the urban sector (Table 1.3) varied between 2 and 7 approximately, with higher values for the lower expenditure classes compared to those for the middle and higher expenditure classes. This indicates a greater responsiveness of demand for clothing to increasing expenditure among the lower expenditure groups. The expenditure elasticity did not vary much across different expenditure classes in the rural sector, ranging between 2.32 and 3.44 (Table 1.4). For the year 1993–94, the expenditure elasticity was higher for the lower deciles compared to upper deciles for both the rural and the urban areas, indicating that lower income people tend to spend a greater proportion of their additional expenditure on clothing. However, during 2004–05, the expenditure elasticity showed little variation across deciles. The rapid increase in the prices of foodgrains and a reduction in public provision of health and transport due to increasing privatisation meant an increase in their relative expenditure on medicines, conveyance, etc. discussed further in this chapter. This seems to have lowered the expenditure elasticity of demand for clothing in the lower expenditure groups.

Table 1.3 Expenditure Elasticity of Per Person Demand for Clothing during 1983, 1993–94, and 2004–05 (Urban)

Expenditure class	1983	1993–94	2004–05
1	0.29	3.11	1.89
2	6.96	3.42	5.24
3	0.24	2.34	1.32
4	6.01	3.91	0.36
5	3.66	1.74	3.76
6	3.52	3.55	1.26
7	2.53	2.68	1.44
8	2.81	2.27	1.24
9	3.44	2.05	1.80
10	2.46	1.65	0.97
11	1.81	1.39	1.32
12	2.11		
13			

Source: Computed based on figures from NSSO (1986, 1996, and 2006).

Table 1.4 Expenditure Elasticity of Per Person Demand for Clothing during 1983, 1993–94, and 2004–05 (Rural)

Expenditure class	1983	1993–94	2004–05
1	0.73	1.84	2.16
2	2.64	3.27	3.06
3	3.44	3.55	2.67
4	2.64	2.51	2.52
5	2.87	4.06	2.24
6	2.91	3.28	2.62
7	2.95	2.25	1.93
8	2.93	2.65	2.06
9	2.43	2.23	2.32
10	2.55	2.81	1.46
11	2.32	0.95	1.20
12	0.93		
13			

Source: Computed based on figures from NSSO (1986, 1996, and 2006).

This conjecture seems to be supported by the evidence on trends over time. The NSS data point to important shifts in the pattern of consumer expenditure away from food products towards non-food products during period 1 (between 1983 and 1993–94; see Tables 1.5 and 1.6). The share of non-food products increased by about 2.5 percentage points for the rural areas and 4.5 percentage points for the urban areas. However, the share of clothing saw a fall of about 3 percentage points in both the rural[9] and the urban areas[10] during this period.

Table 1.5   Percentage Distribution of MPCE (Rural)

Item	1983	1993–94	2004–05
Food (total)	65.6	63.2	55
Pan, tobacco, and intoxicants	3	3.2	2.7
Clothing	8.6	5.4	4.5
Footwear	1	0.9	0.8
Fuel and light	7	7.4	10.2
Misc. goods and services	12.5	17.3	23.4
Durable goods	2.3	2.7	3.4
Non-food (total)	34.4	36.8	45
Total expenditure	100	100	100

Source: NSSO (2006: 68–9).

Table 1.6   Percentage Distribution of MPCE (Urban)

Item	1983	1993–94	2004–05
Food (total)	59.1	54.7	42.5
Pan, tobacco, and intoxicants	2.4	2.3	1.6
Clothing	7.6	4.7	4
Footwear	1.1	0.9	0.7
Fuel and light	6.9	6.6	9.9
Misc. goods and services	20.5	27.5	37.2
Durable goods	2.3	3.3	4.1
Non-food (total)	40.9	45.3	57.5
Total expenditure	100	100	100

Source: NSSO (2006: 68–9).

[9] Declined from 8.6 per cent to 5.4 per cent.
[10] Declined from 7.6 per cent to 4.7 per cent.

Much of the increase in the share of the non-food items (total) was a consequence of increasing share of miscellaneous goods and services, which is a heterogeneous group of all items other than food, paan, tobacco, intoxicants, fuel and light, clothing, footwear, and durable goods, and includes educational and medical expenses, expenditure on amusement, goods for personal care and effect, toiletries, consumer services, and conveyance. The share of these miscellaneous goods and services, including rents and taxes, increased by about 5 percentage points[11] in the rural and by 7 percentage points[12] in the urban areas.

A detailed analysis of demand for clothing in absolute terms using NSS data points to an increase in the demand for clothing during period 1 (from 1983 to 1993–94) in both the urban and the rural areas. Average MPCE on clothing at current prices increased at 5.5 per cent per annum for the urban and at 4.6 per cent per annum for the rural. However, after adjusting for increases in the prices of textiles as captured by the Wholesale Price Index (WPI) for textiles with 1983 as base, it is observed that the total real demand for clothing actually declined both in the urban as well as the rural areas (Tables 1.8 and 1.10). On per capita basis, the NSS data indicate that the average real MPCE on clothing fell by about Rs 2.5 in both the urban and the rural areas (all classes combined; Tables 1.7 and 1.9).

This trend of decline in real per capita demand for clothing during period 1 seems to have been reversed during period 2, from 1993–94 to 2004–05 (Tables 1.7 and 1.9). This reversal is observed for both the areas, with the growth rate of average real MPCE on clothing in the urban areas (3.94 per cent per annum for all classes) being much higher than that in the rural areas (2.46 per cent per annum for all classes). In absolute terms, while the average real MPCE on clothing in the urban areas increased by about Rs 5 and was far higher than the 1983 level, it increased by only Rs 2.20 in the rural areas and despite the rise in real per capita demand for cloth, it remained slightly lower than the 1983 level.

Since it may be argued that the WPIs of textiles do not reflect the increase in the prices to the consumers, real demand for clothing is also calculated using consumer price indices (CPIs) as deflators.

---

[11] Increased from 12.5 per cent to 17.3 per cent.
[12] Increased from 20.5 per cent to 27.5 per cent.

Table 1.7 Expenditure Group-wise Average Real MPCE on Clothing with Base Year 1983 (Rs) (Urban)

Year	1983	1993–94	2004–05
Bottom 40 per cent	2.06	1.64	4.18
Middle 40 per cent	8.62	7.51	13.04
Top 20 per cent	41.23	32.90	43.61
All classes	12.52	10.17	15.56

Sources: Computed based on figures from NSSO (1986, 1996, and 2006) and Office of Economic Advisor, GoI (for figures before 1993–94: Index Numbers of Wholesale Prices in India; for figures of 1993–94 onwards: http://www.eaindustry.nic.in/download_data_9394.asp [last accessed on 11 February 2016]).
Notes: 1. Average of the monthly WPIs for textiles for the agricultural years 1993–94 and 2004–05 are used as deflator.
2. The findings reported in the survey reports, with respect to value (Rs) of consumption of broad groups of items per person for a period of 30 days for urban areas by monthly per capita expenditure classes, are used for calculation.

Table 1.8 Expenditure Group-wise Total Real Monthly Consumer Expenditure on Clothing with Base Year 1983 (Rs million) (Urban)

Year	1983	1993–94	2004–05
Bottom 40 per cent	133.7	126.4	415.5
Middle 40 per cent	558.8	579.0	1,296.2
Top 20 per cent	1,335.7	1,268.2	2,167.5
All classes	2,028.3	1,960.1	3,866.7

Source: Computed based on figures from Table 1.7 and NSSO (1986, 1996, and 2006).
Note: The findings reported in the survey reports, with respect to percentage distribution of estimated number of households and total persons per household, by monthly per capita expenditure classes at the all-India level for urban areas, are used for calculation.

The consumer price index numbers for agricultural labourers (CPI-AL) for clothing, bedding, and footwear is used for deflating demand for clothing in the rural areas. The consumer price index numbers for

Table 1.9 Expenditure Group-wise Average Real MPCE on Clothing with Base Year 1983 (Rs) (Rural)

Year	1983	1993–94	2004–05
Bottom 40 per cent	1.95	1.24	2.55
Middle 40 per cent	6.22	4.79	7.57
Top 20 per cent	31.96	23.89	26.71
All classes	9.66	7.17	9.37

Sources: Computed based on figures from NSSO (1986, 1996, and 2006) and Office of Economic Advisor, GoI (for figures before 1993–94: Index Numbers of Wholesale Prices in India; for figures of 1993–94 onwards: http://www.eaindustry.nic.in/download_data_9394.asp [last accessed on 11 February 2016]).
Notes: 1. Average of the monthly WPIs of textiles for the agricultural years 1993–94 and 2004–05 are used as deflator.
2. The findings reported in the survey reports, with respect to value (Rs) of consumption of broad groups of items per person for a period of 30 days for rural areas by monthly per capita expenditure classes, are used for calculation.

Table 1.10 Expenditure Group-wise Total Real Monthly Consumer Expenditure on Clothing with Base Year 1983 (Rs million) (Rural)

Year	1983	1993–94	2004–05
Bottom 40 per cent	407.0	290.1	747.8
Middle 40 per cent	1,296.2	1,120.6	2,219.8
Top 20 per cent	3,329.9	2,794.6	3,916.2
All classes	5,033.2	4,193.7	6,869.2

Source: Computed based on figures from Table 1.9 and NSSO (1986, 1996, and 2006).
Note: The findings reported in the survey reports, with respect to percentage distribution of estimated number of households and total persons per household, by monthly per capita expenditure classes at the all-India level for rural areas, are used for calculation.

industrial workers (CPI-IW) for clothing, bedding, and footwear is used to deflate the demand for clothing in the urban areas. The consumer price index for urban non-manual employees (CPI-UNME) for clothing, bedding, and footwear is also used for the urban areas. Similar results (reported in the Tables A.1, A.2, and A.3 in

Appendix A) are indicated when the CPIs are used as deflators, except that the MPCE now appears to have almost stagnated (slight decline) in the rural areas during period 2.[13]

To analyse the source of decline in demand for clothing during period 1 and its increase during period 2, the entire population is divided into three sections—bottom 40 per cent, middle 40 per cent, and top 20 per cent—for both the rural and the urban areas, according to their MPCE. The average real MPCE on clothing for these three sections of the population is calculated for the years 1983, 1993–94, and 2004–05, using the WPI for textiles with base 1983 as the deflator. The average real MPCE is also calculated for all the three sections of population using the CPI-AL as the deflator for the rural sector and the CPI-UNME for the urban sector with base 1983. The deflators used are not the appropriate measures of the consumer price changes affecting the households in all MPCE classes in the rural/urban areas. Therefore, the conclusions reached are wanting to that extent. The comparison rests on the assumption that the impact of inflation on the incomes and expenditures of those in different expenditure deciles is the same.

A comparison of the results for 1983 and 1993–94 for the urban areas indicates that during period 1, while the total real demand for clothing fell substantially in the top 20 per cent of the population, it increased in the middle expenditure group and declined slightly in the lower expenditure group (Table 1.8). The average real MPCE on clothing (Table 1.7) fell substantially in the higher expenditure group (from Rs 41.23 in 1983 to Rs 32.90 in 1993–94). It declined slightly in the middle and the lower expenditure groups (falling by Re 1 in the middle and by Re 0.32 in the lower expenditure group), which recorded an increase in their total real expenditure on clothing due to the increase in population.

In the rural areas also, much of the decline (64 per cent) observed in the total real demand for clothing during period 1 occurred in the higher income group (Table 1.10). There was a decline in the total demand for clothing in the lower and middle expenditure groups as

---

[13] This is due to decline in MPCE on clothing in the top 20 per cent of population. The other two groups of population show an increase during period 2.

well by 14 per cent and 21 per cent respectively. The average real MPCE on clothing in the higher expenditure group fell substantially, from about Rs 32 in 1983 to about Rs 24 in the year 1993–94 (Table 1.9). The real MPCE on clothing declined by a small amount of Rs 1.4 and Re 0.7 in the rural middle and lower income groups respectively.

Overall, the results indicate that much of the decline during period 1 was accounted for by the rich, who, given their high marginal propensity to save, saved a large proportion of their income. This was reflected in the slow growth of the overall average real MPCE of the rural rich (at a rate of less than 1 per cent per annum; Table 1.11). The overall average real MPCE grew faster at about 1.5 per cent per annum for the urban rich (Table 1.12). But the rich in the urban, as well as the rural, areas seem to have distributed their additional consumer expenditure across a range of competing luxuries, as suggested in the NSS consumer expenditure reports by the rise of consumer services, goods for personal care, and amusement expenditure, while textiles being necessities, did not record any increase.

The NSS data indicate that the overall average real MPCE in the bottom 40 per cent of the population grew as well during period 1

Table 1.11   Expenditure Group-wise Average Real MPCE with Base Year 1983 (Rs) (Rural)

Year	1983	1993–94	2004–05	Rate of growth per annum (Period 1: 1983 to 1993–94)	Rate of growth per annum (Period 2: 1993–94 to 2004–05)
Bottom 40 per cent	64.72	70.68	79.58	0.0088	0.0108
Middle 40 per cent	104.4	117.95	132.51	0.0123	0.0106
Top 20 per cent	223.93	237.35	286.11	0.0058	0.0171
All classes	112.45	123.16	141.90	0.0091	0.0130

Sources: Computed based on figures from NSSO (1986, 1996, and 2006) and GoI, Ministry of Labour and Employment for CPIN.

Note: CPI-AL is used as deflators.

Table 1.12　Expenditure Group-wise Average Real MPCE with Base Year 1983 (Rs) (Urban)

Year	1983	1993–94	2004–05	Rate of growth per annum (Period 1: 1983 to 1993–94)	Rate of growth per annum (Period 2: 1993–94 to 2004–05)
Bottom 40 per cent	86.49	89.38	94.88	0.0033	0.0054
Middle 40 per cent	153.08	169.47	188.79	0.0102	0.0099
Top 20 per cent	341.00	394.28	472.43	0.0146	0.0166
All classes	164.03	182.26	207.55	0.0106	0.0119

Sources: Computed based on figures from NSSO (1986, 1996, and 2006) and RBI (2012) for CPIN.
Note: CPI-UNME is used as deflators.

(Tables 1.11 and 1.12). The middle 40 per cent of the population also recorded increases in overall average real MPCE of 1.23 per cent and 1.02 per cent per annum in the rural and urban areas, respectively, during period 1 (Tables 1.11 and 1.12). However, there were other factors that restricted the increase in demand for clothing in these expenditure groups.

The economy was characterised by a significant reduction in poverty, some decline in inequalities, coupled with a reasonable rate of growth of national income at 5 per cent per annum. The headcount ratio, based on official national poverty line, declined during this period from 45.6 per cent and 40.8 per cent in 1983 to 37.2 per cent and 32.4 per cent in 1993–94 for the rural and the urban areas respectively (Sen and Himanshu 2004). The inequalities increased in the urban areas with Gini ratio increasing from 33.9 per cent in 1983 to 34.4 per cent in 1993–94. However, the rural areas experienced a decline in inequalities with Gini falling from 30.4 per cent in 1983 to 28.6 per cent in 1993–94. Clearly, the rapid growth of the 1980s was accompanied by decline in inequality. Indian poverty, which had no trend up to 1973–74, declined quite significantly during period 1.

Overall, these were favourable changes for the bottom 40 per cent of population, but any small increase in the incomes of those who were underfed, undernourished, and at the margins of subsistence led to increases in the consumption of food, which became relatively cheaper as its prices were rising less rapidly than the general rate of inflation. The NSS data on consumer expenditure indicate that though the average real MPCE on food among the bottom 40 per cent of the population in the urban areas grew slowly (0.12 per cent per annum), it grew fast at 0.57 per cent per annum among the bottom 40 per cent of the population in the rural areas.[14] In terms of percentage of MPCE on food, though there was some decline for the bottom 40 per cent of the population in the urban areas[15] during this period, there was an increase of about 6 percentage points for the bottom 40 per cent of the rural population. Although their real MPCE grew at a higher rate when compared with their real MPCE[16] on food in both the rural and the urban areas,[17] there were other reasons like the decline in public expenditures on health and education which led to an increase in reliance on paid services offered by private providers and restricted any increase in demand for clothing in the lower as well as middle expenditure groups during period 1. For example, public health expenditure as a percentage of GDP peaked around the mid-1980s and then declined subsequently. It increased

[14] 'CPI-IW for food', constructed for the agricultural year (July to June for which the consumption expenditure survey was conducted) using monthly price indices, is used as deflator for the urban areas and 'CPI-AL for food' is used as deflator for the rural areas. The average real MPCE on food (with base year 1983) increased from Rs 61.25 in 1983 to Rs 62.00 in 1993–94 for the bottom 40 per cent of the urban population. The average real MPCE on food (with base year 1983) increased from Rs 48.57 in 1983 to Rs 51.40 in 1993–94 for the bottom 40 per cent of the rural population.

[15] Declined by 2.5 percentage points.

[16] Real MPCE refers to their overall average real MPCE (as shown in Tables 1.11 and 1.12).

[17] Real MPCE for the bottom 40 per cent of the population grew at 0.88 per cent per annum in the rural areas (using 'CPI-AL, General Index' as deflator). It grew at 0.95 per cent per annum in the urban areas (using 'CPI-IW, General Index' as deflator).

from 1.07 per cent in 1980–81 to 1.32 per cent in 1985–86, and fell thereafter to 0.88 per cent by 1991–92. As a percentage of government expenditure, this implied a fall from 3.29 per cent in 1980–81 (which remained the same in 1985–86) to 3.11 per cent by 1991–92 (Duggal 2007).

Similarly, the share of education expenditure of the education departments (together with the other departments) in the total budgeted expenditure of central and state government grew fast from about 10–11 per cent in the first half of the 1980s to 13.64 per cent in 1989–90, but declined afterwards. As a percentage of the gross national product (GNP), this meant an increase from around 3 per cent in the early 1980s to 4.21 per cent in 1990–91, and then a fall to less than 4 per cent in the early 1990s (Ministry of Human Resource Development [MHRD] 1995). People were required to spend more on the purchase of crucial goods and services and this seems to have affected their demand for clothing.

In addition to this, textiles continued to be relatively expensive[18] during period 1 and became cheaper only after the mid-1990s. The continuing high prices of textiles (discussed in the next section) also restricted the increase in demand for textiles in the lower and middle expenditure groups. Overall, given the context of a slowly growing economy during period 1, the necessary inducement in the form of increased demand that was crucial for the revival of the textile industry was not forthcoming.

This trend of decline in per capita demand for clothing during period 1 was reversed during period 2, stretching from 1993–94 to 2004–05 (Tables 1.7 and 1.9). With rapid economic growth and the associated increase in per capita incomes during this period, a shift in the pattern of consumer expenditure away from food towards non-food products is expected. People are expected to spend relatively more on non-food products as their incomes increase. Accordingly, the shift in the pattern of consumer expenditure, which had been observed during period 1, not only continued, but intensified during period 2, with a much greater fall in the share of food and a corresponding rise in the share

---

[18] Compared to the general rate of inflation indicated by the WPI for all commodities.

of non-food products[19] (Tables 1.5 and 1.6). Though textiles was not the major beneficiary and the share of textiles continued to fall during period 2, the fall[20] was less pronounced in this period and the textile industry benefited in terms of an absolute increase in expenditure. While the increasing share of non-food products during period 1 was led by miscellaneous goods and services, during 1993–94 to 2004–05 (that is, period 2), fuel and light along with miscellaneous goods and services contributed to further increase in the share of non-food products. The share of miscellaneous goods and services increased by about 10 percentage points for the urban sector and 6 percentage points for the rural sector during this period. The share of fuel and light increased by about 3 percentage points both for the rural and urban sectors.

A comparison of the results for the 50th (1993–94) and 61st (2004–05) rounds of NSS indicates an increase in the real average monthly expenditure on clothing across all three sections of the population in the urban and the rural areas (Tables 1.8 and 1.10). The top 20 per cent of the population accounted for a major proportion of the total increase in real demand for clothing in the rural and the urban areas (about 42 and 47 per cent respectively). The absolute increase in the average real MPCE on clothing in this expenditure group in the urban areas was as high as about Rs 11 compared to about Rs 3 in the rural areas (Tables 1.7 and 1.9).

The middle 40 per cent of the population accounted for about 41 per cent and 38 per cent of the total increase in the rural and the urban areas respectively. The real MPCE on clothing in the middle expenditure group increased by Rs 5.5 in the urban areas against Rs 2.8 recorded in the rural areas. The bottom 40 per cent of the population accounted for only about 17 per cent and 15 per cent of the total increase in real demand for clothing in the rural and the

[19] According to the NSS data on the distribution of MPCE, there was a fall in the share of food by about 8 percentage points for the rural sector and by 12 percentage points for the urban sector during period 2, from 1993–94 to 2004–05. Correspondingly, the share of non-food increased by 8 percentage points for the rural sector and 12 percentage points for the urban sector.

[20] The share of clothing saw a fall from 4.7 per cent in 1993–94 to 4 per cent in 2004–05 for the urban sector and from 5.4 per cent in 1993–94 to 4.5 per cent in 2004–05 for the rural sector.

urban areas respectively. Their real MPCE on clothing increased by about Rs 1.3 and Rs 2.5 in the rural and the urban areas respectively.

Clearly, the rich, constituting the top 20 per cent of the population, led the growth in demand for the textile industry during period 2. This section of the population gained immensely as inequalities, which had declined somewhat during period 1, increased quite sharply in both the rural and the urban areas. The Gini ratio in the rural areas, which declined from 30.4 per cent in 1983 to 28.6 per cent in 1993–94, increased to 30.5 per cent in 2004–05. The Gini ratio in the urban areas, which rose from 33.9 per cent in 1983 to 34.41 per cent in 1993–94, continued to rise and reached 37.6 per cent in 2004–05 (Himanshu 2007). The urban rich spent more in general, with their average real MPCE increasing at a higher rate (at 1.66 per cent per annum) during period 2 compared to period 1 (Table 1.12). Their real expenditure on clothing increased at more than 2 per cent per annum. The overall real consumer expenditure by the urban rich had increased during period 1 as well, but failed to generate growth in the demand for clothing. The rural rich also increased real spending on clothing in period 2.

The fast growth in incomes among the rich, which accounted for a major proportion of the increase in real demand for T&C, resulted in increase in demand for classic and ethnic cotton textiles, which experienced continuous increases in their prices and became more expensive than synthetic and blended textiles and were considered largely as items of luxury during period 2.[21] According to the Textiles Committee's Market Research Wing, GoI, while the monthly per capita consumer purchases (MPCP) of cotton textiles, as a percentage of their total MPCP of textiles, at 1993–94 prices, declined at the all-India level among the lower and the middle income groups, it remained stable for the higher income group. For the lower income group, the MPCP of cotton textiles as a percentage of their total MPCP of textiles declined from between 37 per cent and 44 per cent in 1990 to between 20 per cent and 26 per cent in 1998. For the middle income group, the decline was from between 20 per cent and 32 per cent in 1990 to around 20–1 per cent in 1998. The higher income group continued to spend about 21–22 per cent of their real MPCP of textiles on cotton T&C (Tables 1.13 and 1.14).

[21] As explained later in detail in Chapter 2, 'Availability and Cost of Raw Materials' and Chapter 4, 'Structural Changes in the Indian Textile Industry'.

Table 1.13   Real Per Capita Purchase of Textiles during 1990 at 1993–94 Prices, All-India

Income Groups		Cotton (%)	Non-cotton and blended (%)	Total
Low income group	Less than Rs 6,000	44.38	55.62	100
	6,000–10,000	37.41	62.59	100
Middle income group	10,000–20,000	32.64	67.36	100
	20,000–40,000	20.53	79.47	100
High income group	40,000–60,000	20.08	79.92	100
	60,000 and above	23.33	76.67	100

Sources: Computed based on figures from Textiles Committee (1992) and Office of Economic Advisor, GoI (for figures before 1993–94: Index Numbers of Wholesale Prices in India; for figures of 1993–94 onwards: http://www.eaindustry. nic.in/download_data_9394.asp [last accessed on 11 February 2016]).
Note: The WPIs for cotton textiles and man-made textiles are used for deflating cotton and non-cotton and blended textiles respectively.

Table 1.14   Real Per Capita Purchase of Textiles during 1998 at 1993–94 Prices, All-India

Income Groups		Cotton (%)	Non-cotton and blended (%)	Total
Low income group	Up to Rs 20,000	26.08	73.92	100
	20,000–25,000	26.86	73.14	100
	25,000–50,000	20.16	79.84	100
Middle income group	50,000–100,000	20.51	79.49	100
	100,000–200,000	20.07	79.93	100
	200,000–400,000	20.52	79.48	100
High income group	400,000 and above	21.65	78.35	100

Sources: Computed based on figures from Textiles Committee (2000) and Office of Economic Advisor, GoI (for figures before 1993–94: Index Numbers of Wholesale Prices in India; for figures of 1993–94 onwards: http://www.eaindustry.nic. in/download_data_9394.asp [last accessed on 11 February 2016]).
Note: The WPIs for cotton textiles and man-made textiles are used for deflating cotton and non-cotton and blended textiles respectively.

The increase in demand for cotton textiles by the higher income groups led to stabilisation of the long-term decline in the per capita demand for cotton textiles. The per capita household demand for cotton textiles, which fell at the all-India level from 12.5 m in the early 1970s to about 10 m in the early 1980s and further to about 7.5 m in the early 1990s, stabilised around 7–7.5 m during the rest of the 1990s and crossed 8 m by 2004–05 (Textiles Committee various years). The increased demand for cotton textiles[22] by the higher income groups since the 1990s was reflected in an increase in demand for a variety of cotton textiles. The data from the Textiles Committee, GoI, indicate an increase in the share of per capita purchase of household varieties of cotton, which include bedcovers, bedsheets, chaddars, towels, and Turkish towels, at the all-India level. Their share in the per capita purchase of all textiles rose from 3.67 per cent in 1990 to 4.43 per cent in 1998, and increased slightly to 4.55 per cent in 2006 (Textiles Committee 1992, 2000, and 2007). Similar increase was recorded in the share of woven and knitted ready-made garments of cotton. The growth in demand for cotton textiles, however, was not widespread and remained limited to the urban areas where incomes increased much faster during the period of reforms. The per capita household demand for cotton textiles in the urban areas grew from about 7.65 m in 1993 to 10.1 m in 1998. Rural areas, which hardly observed any growth in incomes, on the other hand, saw a fall in the per capita demand for cotton textiles from 7.58 m in 1993 to 5.1 m in 1998. The per capita demand for cotton textiles in the urban areas crossed 11 m by 2002 and remained around that level till 2006. The rural areas showed some improvement in their per capita demand for cotton textiles, with the figure fluctuating around 6.5 m from 2002 to 2006 (Textiles Committee various years).

In addition to the top 20 per cent, the middle 40 per cent of the population also accounted for a substantial proportion of the total increase in real expenditure on clothing. This class seems to have spent more, in general, during period 2 (Tables 1.11 and 1.12), but the rate of increase in their overall spending was slightly higher

---

[22] In absolute terms.

in period 1—a period that saw their demand for clothing declining. Further, privatisation of essential goods and services, which restricted increase in demand for clothing during period 1 in the middle (and lower) expenditure groups, continued in period 2. For example, due to increasing privatisation, public health financing as a percentage of government expenditure, which was 3.11 per cent by 1991–92, fell further to 3.04 per cent in 2000–01 and to 2.77 per cent in 2005–06 (Duggal 2007). People were spending more on commercial fuel as a source of energy for cooking. According to the figures published in NSS Report No. 464 on energy used by Indian households, the percentage of rural households using firewood and chips as a primary source of energy for cooking declined by 2.7 percentage points from 1993–94 to 1999–2000. The decline for the urban households was about 8 percentage points during the same period.[23] Consequently, the percentage of rural households using liquefied petroleum gas (LPG) as a primary source of energy for cooking increased from 1.9 per cent in 1993–94 to 5.4 per cent in 1999–2000. The proportion of urban households using LPG increased from 29.6 per cent to 44.2 per cent. Overall, it suggests that some of the factors that restricted the demand for textiles among this class of population during period 1, prevailed during period 2, which was a period of high growth, as well. Therefore, the explanation for the increase in demand for clothing in the middle income group in this period 2 needs to be based on other factors, mainly the falling prices of textiles, besides their increasing real income.

The analysis of NSS data indicates that there was hardly any increase in the demand for clothing in the bottom 40 per cent of population, which accounted for 15 per cent and 17 per cent of the total increase in real demand for clothing in the urban and the rural sectors respectively. Their MPCE on clothing continued to

[23] The percentage of rural households using firewood and chips as a primary source of energy for cooking declined from 78.2 per cent in 1993–94 to 75.5 per cent in 1999–2000. The percentage of households using firewood and chips declined from 30 per cent in 1993–94 to 22.3 per cent in 1999–2000 in the urban households.

remain much lower compared to the middle and rich sections of population (Tables 1.7 and 1.9). Though the economy achieved a higher rate of growth of national and per capita income, the benefits of growth remained limited to a small section of society. The economy followed a peculiar pattern of unbalanced growth which was led by the service sector. While incomes grew fast in the service sector, the agricultural sector registered a setback. The share of the service sector in GDP at constant prices increased from 41 per cent in 1980–81 to about 44 per cent by 1990–91. It then increased rapidly to 56 per cent by 2005–06. The share of the industrial sector almost stagnated around 16–19 per cent during the entire period. However, the share of the agricultural sector, which continues to be the major source of employment, fell from about 32 per cent in 1980–81 to 26 per cent by 1990–91. It fell further to 17 per cent by 2005–06.[24]

Further, the headcount ratio of poverty continued to decline from 37.2 and 32.6 per cent in 1993–94 to 28.7 and 25.9 per cent in 2004–05 in the rural and the urban areas respectively. However, the pace of poverty reduction during this period was much lower than the actual pace of reduction during the 1970s and 1980s.[25] The income inequalities also worsened during this period. In addition to this, the fast growth of the economy was associated with falling employment elasticity of production and growing unemployment.[26]

Overall, widening income inequalities, the reduced pace of poverty decline, increasing unemployment, and rising prices of foodgrains since the 1990s meant reduced real incomes of the poor. Further, the report on nutritional intake from the NSSO 55th round (1999–2000) has shown an increase in the proportion of people reporting inadequate nutrition during the period under consideration, implying an increase in nutrition poverty. The average intake of calorie and protein per capita per diem fell for rural India as a whole, and only marginal improvements were reported

---

[24] Computed based on figures from Reserve Bank of India (RBI) (2006).
[25] Based on URP, official poverty line. Refer Himanshu (2007).
[26] For details, see 'Introduction'.

for urban India between 1993–94 and 1999–2000. The results on nutritional intake based on the 61st round of the NSSO (2004–05) indicate a further deterioration in the average per capita intake of calories in both the rural and the urban areas from 1999–2000 to 2004–05. The average daily intake of protein in the rural areas also declined further during this period, though it remained almost stable in the urban areas. In addition to this, according to the NSS data on consumer expenditure, though the average real MPCE on food continued to increase for the bottom 40 per cent of the population (both in rural and urban areas) during period 2,[27] the percentage of MPCE on food declined substantially (by 10 per cent in the urban areas and by about 16 per cent in the rural areas). This shift away from food by the poor has been explained by several studies as a result of an increase in their relative expenditure on fuel, medicines, rent, and conveyance, because of reduced public provision of these services due to increased privatisation (Sen and Himanshu 2004).

[27] The average real MPCE on food (with base year 1983) increased from Rs 48.57 in 1983 to Rs 51.40 in 1993–94, which increased to Rs 54.04 in 2004–05 for the bottom 40 per cent of the rural population. The average real MPCE on food (with base year 1983) increased from Rs 61.25 in 1983 to Rs 62.00 in 1993–94 and further to Rs 62.60 in 2004–05 for the bottom 40 per cent of the urban population.

Per Capita Expenditure on Food at 1983 Prices Deflated by CPIN-AL for Food—Rural (Rs)

Year	Bottom 40 Per Cent	Middle 40 Per Cent	Top 20 Per Cent	All Classes
1993–94	51.40	80.5	126.15	78.16
2004–05	54.04	83.07	131.3	81.06

Per Capita Expenditure on Food at 1983 Prices Deflated by CPI-IW for Food (constructed for agricultural year July to June using monthly prices)–Urban (Rs)

Year	Bottom 40 Per Cent	Middle 40 Per Cent	Top 20 Per Cent	All Classes
1993–94	62.00	102.98	175.55	101.25
2004–05	62.60	101.20	169.19	99.16

Source: Computed based on figures from NSSO (1996 and 2006).

Under these circumstances, even this small increase in the real average expenditure on clothing by the bottom 40 per cent of the population seems surprising. It indicates that inequalities were increasing not only at the economy level but also differences were widening in the standards of living of those who constituted this bottom 40 per cent of the population, which are not revealed by the average figures. On the one hand, a large number of farmer suicides were reported due to the agricultural crisis during the period, pointing to the deteriorating standard of living of many in the lower expenditure class. On the other hand, there is evidence which points to an improved scenario after 1999 in the states that traditionally had higher than national average poverty (Himanshu 2007). These include states like Bihar, Assam, Odisha, Chhattisgarh, and West Bengal. Both non-income indicators as well as employment and income indicators showed improvements in these states after 1999. Their performance on total state domestic product (SDP) growth and agricultural SDP growth improved in this period compared to the previous period. Further, according to the NSS report on calorie intake, 61st round, the per capita per day intake of calorie was higher in the rural areas of Bihar, Assam, and West Bengal, compared to the national average for the rural areas. Higher than the national average calorie intake was reported in the urban areas of Assam, Bihar, Odisha, and Chhattisgarh. According to Himanshu (2007), Odisha, Haryana, Bihar, and Madhya Pradesh showed the highest diversification in non-farm employment. West Bengal, Gujarat, and Assam showed absolute decline in unemployment, which was increasing generally since the 1990s. The unemployment rate declined from 5.1 per cent during 1993–2000 to 1.4 per cent during 1999–2005 in Bihar. Clearly, while deteriorating circumstances led some of them, who belonged to the lower expenditure group, to reduce their expenditure on even the prime necessity, that is food, the improved scenario led others to increase their real expenditure to meet the requirements of basic necessities of life, including food and clothing. Overall, it meant that the fall in demand for these necessities by the former group was more than balanced by the rise in demand by the latter group. A small proportion of the growth in demand for textiles was thus accounted for by the bottom 40 per cent of the population.

Overall, the fast growth of the economy during period 2 provided the necessary inducement in the form of increased demand that was crucial for the revival of the textile industry. The increasing demand for textiles was led by the rich and middle income groups of the population.

Role of Prices in Consumer Demand

Prices of Textiles

Most Indian consumers are highly price sensitive. The average Indian household spends about 50 per cent of its income on food and as a result, spends discretionary income carefully. Price-sensitive lower and middle income households continue to account for the bulk of India's more than one billion consumers. Going by the WPI, absolute prices of textiles were increasing continuously since 1980–81 (Figure 1.4). However, in the current scenario where incomes as well as all other prices are increasing, what matters are relative prices rather than absolute prices. The prices of textiles relative to the general price level were falling during the 1990s. That is, relatively speaking, textiles were getting cheaper in comparison to other commodities during the period under consideration (Figure 1.5). The ratio of the WPI of textiles to the WPI of all commodities at 1993–94 prices, which was greater than unity up to the mid-1990s,[28] declined considerably thereafter. For example, the ratio declined from 1.06 in 1995–96 to 0.79 in 1999–2000. It continued to decline further to 0.57 by 2008–09. This was mainly because prices of synthetic textiles declined significantly after the mid-1990s. The WPI of synthetic textiles (with base year 1993–94) declined to 81.7 in 1998–99 (Figure 1.4). On the other hand, the price of cotton textiles continued to remain high, with the index fluctuating around 144 (base year 1993–94) during this period. As a result, the ratio of the WPI for synthetic textiles to the WPI for cotton textiles declined to 0.56 in 1998–99 and remained around that level in subsequent years. Though this ratio had started declining during the 1980s, synthetic textiles remained more expensive relative to cotton textiles during the 1970s and 1980s and became relatively cheaper only since the

[28] Exceptions are 1986–87 and 1987–88.

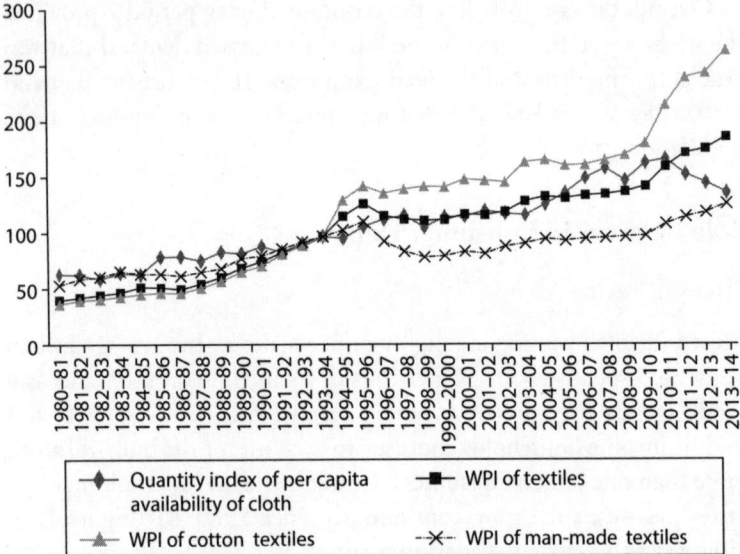

Figure 1.4   Quantity Index of Per Capita Availability of Cloth and WPIs of Textiles with Base Year 1993–94

Sources: Computed based on figures from Office of Economic Advisor, GoI (for figures before 1993–94: *Index Numbers of Wholesale Prices in India*; for figures of 1993–94 onwards: http://www.eaindustry.nic.in/download_data_9394.asp [last accessed on 11 February 2016])   for the WPIs; Office of Textile Commissioner (1996) for figures up to 1984–85 and CITI, *Handbook of Statistics on Textile Industry* (2008) for figures from 1985–86 to 2005–06; and www.txcindia.gov.in (last accessed on 5 September 2015) for later years, for per capita availability of cloth.

mid-1990s. Previously, synthetic textiles were largely imported, attracting very high import duties (as high as 200 per cent) because they were considered as items of luxury and were only affordable for the rich.

Synthetic textiles became cheaper since the mid-1990s as the synthetic fibre and yarn that are the intermediates for these products became available at lower prices as a consequence of the continuous cuts in import[29] and excise[30] duties associated with liberalisation. Duties were also lowered on the raw materials, like

[29] For details, see Chapter 2, 'Availability and Cost of Raw Materials'.
[30] For details, see Chapter 2, 'Availability and Cost of Raw Materials'.

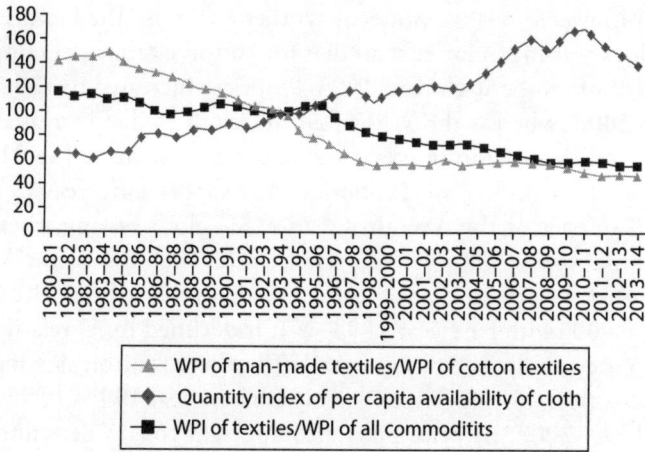

Figure 1.5   Quantity Index of Per Capita Availability of Cloth, Ratio of WPI of Textiles to WPI of All Commodities, and Ratio of WPI of Man-made Textiles to WPI of Cotton Textiles with Base Year 1993–94

Sources: Computed based on figures from Office of Economic Advisor, GoI (for figures before 1993–94: *Index Numbers of Wholesale Prices in India*; for figures of 1993–94 onwards: http://www.eaindustry.nic.in/download_data_9394.asp [last accessed on 11 February 2016]) for the WPIs; Office of Textile Commissioner (1996) for figures up to 1984–85 and CITI, *Handbook of Statistics on Textile Industry* (2008) for figures from 1985–86 to 2005–06; and www.txcindia.gov.in (last accessed on 5 September 2015) for later years, for per capita availability of cloth.

dimethyl terephthalate (DMT), purified terephthalic acid (PTA), and monoethylene glycol (MEG), which are used to produce these intermediates.[31] The increased competition from imports due to tariff reductions resulted in lowering of the prices of polyester staple fibre (PSF) and polyester filament yarn (PFY) in the domestic market, from around the middle of the 1990s. The reduction in their prices increased the use of these intermediates by fabric producers, which encouraged an expansion in the capacity for producing PSF and PFY. Although the WPI of synthetic cloth did not decline during this period, the benefit of reduced prices of synthetic fibres and filament yarn seems to have been passed on to consumers in the

[31] Discussed in Chapter 2, 'Availability and Cost of Raw Materials'.

form of lowered relative prices of synthetic fabrics. The increase in the index was much lower than that for cotton cloth. For example, the WPI of synthetic cloth at 1993–94 prices increased to 126.3 in 1999–2000, whereas the WPI of cotton cloth (mills) increased to 154.7 and that of cotton grey cloth and canvas increased to 216.6 by that year (Office of Economic Advisor various years). The overall impact of this was that man-made cloth became cheaper in comparison to all types of cotton cloth. The ratio of the WPI of synthetic cloth to that of cotton cloth (mills) fell to 81.64 in 1999–2000 (with base year 1993–94). It declined to 79 relative to cotton grey cloth. The ratio of the WPI of terry cotton shirting to that of cotton shirting fell to 71.64 (with base year 1993–94) by the year 1999–2000. As price plays an important role in determining the demand for textiles of the low and middle income sections of the population, synthetic textiles soon came to be considered as items of mass consumption, easily available domestically at much lower relative prices. The monthly per capita purchase of non-cotton and blended textiles, for the low and middle income groups, as a percentage of their total MPCP of textiles increased substantially during the 1990s (Tables 1.13 and 1.14).

Thus, the overall impact of the policy changes was that synthetic and blended textiles that were relatively much more expensive prior to the mid-1990s became cheaper. As a result of their rapid growth, synthetic and blended cloth now accounted for the bulk of household cloth purchases. Almost the entire increase in the demand for clothing during period 2 was because of increasing demand for synthetic and blended textiles. The per capita availability of synthetic and blended cloth increased at a rate of about 6 per cent per annum, while the per capita availability of cotton cloth almost stabilised. The increase in demand for clothing among the middle income and lower income groups during period 2 seems to be due to the lower prices of synthetic textiles that are also preferred because of their inherent properties like durability, wash-and-wear characteristics, and easy maintenance. Overall, in a rapidly growing economy, there was an increase in income allocated to non-food purchases. Though textile was not the main beneficiary, the combination of some increase in nominal expenditure on textiles and reduced prices led to substantial increase in the real demand for textiles.

However, after 2009–10, the WPI of man-made textiles started rising fast. By 2011–12, the prices of man-made textiles reached levels higher than those attained prior to the mid-1990s. This was mainly a result of rapid increase in the price of polyester due to increase in the prices of intermediates[32] required in its production. Further, excise duty on PSF, PFY, and on the intermediates required in their production, also increased during this period. On the other hand, domestic production of cotton started increasing fast after 2003–04. Although domestic consumption increased, a sharp decline in global trade and increase in world stocks in recent years affected Indian cotton markets also.[33] Although it is not reflected in the WPIs, overall it seems that cotton textiles became less expensive in comparison to synthetic textiles during the recent years. This seems to have reduced demand for synthetic and blended cloth, while demand for cotton textiles has continued to grow. Overall, the rapid decline in the relative prices of textiles after the mid-1990s has slowed down during the recent years. In an overall context, during the recent times when growth of real per capita income decelerated and there was rapid increase in the prices of foodgrains, this affected the demand for textiles adversely.

Prices of Foodgrains

Recognising the interdependence of the demand for a large number of commodities in the consumer's budget, it is suggested in the literature that the demand for textiles, besides depending on income and its own price, also depends on the relative price structure of items like food and fuel. Any change in the relative price structure of these items may affect the demand for different varieties of clothing.

This recognition shifted the focus from the estimation of partial demand relations that served the purpose of measuring income and own price elasticity to the estimation of complete demand systems. In spite of their importance, however, empirical analysts faced difficulties when working with complete systems of demand equations, because of the large number of parameters involved in the estimation.

---

[32] For details, see Chapter 2, 'Availability and Cost of Raw Materials'.

[33] Fibre2Fashion (2012), published in www.citiindia.com.

With the availability of the NSS data on consumer expenditure, numerous empirical works on consumer demand systems have been reported for India. These studies are carried out by utilising the panel data for the rural and the urban areas, and explicitly incorporating the distribution of income. Murty (1983), for example, estimated a two-stage optimisation model for the three income groups of the rural and the urban population. The NSS data on consumer expenditure[34] were used to estimate the household's expenditure on four commodity aggregates (cereal and cereal substitutes; other food; clothing; and other non-food) in the first stage. The outlay on clothing was then allocated across three varieties of clothing (cotton, mixed, and non-cotton) to estimate demand for different types of clothing in the second stage, using the data from the *Consumer Purchases of Textiles*, published by Textiles Committee annually. The prices of cereal and cereal substitutes, other food, and other non-food were also included, besides including the price of clothing, as determinants of demand for clothing. It was found that the cereal group takes a major share of the marginal benefits of the lower income groups. While the marginal benefit shares of cereal group decline, those of clothing and other non-food items increase with a rise in the total expenditure level.

However, while estimating a partial demand model using a linear expenditure system (LES) for cottons, non-cottons, and blended textiles, Goswami (1985) included relative prices of various varieties of textiles and expenditure on textiles. The prices of foodgrains were ignored on account of remarkable stability of the share of household expenditure allocated to textiles despite a steady increase in the prices of foodgrains. There were problems in substituting the variable 'expenditure on textiles' by 'total household expenditure' in the estimation of a complete demand model due to limited data availability on other items of household expenditure across income groups during the period 1974 to 1983. However, Murty and Sukumari (1991) included the prices of food and fuel, in addition to the price of textiles and per capita consumer expenditure, as variables in their estimation of a complete two-stage model using LES for the period 1960–86. The price elasticity of demand for clothing with respect to the price of food was found to be high. Fuel did not emerge as an important variable.

[34] From the 2nd to the 25th rounds of the NSS.

Chandrasekhar (1981) argued that the cyclical fluctuations in the industry were closely linked to fluctuations in agricultural prices. The increase in the prices of foodgrains was accompanied by a decline in the demand for cloth. The increase in the prices of foodgrains forced the allocation of a greater proportion of income to food, and thus constrained the demand for manufactured goods of the net purchasers of food. However, they also increased the revenues of the net sellers of food (mainly the landlords and the upper section of the peasantry), resulting in an increase in their demand for manufactured goods, including textiles. An inverse relationship between the prices of foodgrains and the demand for textiles, which was true of the Indian economy during the mid-1960s to the late 1970s, indicated that the fall in consumption of the former group outweighed the increase in consumption of the latter. Those who gained from an increase in foodgrain prices constituted a very small proportion of the total population. As the marginal propensity to save of these beneficiaries was higher, they chose to save a larger proportion of income distributed in their favour. Hence, substantial increase in the per capita demand of this class, in order to balance for the fall in the case of a much larger section, could not materialise. Further, the additional income that they spent on consumption was distributed across a range of competing luxuries. Since this class demanded more of the higher valued and processed textiles, even if there was a significant increase in the expenditure on textiles, it did not reflect in a significant increase in the consumption in linear metres.

During the 1980s, although foodgrain production was growing at above 3 per cent per annum, the WPI of foodgrains rose from 35 to 63.5 (with 1993–94 as base), though they remained relatively cheaper in comparison with textiles. The increase in incomes of the poor (who spend a major proportion of their income on food) from 1983 to 1993–94, as a result of a fast reduction in poverty and inequalities, resulted in an increase in their consumption of food. In addition, the decline in public expenditures on health and education meant that they were required to rely on paid services.[35] Those who gained from increase in the prices of foodgrains seem to have already

---

[35] As discussed earlier while explaining the fall in real demand for clothing during this period.

met their clothing requirements. They spend their money on miscellaneous goods and services, like educational and medical expenses and consumer services. This is reflected in the increased demand for miscellaneous goods and services in the NSS data. As a result, the demand for clothing declined during the 1980s. The inverse relationship discussed in the literature between price of foodgrains and demand for clothing held true from the early 1980s to the early 1990s, when the increase in the prices of foodgrains was accompanied by a decline in the per capita demand for clothing in all income groups in the rural and the urban areas.

However, from the early 1990s onwards, prices for foodgrains were generally rising fast (Figure 1.6). The ratio of the WPI for foodgrains to the WPI for all commodities was greater than unity throughout the

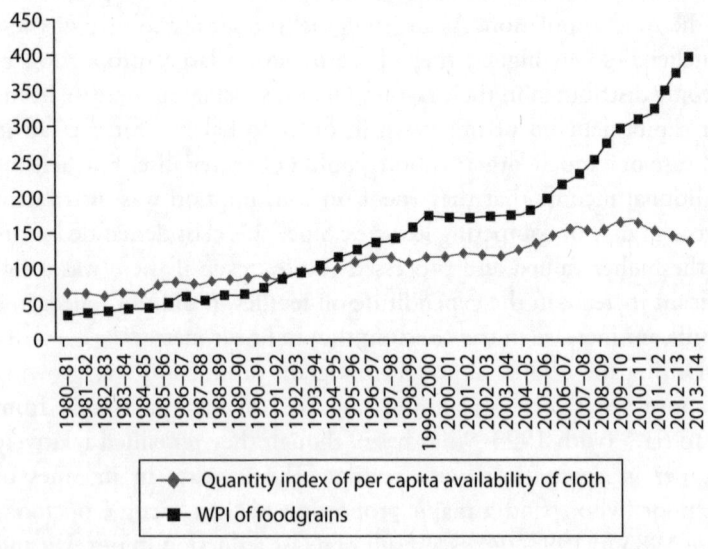

Figure 1.6   Quantity Index of Per Capita Availability of Cloth and WPI of Foodgrains with Base Year 1993–94

Sources: Computed based on figures from Office of Economic Advisor, GoI (for figures before 1993–94: *Index Numbers of Wholesale Prices in India*; for figures of 1993–94 onwards: http://www.eaindustry.nic.in/download_data_9394.asp [last accessed on 11 February 2016]) for the WPIs; Office of Textile Commissioner (1996) for figures up to 1984–85 and CITI, *Handbook of Statistics on Textile Industry* (2008) for figures from 1985–86 to 2005–06; and www.txcindia.gov.in for later years for per capita availability of cloth.

period beginning 1992–93. The growth rate of foodgrain production dropped substantially from 3.38 per cent per annum during the 1980s to 1.75 per cent per annum over the 1990s, and was even lower than the population growth rate of 1.9 per cent in the same period. This was largely the result of a decline in real public investment that occurred in agriculture over a long period. Exports and imports of agricultural products were progressively freed during trade liberalisation. The growing integration of Indian agriculture with world markets meant that domestic trends reflected international price movements. The high international prices of agricultural commodities led to increased exports and resulted in rapid increase in the prices of food in the domestic market up to 1996 (Chandrasekhar and Ghosh 2000). However, things changed after the mid-1990s. The international prices of many agricultural commodities, including foodgrains, started declining sharply after agriculture was opened up to free global trade in the post-World Trade Organization (WTO) era and continued to decline till 2000. There was some increase thereafter but till 2005, prices remained lower than what they were at the beginning of WTO era (National Academy of Agricultural Sciences [NAAS] 2006). This was largely a result of increasing subsidies by presently developed countries.[36] This was the time when the little protection that Indian farmers once enjoyed was lifted following the Uruguay Round Agreement on Agriculture. The process of lifting quantitative restrictions (QRs) was accelerated in 1997 when India lost the balance-of-payment waiver that allowed it to maintain restrictive trade practices and, by 2001, the process was complete. Almost all agricultural products can now be imported subject to a tariff and to sanitary and phytosanitary standards. Since then, tariffs have been lowered continuously—import duties were scrapped in 2007 and 2008 in a number of cases, including for wheat, rice, pulses, and crude vegetable oil (Ministry of Agriculture various years).

With the withdrawal of quantity restrictions and reduction in tariff, there was a surge of cheap subsidised imports of agricultural commodities like cotton, pulses, sugar, and edible oil into India. The dumping of these agricultural commodities reduced domestic prices after the mid-1990s, which affected the growth of foodgrain

[36] Explained in detail in Chapter 2, 'Availability and Cost of Raw Materials'.

production. Indeed, the domestic prices of agricultural commodities declined in the domestiç market despite the reduction in their domestic production. As a result, high levels of minimum support prices were offered to the farmers to provide the incentive to produce more in the later years of the 1990s, which not only pushed up procurement of foodgrains but also increased the food subsidy bill. This ultimately led to subsequent increases in central issue prices of food, which affected the offtake from the public distribution system (PDS). The combination of more procurement with falling offtake from the PDS resulted in high levels of public foodgrain stocks and rising open market prices (Chandrasekhar and Ghosh 2000).

Those who benefited from the fast-rising prices of foodgrains, the rural rich including landlords and upper peasantry, recorded only a small increase[37] in their per capita real demand for clothing, indicating that their demand for clothing has almost reached satiation levels. On the other hand, those who were adversely affected by the rise in prices of foodgrains, quite contrary to what is expected based on the literature relating to earlier periods, did not record any decline in their demand for clothing. Rising foodgrain prices neither led to the allocation of a greater proportion of income to food nor did it constrain the demand for manufactured goods, including clothing, of a large section of population who constituted net purchasers of food. The increasing incomes and lowering of the prices of textiles seem to have more than balanced the fall in demand for clothing due to increase in the prices of foodgrains among the majority of the population. The NSS data indicate that the increase in demand for clothing is not limited to a small rich section of landlords and the upper section of peasantry, but is quite widespread and characterises all sections of the population. This is not to deny that increasing relative prices of foodgrains adversely affected the poor. Some of them were forced to reduce their expenditure on even the prime necessity, food. It is to argue that, overall, increasing relative prices of foodgrains did not impose constraints on these sections increasing demand for the products of the textile industry as they did during the mid-1960s to the 1980s. The inverse relationship between the prices

---

[37] Their real MPCE on clothing increased by about Rs 1.5.

of foodgrains and demand for textiles that had been observed for the Indian economy during previous decades, did not seem to hold during the period from the early 1990s to 2010–11 (Figure 1.6). However, in the more recent period, prices of foodgrains increased at a much higher rate. This increase in prices of foodgrains, during times when growth rate of income decelerated and the decline in the relative prices of textiles also slowed down, seems to have constrained the demand for clothing.

* * *

Thus, the analysis of trends in domestic demand of the Indian textile industry suggests that there has been a reversal of the long-term declining trend after the early 1990s. Much of the decline during period 1, from 1983 to 1993–94, was accounted for by the rich in the rural and the urban areas, who chose to save a large proportion of their income.[38] Further, they increased their spending across a range of competing luxuries, like consumer services, goods for personal care, and amusement expenditure. Textile, being a necessity, did not observe any increase in demand by the rich. Increase in privatisation of the essential services, like health and education, affected the expenditure on clothing of the medium and lower income sections of population. Higher prices of textiles also restricted the clothing demands of these groups. Overall, a slowly growing economy during period 1 could not deliver increased demand.

Though the growing demand for T&C since the early 1990s seems to be true of all expenditure groups, it was led by the rich and the middle income groups. The increase in demand was mainly driven by the rising incomes and the fall in the prices of textiles. The lowered prices of synthetic fibres and filament yarns due to tariff reductions resulted in an increase in their use by the fabric producers. The increased demand led to an expansion in the domestic capacities for producing synthetic fibres and filament yarns, which ultimately led to a much lower relative price of synthetic fabrics which were

---

[38] Their real average overall MPCE increased by less than half per cent per annum during period 1.

widely available domestically. However, demand declined in the recent period as the growth of incomes decelerated and fall in the relative prices of textiles slowed down.

The fast rising prices of foodgrains did not constrain the growing demand for T&C during 1990–91 to 2010–11. The increasing incomes and lowered prices of textiles seem to have more than balanced the fall in demand for clothing due to increased prices of foodgrains. The inverse relationship between the prices of foodgrains and demand for textiles that had been observed for Indian economy during the previous decades, did not hold during this period. The trend seems to be changing in the recent years.

2

Availability and Cost of Raw Materials

The revival of growth in the Indian textile industry since the early 1990s was accompanied by significant changes in the fibre mix used in cloth production. Cotton, which had dominated the industry until then, was no longer the dominant textile fibre. The share of cotton in fabric production, which had come down from about 70 per cent in the 1980s to about 65 per cent in the early 1990s, fell further to 42.6 per cent in 2003–04. However, it started increasing thereafter. The share of cellulosic fibre in the man-made fibres (MMFs) used also came down from 43–7 per cent in the early 1990s to 23–5 per cent by 2005–06 (Indian Cotton Mills Federation [ICMF], *Handbook of Statistics on Cotton Textile Industry* 2004; Confederation of Indian Textile Industry [CITI], *Handbook of Statistics on Textile Industry* 2008).[1] Thus, there was a significant increase in the use of synthetic fibre. The movements in the prices of cotton and non-cotton fibres during the period played a crucial role in bringing about changes in the mix of fibres demanded and produced, away from cotton towards non-cotton and blended textiles. This chapter analyses the movements in the prices of cotton and non-cotton fibres and yarns since 1980–81. An attempt has been made

[1] CITI was formerly called the Indian Cotton Mills Federation (ICMF). The broad basing of the erstwhile ICMF led to CITI. ICMF published *Handbook of Statistics on Cotton Textile Industry*. CITI publishes *Handbook of Statistics on Textile Industry*.

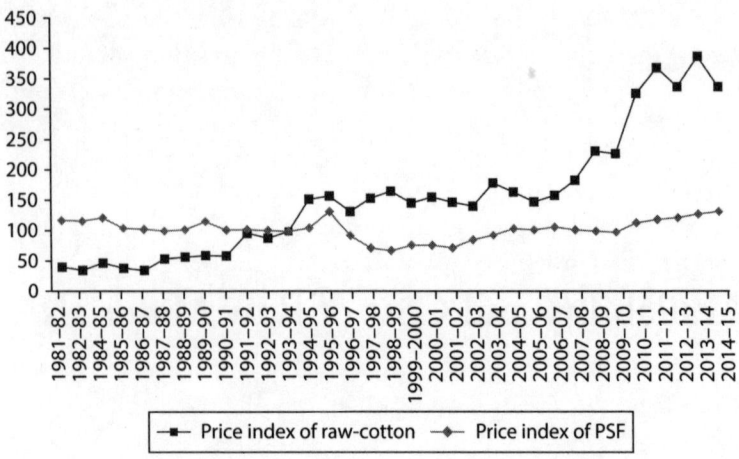

Figure 2.1   Wholesale Price Indices of Fibres with Base Year 1993–94
Sources: Office of Economic Advisor, GoI (for figures before 1993–94: *Index Numbers of Wholesale Prices in India*; for figures of 1993–94 onwards: http://www. eaindustry.nic.in/download_data_9394.asp [last accessed on 11 February 2016]).

to identify the various determinants of the prices of these fibres and to analyse their impact on the relative price movements during the period.

While the price of raw cotton rose after 1980, the prices of synthetic fibres fell considerably after the mid-1990s (Figure 2.1). The Wholesale Price Index (WPI) for raw cotton (with base year 1993–94) increased to 166.9 in 1998–99. The WPI for polyester staple fibre (PSF), on the other hand, came down to 68 in the same year. Though the prices of synthetic fibres increased afterwards, they remained much lower when compared to the prices of cotton. As a result, cotton yarn remained consistently more expensive when compared with the prices of synthetic yarn since the 1980s. The WPI for cotton yarn (with 1993–94 as base year) increased from 141.8 in 1998–99 and to 299.3 by 2014–15. The WPI for polyester yarn declined to 54.6 in 1998–99 and has been fluctuating around 80 in recent years.

Movement in the Prices of Synthetic Fibres

The synthetic fibre industry is a relatively young industry in India. It began with the production of polyester staple fibre (PSF) in 1965, followed by nylon staple fibre (NSF) in 1971, polypropylene staple fibre in 1977, and acrylic staple fibre (ASF) in 1979. The initial exposure of the Indian markets to synthetic fibres was through imports. Domestic production was encouraged following effective import substitution. The apparent consumption, which was rising slowly up to the mid-1980s, picked up somewhat thereafter. The industry faced several problems initially. The prices of synthetic fibres produced in India were much higher in comparison to the prices at which these were available in the international market. The domestic ex-factory price of PSF in 1978 stood at Rs 27.23 per kg when the cost, insurance, and freight (CIF) import price was Rs 11.07 per kg. In 1981, it increased to Rs 40 per kg against the CIF price of Rs 14 per kg; and in 1982, it stood at Rs 38 per kg when the CIF price had fallen to Rs 9.56 per kg (Dhar 1984).

Thus, the synthetic fibre industry was growing under the umbrella of protection. The quantitative restrictions (QRs) were imposed on the imports of synthetic fibres as the domestic producers could not compete with the producers of synthetic fibres in the international market. There was a shift from a regime of QRs to one based on tariffs in 1977. This necessitated higher duties on imports of synthetic fibres, in order to protect domestic producers. The rates of duty had been going up. In addition to the basic import duty and the auxiliary duty, there was also a countervailing duty (CVD), which was equal to the excise duty. For example, the total effective customs duty on PSF, which was 100 per cent in the early 1970s, was increased to 165 per cent by 1981–82, which was further increased to 190 per cent ad valorem plus Rs 9 per kg and a CVD of Rs 25 per kg by 1987–88. The customs duty on polyester filament yarn (PFY), which was 100–10 per cent in the early 1970s, was increased to 205 per cent and a CVD of Rs 78.75 per kg by 1981–82, which was further increased to 225 per cent plus a CVD of Rs 83.75 per kg by 1987–88 (Department of Chemicals and Petrochemicals 1993). Besides this, excise duty was also imposed on the domestic production of synthetic fibres, on the ground that they were inputs into what were essentially luxury fabrics, catering to the needs of the upper income groups. During the first half of the 1980s, the excise duties on PSF and PFY were as high as Rs 45 per kg and Rs 78.75 per kg respectively, which came down after the mid-1980s (Department of Chemicals and Petrochemicals 1993). Though the customs duty on synthetic fibres started coming down after 1987–88,

Table 2.1   Price Comparisons of PSF (1.5D), Rs/kg

Year	Ex-factory price of PSF	Market price of PSF	International CIF price	Landed cost
1985–86	60.0	85.0	20.0	88.9
1986–87	47.5	72.5	14.0	73.9
1987–88	45.5	70.5	16.1	80.5
1988–89	45.3	61.0	18.4	74.1
1989–90	64.6	81.0	19.5	78.0
1990–91	55.4	68.0	18.9	74.6

Source: Department of Chemicals and Petrochemicals (1993: 56).
Note: D stands for Denier.

Table 2.2   Price Comparisons of PFY, Rs/kg

Year	Ex-factory price	Market price	International CIF price	Landed cost
1986–87	81.3	165.0	20.9	166.5
1987–88	93.8	177.5	20.5	150.5
1988–89	75.9	132.0	24.9	132.2
1989–90	99.1	158.0	28.1	144.5
1990–91	104.0	170.0	34.4	162.4

Source: Department of Chemicals and Petrochemicals (1993: 56).

it remained high until 1991–92. This provided adequate protection to the domestic producers by raising the landed cost (inclusive of duties) of the imported synthetic fibres above their CIF price. The prices in the domestic oligopolised market were set at levels almost equal to the landed cost of imports of these synthetic fibres (Tables 2.1 and 2.2).

However, despite this protection, the domestic synthetic fibre industry grew at a slower pace during the 1970s and 1980s. According to *Manmade Fibres Industry Report*, published by INFAC in March 1995, '[t]here have been two three-year waves of capacity addition in the PSF industry.' The first wave, in the 1972–75 period, seems to have occurred as a response of the industry to the New Industrial Licensing Policy of 1970, when new undertakings with investment up to Rs 10 million were exempted from licensing requirements. The new plants which were set up during this period were of small size. They included Calico (1974), ICI (1965), JK Synthetics (1972), Indian Oil Corporation Ltd (IOCL) (1973), and Swadeshi Polytex (1975).[2] The second wave of capacity creation took place in the 1986–89 period. There was some progress towards deregulation of the industry during the 1980s. The NTP (1985) provided greater flexibility in the use of various fibres and projected strong growth prospects for the industry. As a result, the existing players expanded their capacities and new units were set up. New capacities included Reliance (1986), Bongaigaon Refinery & Petrochemicals Ltd (BRPL) (1988), India Polyfibres (1987), JCT Fibres (1989), and Orissa Synthetics (1987). The ICIL (1989), Swadeshi Polytex (1988 and 1989), JCT (1990), and IOCL (1985–86 and 1989) expanded their capacities during this period (INFAC 1995).[3]

The consumption of polyester was modest in the 1960s and 1970s and cellulosic staple fibres dominated the MMF industry up to the first half of the 1980s. However, the growth after the mid-1980s was led by polyester, which was superior in properties. With the growth of the petrochemical industry, the raw materials for synthetics, which turned cheaper, were more easily available than natural wood, which is a non-renewable resource. Further, a wide range of modifications were possible using chemical formulations to generate polymeric fibres suitable for specific applications.

Although the industry was undergoing recession with overall demand for textiles decelerating or stagnating during the pre-1993–94 period,[4] signs of increasing preference for 100 per cent synthetic and blended textiles were observed since the 1970s, which reflected a shift away from cotton towards other textiles. In his study relating to the period 1974–83, Goswami (1985) observed shifts distributed across the top three quarters of households in both rural and urban areas, in spite of large price differential between cotton on the one hand, and synthetic and blended cloth on the other. However, cotton continued

[2] Years in brackets signify when the respective companies expanded their capacity.

[3] Years in brackets signify when the respective companies expanded their capacity.

[4] For details, see Chapter 1, 'Trends in Domestic Demand and Their Implications'.

to dominate, accounting for about 74 per cent of the quantity of textiles purchased across all income groups even in 1983. The lower the household income, the greater was the share of cotton textiles in total cloth purchased. Clearly, the inherent characteristics of synthetics, like durability and wash and wear, seem to have started attracting the consumers. But due to the much higher prices of polyester compared to cotton, the shift remained limited until the mid-1990s. Synthetic textiles till then were considered as items of luxury, which could be afforded mainly by the richer section of society.

The limited demand for synthetic textiles seems to have inhibited the fast growth of the synthetic fibre industry during the period prior to the mid-1990s. Investments were risky due to the limited size of the market. High capital costs in the production of synthetics resulted in plant sizes which were far short of the minimum viable capacity. Inefficient production of synthetic fibres at much smaller scale by the domestic producers led to much higher costs (and then prices) compared to the international producers. The only exception to this experience in the Indian MMFs sector was Reliance Industries Ltd. (RIL), which started as a relatively small unit producing polyester/nylon knitted fabrics in the mid-1960s and accelerated its growth in the late 1970s and 1980s when it started the production of PFY, PSF, purified terephthalic acid (PTA), and paraxylene (INFAC 1995).

The second wave of capacity creation, which occurred during the late 1980s, led to a sharp increase in capacity, where capacity referred to the maximum output that could be produced per year under 'normal working conditions' specified in terms of 'a number of working days in a year' and 'a particular number of shifts working per day' depending on the normal practice of operation in the industry.[5] However, a sharp increase in capacity during the period 1986–89, without a proportionate increase in production, in view of limited demand, led to a fall in capacity utilisation, measured as the actual production as a proportion of installed capacity. According to the Textile Commissioner Office's figures on production and installed capacity, capacity utilisation in

[5] As measured by the Office of the Textile Commissioner (National Council of Applied Economic Research 1966, cited in Chandrasekhar 1981: 172–3).

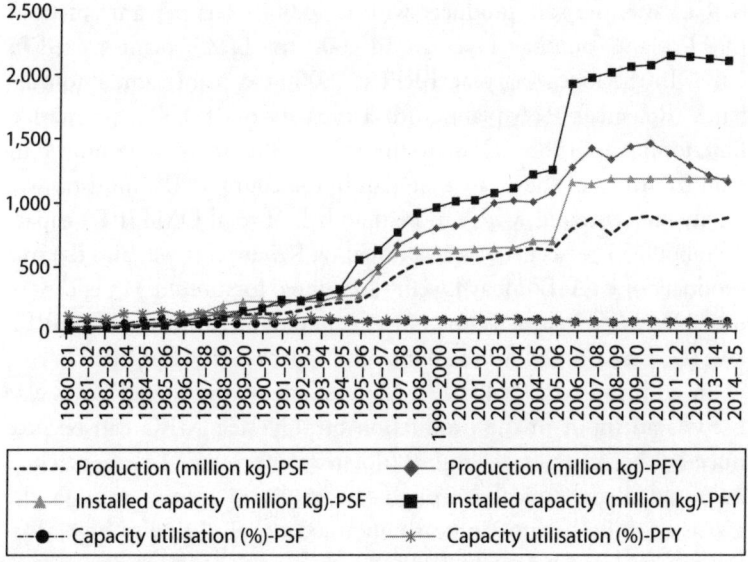

Figure 2.2   Production, Installed Capacity, and Capacity Utilisation of PSF and PFY

Sources: Office of the Textile Commissioner, in CITI, *Handbook of Statistics on Textile Industry* (2008), for 1980–81 to 2005–06; and http://www.texmin.nic.in/ermiu/mmf1.pdf for PSF and http://www.texmin.nic.in/ermiu/mmf2.pdf for PFY (last accessed on 15 February 2009 for 2006–07 and 2007–08; last accessed on 3 December 2013 for 2008–09; and last accessed on 3 August 2015 for later years).

case of PSF fell from about 99 per cent in 1985–86 to about 55 per cent in the late 1980s. For PFY, the fall was from 156 per cent to 99 per cent during the same period (Figure 2.2).

In addition to limited demand, the synthetic fibre industry faced problems with respect to the availability of raw materials at competitive prices during the 1970s and 1980s. Dimethyl terephthalate (DMT) and PTA are alternative raw materials for the production of polyesters, which require paraxylene as the major input in their production, which, in turn, requires naphtha for its production. The production of DMT also requires methanol. The market for these raw materials in the country was an oligopolised market. While DMT was being produced since 1973, the domestic production of PTA started much later in 1988. Until 1984–85, Indian Petrochemicals Corporation Ltd

(IPCL) was the sole producer with a 30,000 tons per annum (tpa) DMT plant. Bombay Dyeing's 145,000 tpa DMT plant started in 1984. In the following year, BRPL's 45,000 tpa plant came into existence. Reliance's PTA plant, with a capacity of 100,000 tpa, started functioning in 1988. Thus by the mid-1990s, there were only four manufacturers of these raw materials in the country. The industry was highly concentrated, where more than half of total DMT/PTA capacity (about 53 per cent) was accounted by Reliance. It was also the sole producer of PTA. Bombay Dyeing accounted for around 31 per cent of total DMT/PTA capacity and 66 per cent of DMT capacity. The BRPL and IPCL accounted for the remaining capacities (INFAC 1995).

In addition to DMT/PTA, Monoethylene glycol (MEG) is also used as an input in the production of polyester. MEG can be produced either as a petrochemical (downstream to an ethylene cracker) or as an alcochemical (through the molasses route); though the molasses route became increasingly uneconomical due to high alcohol and molasses prices. In 1988–89, there were only a few producers of MEG in the country: IPCL–Baroda, National Organic Chemical Industries Ltd (NOCIL), and India Glycols. Demand for MEG increased during the 1980s, in line with growth in production of PSF and PFY, whose consumption grew during the period. However, the production of MEG grew more slowly in the 1980s.[6] The MEG capacity was far lower than demand during this period. Despite the demand–supply gap, the domestic producers of MEG did not expand MEG production. They expanded capacities in other lines of production, which were more profitable.[7] The average capacity utilisation in MEG production remained low (75 per cent). A large proportion of domestic demand, therefore, used to be met through imports. Large-scale imports took place, especially in the late 1980s.

[6] While the production of PSF grew at 21 per cent per annum and that of PFY at 35 per cent per annum during the 1980s, the production of MEG grew only at 8.43 per cent per annum. From 1979–80 to 1985–86, the consumption of MEG grew at a rate of 23 per cent per annum, while the production grew at about 10 per cent per annum. See Department of Chemicals and Petrochemicals (1986) for consumption and Association of Synthetic Fibre Industry (ASFI various years) for production of MEG.

[7] For example, ethylene oxide.

In 1990–91, imports accounted for more than 70 per cent of MEG consumption in India (INFAC 1995). The number of manufacturers of MEG increased to six by the mid-1990s. MEG capacity increased sharply in the early 1990s when IPCL's Nagothane, RIL's Hazira, and subsequently SM Dyechem's plants were set up. Domestic prices of MEG were fixed at low levels during the early 1980s. In 1981–82, the ex-factory price of MEG[8] was Rs 13,560 per metric ton, which increased to Rs 16,250 per metric ton in the year 1987–88. Prices went up much faster afterwards, to around Rs 27,209 per metric ton in 1989–90 and to Rs 33,001 per metric ton in 1991–92.

While earlier the main aim of the policy was to ensure adequate supplies of the raw materials through imports, there was a fundamental change in the direction of import policy during the mid-1980s when the main thrust was towards protecting the domestic DMT industry. Until 1984–85, imports of DMT and PTA were under the Open General Licence (OGL).[9] By the end of 1985, DMT and PTA were put on the Restricted Permissible List. Only those units which had switched over exclusively to PTA were permitted to import PTA (Bureau of Industrial Costs and Prices [BICP] 1997). The PTA was a substitute for domestically produced DMT, whose consumption was fully based on imports until 1988–89. Finally, in order to curb import, the standard customs duties on DMT and PTA were raised from 140 per cent before 1985 to 190 per cent by 1986–87, due to which their imports became uneconomical (Department of Chemicals and Petrochemicals 1993).

Raw materials of PSF account for about 65 per cent of the price realisation (BICP 1997). Hence, price movements of these raw materials have a direct and significant impact on prices. The difference between the indigenous and international prices of major raw materials, for example, DMT, MEG, and PTA, was one important factor accounting for the difference between the domestic ex-factory and the international CIF prices of synthetic fibres during the 1970s and 1980s. According to the Expert Group on Petrochemicals (EGP),

---

[8] Calculated as the average of the monthly ex-factory prices based on figures from ASFI (2000).

[9] OGL category includes commodities which do not require an import licence but can be freely imported on payment of the specified tariffs.

Table 2.3   Prices of Raw Materials, Rs/kg

Year	DMT		PTA		MEG		Paraxylene	
	Ex-factory	CIF	Ex-factory	CIF	Ex-factory	CIF	Ex-factory	CIF
1985–86	19.0	7.2	–	8.1	14.5	5.6	–	5.6
1986–87	21.5	7.1	–	7.2	15.5	5.2	–	5.4
1987–88	21.0	6.9	–	7.9	15.9	4.5	–	8.3
1988–89	21.0	8.8	30.3	11.4	15.9	10.9	23.3	10.0
1989–90	32.0	9.3	32.3	13.1	17.4	13.2	22.0	11.6
1990–91	28.0	10.0	28.4	11.6	25.0	6.9	22.0	7.3

Source: Department of Chemicals and Petrochemicals (1993: 62–4).

Department of Chemicals and Petrochemicals (1993), the cost structure of Indian PSF units varied substantially from that of PSF units located in the Asia-Pacific or in advanced countries. For a 60,000 tpa plant, production costs of PSF in these countries were found to be around Rs 36 per kg, as compared to Rs 72 per kg in India. The significant difference in costs was due to the prices of raw materials.

Up to the end of the 1980s, the average domestic price of feedstock of PSF was consistently higher than the international CIF prices (Table 2.3). As a result, in the case of PSF, nearly one-half of the 200 per cent differential between domestic ex-factory prices and the CIF value of imports was explained by differentials in the cost of raw material. Further, though the excise duty imposed on DMT was nil, it was equal to 8 per cent on MEG in the early 1980s, which continued to increase and was as high as 15 per cent by the end of the 1980s (Department of Chemicals and Petrochemicals 1993). While the shortage of domestically available raw materials led to a higher ex-factory price of polyester compared to the international CIF price, the imposition of tariffs on the raw material continued to raise further the costs of producing PSF, resulting ultimately in higher market prices, the ceiling to which was provided by the landed cost of PSF. Thus, in addition to limited demand, the shortfall in domestic availability of raw materials and heavy tariffs seem to have restricted the growth of the synthetic fibre industry during the 1970s and 1980s.

The overall scenario before the mid-1980s led to a situation where domestic market prices of polyester fibre were 450–600 per cent higher than the CIF prices of comparable international products. Out of this, a major part (around 250–350 per cent) was accounted by the excise duty on the product. Differences in prices paid for raw materials accounted for another 90–120 per cent of the price differential. Utilities and conversion cost accounted for a relatively small share of the difference in domestic and international prices (Department of Chemicals and Petrochemicals 1993). Though the excise duties were lowered from Rs 45 per kg in the early 1980s to Rs 25 per kg by the end of 1985, and further to Rs 16.44 per kg by March 1989 after the NTP, 1985, the market price of PSF remained high and did not change significantly[10] from 1980 to 1993. Users continued to complain of high domestic prices and demanded cheaper imports during this period. Government commissions were instituted to assess the real cost of production and the extent of profits made by the producers.

Things seem to have changed after the early 1990s when there was a substantial increase in the demand for textiles. Although rising incomes and falling relative prices of textiles during the period led to an increase in demand for all types of textiles, much of the increase occurred for synthetic textiles, especially polyester. The fall in customs duties on the intermediates and raw materials for synthetic textiles during the period of liberalisation facilitated the growth in demand for synthetics and resulted in inter-fibre competition that raised the share of polyester in consumption, namely cotton. This increased competition, in turn, lowered the prices of PSF and PFY in the domestic market since the mid-1990s. This led to a substantial increase in the demand for PSF and PFY for producing synthetic fabrics, which became cheaper in comparison with cotton fabrics and no longer remained items of luxury which could be afforded mainly by the rich. The increase in demand for polyester encouraged expansion in its domestic capacity and greater capacity utilisation.[11] This was the third wave of capacity build-up after the early 1970s and the late 1980s, when the capacity grew fast. This resulted in a substantial

[10] Varying around Rs 80 per kg, except for short periods of excess supplies when the prices fell, for example, from Rs 81 per kg in 1985 to Rs 67 per kg in 1987 (ASFI 2000).

[11] See Chapter 1, 'Trends in Domestic Demand and their Implications'.

growth in domestic production (Figure 2.2), which was made widely available at lower prices after the mid-1990s.

For example, the total import duty on PSF, which was 150 per cent ad valorem plus Rs 20.13 per kg specific in 1991–92, was gradually lowered to 47.76 per cent in 2000–01 and further to 8.24 per cent in 2007–08.[12] This led to continuously falling prices of PSF[13] since the mid-1990s. The market price of PSF (1.2D),[14] which was above Rs 100 per kg in the mid-1990s,[15] registered a sharp decline. It fell to Rs 52.67 per kg in 1998–99, and then fluctuated between Rs 46 to Rs 70 per kg up to 2007–08. The reduced price of PSF seems to have pushed up its demand after the mid-1990s. Accordingly, there was an expansion in the capacity for PSF during 1995–96 to 1997–98 and then again, during the year 2006–07 (Figure 2.2). As a result of the fast growth of demand during the period, the increase in capacity for PSF was accompanied by increasing capacity utilisation. According to the figures from the Office of the Textile Commissioner, the capacity utilisation which had declined to 50–8 per cent during the second half of the 1980s, increased substantially to 77–95 per cent during 1995–96 to 2007–08 (Figure 2.2). Overall, this resulted in a substantial growth of production of PSF at an average annual rate of about 11.88 per cent per annum between 1995–96 and 2007–08.

Similarly, the total import duty on PFY, which was 150 per cent ad valorem plus Rs 87.5 per kg specific in 1991–92, was gradually lowered to about 71 per cent by 2002–03 and further to 8.24 per cent in 2007–08, resulting in a continuous fall in the price of PFY after the mid-1990s. The market price of PFY,[16] that was above

---

[12] It has remained at that level in recent years. For duties, refer to CITI, annual reports and ASFI (various years).

[13] Average Mumbai market prices of fibre (ASFI various years).

[14] Denier (D) is a unit of measurement that is used to determine the fibre thickness of individual threads or filaments used in the creation of textiles. Lower the denier number, finer the material and higher the denier number, coarser the material.

[15] Exceptionally high prices in 1994–95 and 1995–96 were due to switch over from specific to ad valorem basis.

[16] Average Mumbai market prices, TECOYA TREND (ASFI various years).

Rs 150 per kg during the first half of the 1990s, observed a sharp decline during the mid-1990s and reached Rs 75 per kg by 2000–01 and stood at Rs 79.35 per kg in 2007–08. The consequent increase in demand led to an expansion in the capacity for PFY at a rate of about 8.5 per cent per annum during 1995–96 to 2005–06, which then grew substantially in the year 2006–07. As a result, the production of PFY grew fast at an average annual rate of about 11.70 per cent per annum during the period (Figure 2.2).

The production declined substantially in 2008–09 as a result of global crisis both for PSF and PFY. It recovered soon and was at its peak in 2010–11. Overall, the growth was slow as far as production of ASF is concerned.[17] Polypropylene staple fibre also emerged as a new fibre during the 1990s and registered growth in production. But it remained far below the installed capacity. The production of nylon filament yarn[18] declined after the mid-1990s. Polypropylene filament yarn, which appeared in the 1990s, registered some increase in its production. Overall, polyester dominated demand and, therefore, the production of synthetic fibres/filament yarn after 1990.

The increased domestic production of polyester after the middle of the 1990s reduced the country's dependence on its imports (Table 2.4). The share of imports in total domestic consumption of PSF, which had crossed 15 per cent before the middle of the 1990s, came down to about 2 per cent by the year 2003–04 and varied around that level up to 2009–10. The share of imports in total domestic consumption of PFY declined from 11.8 per cent in 2002–03 to around 2.11 per cent by 2009–10.

Another impact of the fast growth of the polyester fibre industry after the mid-1990s and the associated economies of scale was that the ex-factory prices of domestically produced synthetic fibre, which far exceeded the international prices during the 1970s and 1980s, registered a fall relative to the latter. A comparison of the domestic ex-factory prices of PSF (1.5D) and ASF (3D) with their CIF prices shows that domestic prices of these fibres were higher than their international prices after 1990, but the difference

[17] See Table B.1 in Appendix B on production of other synthetic fibres.
[18] See Table B.2 in Appendix B on production of other synthetic filament yarns.

Table 2.4   Share of Imports in Total Domestic Consumption of Polyester (%)

Year	PSF	PFY
1991–92	6.06	1.84
1993–94	3.27	7.11
1995–96	15.74	5.33
1997–98	6.44	0.44
1999–2000	2.57	9.19
2001–02	4.86	9.10
2002–03	4.52	11.80
2003–04	1.90	8.50
2005–06	2.53	8.45
2007–08	2.83	6.37
2009–10	1.96	2.11
2011–12	6.24	2.12
2013–14	6.04	2.83

Sources: Computed based on figures from the Office of the Textile Commissioner, in ICMF, *Handbook of Statistics on Cotton Textile Industry* (1996, 2004) for 1991–92 to 2002–03; and http://www.texmin.nic.in/ermiu/mmf1.pdf for PSF and http://www.texmin.nic.in/ermiu/mmf2.pdf for PFY (last accessed on 11 January 2009 for 2003–04 to 2007–08 and last accessed on 4 December 2013 for later years).

between the two is getting narrower in the case of PSF after the mid-1990s (Table 2.5). Polyester staple fibre, which had been in the negative list as a restricted item in the export–import policy for 1992–97, was placed under OGL with effect from February 1995. Since import of intermediates is under OGL, the domestic prices, by and large, aligned themselves with the trends in international prices. There were fluctuations in the international prices of these fibres during the 1990s and afterwards, and fluctuations in the domestic prices corresponded roughly to these fluctuations in the international prices.

During liberalisation, not only the customs duties, as discussed earlier, but also the excise duties were lowered on synthetic fibres and their raw materials. Therefore, a more meaningful analysis of price movements requires a comparison of market prices (ex-factory prices including total effective excise duty) of domestically produced fibres and landed prices (CIF prices including total effective customs duty) of imported fibres. The specific excise duty imposed on PSF

Table 2.5 Comparison of Domestic Ex-factory and International CIF Prices of Synthetic Fibres, Rs/kg

Year	Ex-factory price of PSF (1.5D)	CIF price of PSF (1.5D)	Ex-factory price of ASF (3D)	CIF price of ASF (3D)
1993–94	63.93	32.93	81.30	60.64
1995–96	84.71	59.09	90.25	75.26
1997–98	46.55	35.31	86.25	63.18
1999–2000	52.46	33.41	74.25	50.87
2001–02	39.09	34.00	73.50	50.41
2003–04	50.95	44.21	81.30	60.84
2005–06	56.22	52.68	NA	84.12
2006–07	59.03	49.43	109.26	83.68

Sources: Computed based on figures from ASFI (various years) for prices; and RBI (2013) for exchange rates.

Notes: 1. Annual ex-factory prices of fibres are calculated from the annual market prices after adjusting for excise duty.

2. Annual CIF prices of imported fibres are calculated as the average of the monthly prices.

3. Exchange rates are used to convert CIF prices from dollars into rupees.

was reduced from Rs 16.44 per kg in 1989–90 to Rs 12.65 per kg in 1993–94. Since 1994–95, an ad valorem duty at the rate of 23 per cent replaced specific duty. In case of ASF also, the excise duty, which was increasing in the early 1990s, was replaced by an ad valorem duty at the same rate of 23 per cent. The excise duty on PSF and ASF was then lowered gradually to 18.4 per cent in 1999–2000 and then, subsequently, to 8.24 per cent in March 2007. As a result of imposition of excise duties, the market price of these fibres was higher than the ex-factory price. The excise duty imposed on the domestically produced raw materials was also lowered from 1997–98 onwards. The rates on all the inputs were lowered from 20 per cent in 1996–97 to 16 per cent in 1999–2000, which were lowered subsequently to 8.16 per cent for DMT and PTA and to 12.24 per cent for MEG in March 2006. Overall, the excise duty on polyester and its inputs have been lowered, but the extent of the fall was not as significant as it was for the customs duties, which registered a much greater fall during the period.

Table 2.6   Market and Landed Prices of Synthetic Fibres (Rs/kg)

Year	Market price of PSF (1.5D)	Landed price of PSF (1.5D)	Market price of ASF (3D)	Landed price of ASF (3D)
1993–94	76.58	73.58	96.25	127.13
1994–95	102.33	92.40	89.79	123.20
1995–96	104.19	105.40	111.01	134.23
1996–97	72.53	71.57	105.78	109.51
1997–98	56.19	57.53	104.36	102.95
1998–99	52.51	49.91	91.96	86.72
1999–2000	62.11	55.54	87.62	84.57
2000–01	61.45	56.36	98.53	94.64
2001–02	46.28	50.24	86.73	74.49
2002–03	55.77	65.22	88.85	94.68
2003–04	60.33	65.32	95.93	89.90
2004–05	67.06	73.72	112.29	105.66
2005–06	65.40	69.34	NA	110.72
2006–07	68.66	62.68	118.00	99.28

Sources: Computed based on figures from ASFI (various years) for prices and CITI, Annual Reports (various years) for duties.
Notes: 1. The landed prices of imported fibres are calculated from their CIF prices after adjusting for their total effective customs duties.
2. The market prices are not available for PSF (1.5D) after 2006–07.

A comparison of market prices and landed prices of imported fibres (Table 2.6) shows that the reduction in tariffs has reduced the gap between the domestic and international prices, both in case of PSF and ASF required to produce synthetic fabrics. Any increase in the tariffs increases the price at which these fibres are made available to the producers of man-made fabric and vice versa. It is evident that the duty structure is devised to bring the market prices of the fibres closer to the landed prices. There are fluctuations in the domestic market prices and landed prices of these fibres. The sudden increase in prices of these fibres after 1994–95 was due to excise duty rationalisation from a specific to ad valorem basis. A steep decline in the market price of PSF in 1996–97, the excise duty remaining unchanged (for this year and/or the last two years), seems to be the result of sudden fall of the price of this product in the international market.

The growth in the domestic production of polyester during the period was made possible by ensuring easy availability of raw materials required in the production of synthetic fibres via increase in their domestic production. The much higher domestic ex-factory prices of DMT and PTA compared to the international CIF prices seem to suggest, at a first glance, that perhaps the domestic production of these raw materials is less efficient compared to the international production or that the domestic producers are not utilising the resources at their disposal as effectively as the producers in the international market. However, since one of the reasons for the high cost (and high price) of these domestically produced raw material is the high cost of paraxylene, their main input, therefore, to account for the differences in the input prices, the domestic resource cost (DRC), which contrasts value added domestically with value added internationally, provides a better measure of efficiency of domestic production of DMT and PTA.

The DRC ratios for DMT and PTA, as calculated by the BICP (1994) for the year 1993–94, showed that if inputs were made available to domestic producers at international prices, domestic production of both DMT and PTA was almost as efficient as international production. The DRC ratio of DMT and PTA varied in the range of 1.04–1.25. However, the domestic production of paraxylene was found to be unfavourable with its DRC ratio varying in the range of 1.87–2.12. One of the reasons for the high cost of domestically produced paraxylene, according to the study, was the high cost of naphtha. The international CIF price of naphtha was Rs 5,670 per metric ton, while the cost of domestic naphtha at the factory site was much higher at Rs 7,216 per metric ton. Domestic price of paraxylene at the then existing domestic prices of naphtha were 45–9 per cent higher than the international prices in 1993–94. The domestic prices were estimated to continue to be higher by 35–9 per cent if naphtha was made available at the international prices. According to this study, another reason for the inefficiencies in paraxylene production was small capacities in comparison to the surplus-producing countries.

Although the domestic production of both DMT and PTA was almost as efficient as the international production, there was a shift in the domestic production of raw materials towards PTA since the

1990s. This was due to a clear shift towards increased use of PTA in the production of polyester in place of DMT—a shift which was similar to the trend in the rest of the world. The preference for PTA was because of product quality and efficiency norms in polyester production, which are superior when PTA is used as feedstock. The growing popularity of PTA was due to a variety of factors. First, the molecular weight of DMT (194) is much higher than that of PTA (166): nearly 17 per cent more DMT in terms of weight is required per ton of polyester. Second, since the yield of PTA from paraxylene (94 per cent) is much higher than the yield of DMT (87 per cent), the requirement of paraxylene per ton of polymer is about 7.5 per cent lower (INFAC 1995). Third, PTA requires to be combined with a lower volume of MEG per ton, leading to a further saving in polyester raw material costs. Fourth, the energy costs per ton of PTA are estimated to be about 40 per cent less than the energy cost for every ton of DMT produced. And finally, a polyester plant based on DMT requires a methanol recovery unit, making it more expensive than one based on PTA. Overall, PTA has a tremendous competitive advantage vis-à-vis DMT making it a more acceptable raw material (INFAC 1995).

The increasing preference for PTA over DMT in domestic production was reflected in the growth of installed capacity and the production of these raw materials. While the production of DMT declined fast,[19] the production of PTA grew at about 19.27 per cent per annum from 1995–96 to 2007–08. The production of MEG also grew at a high rate of about 15.17 per cent per annum from 1995–96 to 2007–08. But, there was hardly any increase (from 145,000 tons in 1990–91 to 324,000 tons in 1998–99) in the installed capacity of paraxylene, the production of which was unfavourable with respect to the international production. The consumption of PTA and its main input, paraxylene, grew fast. But the slow growth in the domestic production of paraxylene could not meet its increased demand. As a result, while the dependence on imports declined substantially in the case of PTA and MEG after the mid-1990s, it continued to rise for paraxylene (Table 2.7).

[19] The production of DMT declined at the rate of about -28.72 per cent per annum from 1995–96 to 2007–08 (ASFI various years). See Table B.3 in Appendix B.

The share of imports in the consumption of paraxylene was around 20–35 per cent up to the mid-1990s (Table 2.7). The dependence on imports of paraxylene reached its peak after the mid-1990s when about 70 per cent of the consumption was met by imports.

However, the situation changed by the end of the 1990s when the installed capacity and the production of paraxylene increased substantially. The capacity increased from 1,723 thousand tons in 2000–01 to 2,086 thousand tons in 2006–07, and the production grew at a much higher rate of 7.04 per cent per annum during the period (Department of Chemicals and Petrochemicals 2007). As a result, the share of imports in the consumption declined to about 12 per cent by 2006–07 (Table 2.7).

Since the availability of raw materials, for example, paraxylene, PTA, and MEG, continued to fall short of their growing consumption requirements, imports were permitted under OGL. Therefore,

Table 2.7 Share of Imports in Total Consumption of Raw Materials (%)

Year	Paraxylene	PTA	MEG
1990–91	22.11	18.72	71.82
1992–93	10.10	7.20	13.16
1994–95	33.12	19.69	21.17
1996–97	39.64	49.63	39.94
1998–99	72.86	9.36	7.10
1999–2000	46.15	2.55	10.46
2002–03	14.34	0.07	3.69
2004–05	22.71	1.42	15.93
2006–07	11.65	6.91	16.83
2008–09	12.40	7.91	36.18
2010–11	18.54	18.92	52.04
2011–12	19.56	15.30	40.58
2012–13	24.09	15.66	39.84
2013–14	30.59	21.95	45.04

Sources: Computed based on figures from Department of Chemicals and Petrochemicals (2001: 20–2, 41) up to 1999–2000 and http://chemicals.nic.in/stat0107.pdf (last accessed on 10 February 2009) for 2002–03 and 2004–05 and http://www.chemicals.nic.in/Chemicals%20&%20Petrochemicals%20Statistics%20At%20A%20Glance%20%202014.pdf (last accessed on 17 December 2013) for later years.

the domestic prices of these raw materials tended to be in line with their international prices after accounting for the customs duties. The period since the 1990s saw substantial fall in the customs duty on the raw materials required in the production of polyester. The rates of customs duty were lowered substantially from 191.25 per cent in 1991–92 to 44.77 per cent by 2001–02 for MEG, DMT, and PTA, and further to 5.55 per cent for DMT and PTA by December 2007. The import duty on paraxylene was also reduced from 85 per cent in 1992–93 to 40 per cent in 1993–94, which came down to 9.72 per cent by 2000–01 and down to 0.38 per cent in March 2008.[20] As a result of falling import duties, the difference between the CIF and international landed prices (close to market prices) of raw materials, which was very high during the 1970s and 1980s, narrowed during the 1990s and after.

The growing domestic production of the raw materials since the 1990s was accompanied by the lowering of their ex-factory prices after the mid-1990s. As a result, domestic ex-factory prices of the raw materials like DMT, PTA, and MEG, which were consistently far higher than their international CIF prices up to the early 1990s, fell during the rest of the 1990s. A comparison of the domestic ex-factory and the international CIF prices[21] of DMT, PTA, and MEG since the 1990s indicates that average domestic ex-factory prices, which were almost twice the international CIF prices, declined after the mid-1990s (Table 2.8). For DMT and PTA, the ratio of the ex-factory price to the CIF price was reduced substantially towards the end of the 1990s (Table 2.9). By 2006–07, the ratio for PTA fell to 1.16. It was reduced to 1.02 by 2012–13. In the case of MEG, it declined from 2.44 in the year 1992–93 to 1.32 in 2006–07. Falling ex-factory prices and reduced excise duties on these raw materials of PSF resulted in a fall in the market prices of these raw materials.

The overall impact of the decline in import duties on synthetic fibres as well as on the raw materials required in their production, starting in the 1990s, was that the protection given to the synthetic

---

[20] The duties have remained the same since then (ASFI various years).

[21] Converted into rupees/metric ton using the exchange rate.

Table 2.8 Ex-factory and CIF Prices of Raw Materials (Rs/metric ton)

Year	Annual ex-factory price of DMT	Annual CIF price of DMT	Annual ex-factory price of MEG	Annual CIF price of MEG	Annual ex-factory price of PTA	Annual CIF price of PTA
1992–93	32,666.67	16,537.69	25,625.00	10,510.05	33,625.00	14,369.66
1994–95	42,704.17	24,608.97	37,500.00	16,890.05	49,858.33	25,851.84
1996–97	30,229.17	22,720.00	31,393.75	17,661.25	36,625.00	23,681.46
1998–99	22,500.00	19,615.60	25,245.83	15,908.10	22,991.67	17,810.06
2000–01	28,366.67	21,252.58	36,450.00	23,670.02	33,066.67	21,665.64
2002–03	34,375.00	32,464.98	33,808.33	25,992.15	34,837.50	29,359.63
2004–05	44,420.83	NA	55,416.67	44,995.80	44,141.67	36,230.02
2006–07	NA	NA	48,484.50	36,810.31	44,710.75	38,597.13
2008–09	NA	NA	39,537.5	37,477.35	43,183.33	40,638.48
2010–11	NA	NA	30,400.00	25,992.00	43,100.00	37,255.20
2012–13	NA	NA	59,500	60,123.05	61,500.00	60,123.05

Sources: Computed based on figures from ASFI (various years) for prices; and RBI (2013) for exchange rates.

Notes: 1. Annual prices of the domestic and imported raw materials are constructed as the average of the monthly prices.

2. Prices of imported raw materials are converted from dollars into rupees using the exchange rate.

Table 2.9 Ratio of Domestic Ex-factory to International CIF Prices of Raw Materials of PSF

Year	DMT	MEG	PTA
1992–93	1.98	2.44	NA
1994–95	1.74	2.22	1.93
1996–97	1.33	1.78	1.55
1998–99	1.15	1.59	1.29
2000–01	1.33	1.54	1.53
2002–03	1.06	1.30	1.19
2004–05	NA	1.23	1.21
2006–07	NA	1.32	1.16
2008–09	NA	1.05	1.06
2010–11	NA	1.17	1.16
2012–13	NA	0.99	1.02

Source: Computed from Table 2.8.

fibre industry declined considerably. The effective rate of protection (ERP), which is the ratio of the difference between value added at domestic prices and value added at international prices to the value added at international prices, for producing PSF using PTA and MEG, which was as high as 124 per cent in 1994–95, declined to around 60–5 per cent after the 1990s (Table 2.10). This suggests that after accounting for any duties on inputs, in 1994–95, the value added in the production of PSF, allowable due to the duty structure, was about 124 per cent higher than what it would have been if the international prices of inputs and outputs prevailed. However, there was a substantial fall in this rate during the 1990s and by 2005–06, the ERP was a mere 32 per cent.

The ERP for the production of PSF using DMT and MEG, which was equal to 135 per cent in 1994–95 and increased to 253 per cent in 1998–99, turned negative recently (Table 2.11). The cost of inputs used exceeded the value of output produced via this route both at home and internationally, depicting the unprofitability of using DMT as a substitute for PTA.

Several factors affected the input prices during the 1990s and after: the buoyancy of the polyester market; the international prices and customs duties on DMT and PTA; and prices of their basic inputs.

Table 2.10 ERP in the Production of PSF Using PTA and MEG

Year	Domestic GVA (V* or GVA of producing one kg of PSF at landed prices) (Rs/kg)	Global GVA (V or GVA of producing one kg of PSF at CIF prices) (Rs/kg)	Domestic GVA/ Global GVA (Rs/kg)	ERP or (V*/V)–1	ERP (%)
1994–95	34.76	15.51	2.24	1.24	124
1996–97	28.32	15.70	1.80	0.80	80
1998–99	14.18	7.06	2.01	1.01	101
2000–01	11.81	9.18	1.29	0.29	29
2002–03	11.91	7.32	1.63	0.63	63
2004–05	4.54	3.31	1.37	0.37	37
2005–06	9.73	7.39	1.32	0.32	32

Sources: Computed based on figures from ASFI (various years) for CIF prices; and CITI, Annual Reports (various years) for customs duties.

Notes: 1. One kg of PSF requires 0.9 kg of PTA and 0.4 kg of MEG (as reported in INFAC [1992: 52]).

2. Domestic gross value added (GVA) is calculated using the landed prices of PSF, PTA, and MEG; and Global GVA is calculated using the CIF prices of PSF, PTA, and MEG.

3. The derivation of CIF and landed price of PSF is explained in the notes of Tables 2.5 and 2.6. The derivation of CIF prices of PTA and MEG is explained in the notes of Table 2.8. The derivation of the landed prices of PTA and MEG is explained in the notes of Table 2.12.

Until 1990–91, domestic pricing of DMT and PTA was largely influenced by domestic market conditions and did not respond quickly to changes in international prices. In the early 1990s, domestic prices were lower mainly due to the easy supply conditions and resistance from the polyester market. Later, the variations in the domestic prices of DMT and PTA depended directly on changes in their landed costs (Table 2.12). Domestic prices of MEG, which were fixed at low levels during the early 1980s and went up much faster in the late 1980s up to 1991–92, were also strongly linked to international prices and customs duties.

Table 2.11   ERP in the Production of PSF Using DMT and MEG

Year	Domestic GVA (V* or GVA of producing one kg of PSF at landed prices) (Rs/kg)	Global GVA (V or GVA of producing one kg of PSF at CIF prices) (Rs/kg)	Domestic GVA/ Global GVA	ERP or (V*/V)–1	ERP (%)
1994–95	27.45	11.70	2.35	1.35	135
1996–97	22.71	12.02	1.89	0.89	89
1998–99	5.33	1.51	3.53	2.53	253
2000–01	5.84	5.30	1.10	0.10	10
2002–03	–1.54	–1.97	0.78	–0.22	–22
2003–04	–0.74	–1.42	0.52	–0.48	–48

Sources: Computed based on figures from ASFI (various years) for CIF prices; and CITI, Annual Reports (various years) for customs duties.

Notes: 1. One kg of PSF requires 1.1 kg of DMT and 0.4 kg of MEG (as reported in INFAC [1992: 52]).

2. Domestic GVA is calculated using the landed prices of PSF, DMT, and MEG; and Global GVA is calculated using the CIF prices of PSF, DMT, and MEG.

3. The derivation of CIF and landed price of PSF is explained in the notes of Tables 2.5 and 2.6. The derivation of CIF prices of DMT and MEG is explained in the notes of Table 2.8. The derivation of the landed prices of DMT and MEG is explained in the notes of Table 2.12.

4. As the prices of DMT are not available after 2003–04, the ERP can be calculated up to 2003–04 only.

However, the scenario changed after 2010–11 when polyester became expensive. The average Bombay market price of PSF (1.2D), for example, which varied between Rs 61 per kg and Rs 74 per kg after the middle of the 1990s, increased to Rs 99.16 per kg in 2011–12 and remained high at Rs 98.01 per kg during 2012–13 (ASFI various years). This was mainly due to increase in the prices of raw materials (PTA and MEG) required in the production of polyester (Table 2.8). Further, there were increases in the excise duty on polyester and the raw materials required in its production in the recent period. In order to stimulate the economy after the

Table 2.12 Domestic Market Price and Landed Price of Raw Materials of PSF (Rs/metric ton)

Year	Market price of DMT	Landed price of DMT	Market price of MEG	Landed price of MEG	Market price of PTA	Landed price of PTA
1990–91	33,567.50	NA	26,043.75	NA	NA	NA
1992–93	38,301.67	40,719.10	30,045.31	25,877.85	39,425.31	NA
1994–95	51,245.00	47,249.22	45,000.00	32,428.89	59,830.00	49,635.54
1996–97	36,275.00	34,625.28	37,672.50	26,915.75	43,950.00	36,090.54
1998–99	26,550.00	31,294.73	29,790.08	25,379.78	27,130.17	28,414.16
2000–01	32,905.33	32,690.72	42,282.00	36,409.23	38,357.33	33,326.08
2002–03	39,875.00	32,610.33	39,217.67	37,628.83	40,411.50	42,503.94
2004–05	51,670.31	NA	64,460.66	61,518.30	51,345.97	49,533.70
2006–07	NA	NA	54,419.00	43,742.90	48,359.15	45,806.10
2008–09	NA	NA	44,424.00	39,605.94	46,742.00	45,820.87
2010–11	NA	NA	33,531.00	27,468.35	47,539.00	42,599.77
2011–12	NA	NA	53,698.00	31,827.78	58,827.00	48,519.26
2012–13	NA	NA	66,854.00	63,538.04	69,101.00	63,459.88

Sources: Computed based on figures from ASFI (various years) for prices; and CITI, Annual Reports (various years) for duties.

Notes: 1. Annual market prices are obtained as the average of the monthly ex-factory prices for domestic raw materials after adjusting for the excise duties imposed.

2. Annual landed prices of imported raw materials are obtained as the average of the monthly CIF prices of raw materials after adjusting for the import duties.

3. Prices of imported raw materials are converted from dollars into rupees using the exchange rate.

global crisis in December 2008, the three major ad valorem rates of CENVAT, 14 per cent, 12 per cent, and 8 per cent, applicable to non-petroleum products were reduced by 4 per cent each. However, in budget 2009–10, the mandatory CENVAT on MMFs and filament yarn as well as on their intermediates was increased from 4 per cent to 8 per cent. In budget 2010–11, the general rate of excise duty was increased to 10 per cent, which was then increased to 12 per cent in budget 2012–13. These recent increases in excise duty on polyester and the raw materials required in its production made polyester more expensive. Another impact of the recent increase in excise duty was that the domestic production of polyester and its raw materials became more expensive in comparison to their imports. The share of imports in total domestic consumption of polyester, however, increased after 2009–10 to about 6 per cent and 2.8 per cent in case of PSF and PFY respectively (Table 2.4). The share of imports also increased in consumption of PTA, MEG, and paraxylene in recent years (Table 2.7).

The increase in price reduced the demand for polyester. As a result of increase in price of polyester, man-made textiles became expensive. There was a fall in demand for man-made textiles in the recent years, which further affected the demand for polyester. As a result, the rate of growth of production slowed down after 2010–11 for PSF. The capacity utilisation for PSF remained low (around 70–5 per cent) during the period. For PFY, the production started falling after 2010–11 (Figure 2.2). The capacity utilisation in the case of PFY declined to around 55–60 per cent in the recent years.

Overall, things seem to have changed since the early 1990s, with substantial increase in the demand for textiles resulting from growth of income and fall in the relative prices of textiles. Reduction in the customs duties on the synthetic fibres as well as on their raw materials during the period of liberalisation increased competition and lowered their prices. This led to reduced prices of synthetic textiles, which facilitated the growth in their demand and thus production of synthetic textiles. The dependence of the synthetic fibre industry on the imported fibres and raw materials declined due to a fast expansion in the domestic capacities for synthetic fibres and their raw materials since the 1990s. However, some of these trends which were favourable for the growth of India's textile industry changed in the recent years. Synthetic textiles became expensive, thereby reducing the demand for synthetic and the overall textiles. The growth in the domestic production of polyester was adversely affected. The share of imports in domestic consumption of synthetic fibres and their raw materials increased.

Movement in the Prices of Cotton

Although the revival of the textile industry since the early 1990s was mainly led by the increase in per capita demand for synthetic textiles, it was also accompanied by the stabilisation of the long-period decline in the per capita demand for cotton textiles. However, the supply of cotton during the period could not match the increase in its demand, leading to an imbalance between the demand and the supply of cotton. This imbalance between the demand and supply of cotton during the 1990s caused the prices of cotton to rise (Table 2.13).

The data point to an increase in the prices of almost all the varieties of cotton since the 1990s. The main reason behind the supply of cotton falling short of its demand after the early 1990s was the slowdown in the growth of cotton production. According to the data from the Directorate of Cotton Development, GoI, the compound

Table 2.13 Average Prices of Selected Cotton Varieties (Rs per candy, ex-Mumbai)

Year	V-797	LRA-5166	MCU-5	DCH-32
1992–93	8,608	10,836	15,924	20,585
1994–95	16,188	20,451	25,496	30,190
1996–97	13,324	18,007	25,622	30,495
1998–99	17,129	20,324	27,545	32,319
2000–01	15,038	19,759	26,841	34,916
2001–02	12,110	15,515	21,630	29,425
2002–03	16,370	21,265	26,685	33,875
2003–04	18,240	19,421	27,421	32,835
2004–05	15,784	17,452	24,906	39,503
2005–06	13,310	18,627	23,179	41,400

Source: Computed based on monthly prices from ICMF, *Handbook of Statistics on Cotton Textile Industry* (2004) and CITI, *Handbook of Statistics on Textile Industry* (2008).

growth rate of cotton production declined from 5.6 per cent per annum during the 1980s to 4.2 per cent per annum from 1990–91 to 2003–04 (Figure 2.3). This was the combined result of a slowdown in the growth of cotton yield per hectare during the respective period and a fall in area under cotton cultivation after the mid-1990s. The compound annual average growth rate of yield per hectare declined from 5.8 per cent during the 1980s to 2.47 per cent from 1990–91 to 2002–03. However, the scenario changed thereafter. The fast-rising domestic demand for cotton textiles due to fast growth of incomes, along with fast growth of exports of cotton textiles and clothing (T&C), resulted in increased production of cotton. This increase in production after 2003–04 to 2006–07 was the combined result of increased area under cotton cultivation and higher productivity (Figure 2.3).

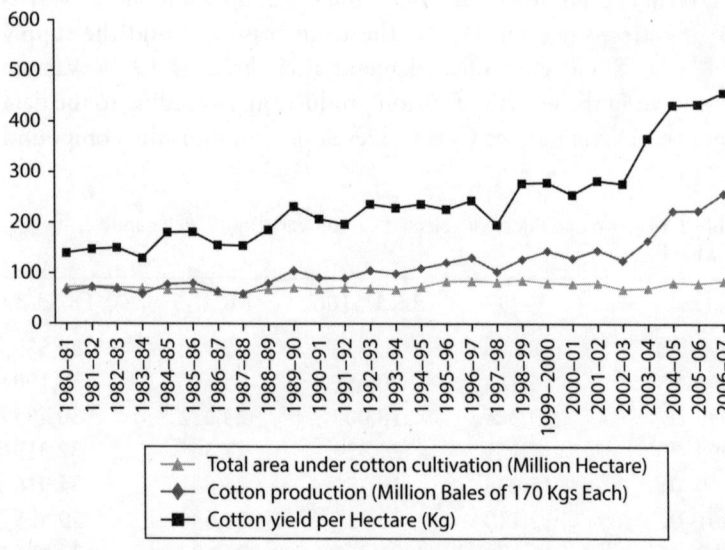

Figure 2.3   Area under Cotton Cultivation (million hectare), Cotton Yield Per Hectare (kg), and Production of Cotton (million bales of 170 kg each)

Source: Directorate of Cotton Development, in CITI, *Handbook of Statistics on Textile Industry* (2008: 44).

Notes: 1. Figures are estimated figures for 2006–07. Up to 1995–96, cotton year ended 31st August. From 1996–1997 onwards, cotton year ended 30th September.

Further, according to the figures from the Cotton Advisory Board, the production of cotton continued to increase at compound annual growth rate of 4.85 per cent during 2006–07 to 2013–14. The increase in the more recent period was mainly due to increase in area under cotton cultivation. The cotton yield per hectare continued to fluctuate during this period.

According to *All India Reports on Input Surveys*, though the rate of application of fertiliser nutrients nitrogen (N), phosphorous (P), potassium (K), and farmyard manure, calculated as kilograms of fertiliser nutrients (or farmyard manure) applied per hectare of land, increased for all size groups under cotton (Table 2.14), the area treated with fertilisers as well as the gross cropped area declined from 1991–92 to 1996–97 (Tables 2.15 and 2.16). The percentage decline in the area treated with fertilisers and the gross cropped area was more prominent in the unirrigated areas compared to the irrigated areas for semi-medium, medium, and large size holdings. The marginal and small size holdings saw slight increase in irrigated area treated with fertilisers as well as in irrigated cropped areas (Tables 2.15 and 2.16).

The slowdown in the growth of cotton production from 1990–91 to 2003–04 was part of a deeper agrarian crisis, which is partly explained by the movement of international prices. International cotton prices have witnessed a sharp and steady decline ever since agriculture was opened up to free global trade in the post-WTO era. This is mainly because of price distortions created by subsidies given to farmers in rich countries, especially the United States (US) and the European Union (EU). These subsidies have helped their farmers to grow surplus cotton, creating a glut in the international market and causing international prices to crash.

As can be seen from Table 2.17, the index of international commodity prices of cotton with 1990 as the base year (equal to 100) declined after the mid-1990s. It declined to 64.35 in 1999 and further to 58.14 in 2001. This trend of decline in world prices after mid-1990s was not limited to cotton and was experienced by almost all important agricultural commodities, including cash crops and foodgrains (Chandrasekhar and Ghosh 2000). As India opened up its agricultural sector and both exports and imports of agricultural products were freed, these international price movements led to a sharp

Table 2.14 Percentage Change in the Rate of Application of Fertiliser Nutrients (N, P, K) and Farmyard Manure in Irrigated and Unirrigated Areas under Cotton—from 1991–92 to 1996–97

Size Group (ha)	Nitrogen		Phosphorous		Potassium		Farmyard manure	
	Irrigated	Unirrigated	Irrigated	Unirrigated	Irrigated	Unirrigated	Irrigated	Unirrigated
1 Marginal (below 1)	122.21	49.11	126.04	64.54	519.03	110.74	9.97	47.30
2 Small (1–1.99)	63.42	27.37	105.93	49.36	234.80	130.67	38.45	111.05
3 Semi-medium (2–3.99)	45.93	28.74	101.99	68.74	271.82	80.47	23.28	104.98
4 Medium (4–9.99)	36.26	26.53	73.32	52.43	154.92	72.06	48.60	1606.40
5 Large (10 and above)	26.25	3.99	94.55	16.33	-43.90	54.45	33.02	644.22
6 All size groups	47.20	32.02	104.69	59.52	248.44	96.74	42.35	82.13

Source: Computed based on figures from GoI (2000, 2007).

Note: ha: hectare.

Table 2.15 Area Treated with Fertilisers under Cotton from 1991–92 to 1996–97 (000' ha)

Size Group (ha)	1991–92			1996–97			Percentage change from 1991–92 to 1996–97		
	Irrigated	Unirrigated	Total	Irrigated	Unirrigated	Total	Irrigated	Unirrigated	Total
1 Marginal (below 1)	96	243	339	106.9	228.54	335	11.32	-5.95	-1.06
2 Small (1–1.99)	209	727	936	232.8	386.29	619	11.36	-46.87	-33.86
3 Semi-medium (2–3.99)	413	1031	1444	409.2	570.14	979	-0.93	-44.70	-32.18
4 Medium (4–9.99)	841	1213	2054	646.8	609.61	1256	-23.09	-49.74	-38.83
5 Large (10 and above)	471	389	860	380.5	215.47	596	-19.21	-44.61	-30.70
6 All size groups	2030	3602	5632	1776	2010	3786	-12.51	-44.20	-32.77

Source: Computed based on figures from GoI (2000, 2007).
Note: ha: hectare.

Table 2.16 Percentage Change in Gross Cropped Area under Cotton from 1991–92 to 1996–97

S. No.	Size Group (ha)	Gross Cropped Area (000' ha), 1991–92		Gross Cropped Area (000' ha), 1996–97		Percentage Change in Gross Cropped Area, 1991–92 to 1996–97	
		Irrigated	Unirrigated	Irrigated	Unirrigated	Irrigated	Unirrigated
1	Marginal (below 1)	109	283	110.94	259.68	1.78	-8.24
2	Small (1–1.99)	221	874	240.64	460.89	8.89	-47.27
3	Semi-medium (2–3.99)	446	1271	421.77	721.19	-5.43	-43.26
4	Medium (4–9.99)	897	1610	673.38	868.16	-24.93	-46.08
5	Large (10 and above)	525	580	397.96	334.26	-24.20	-42.37
6	All size groups	2198	4618	1844.7	2644.18	-16.07	-42.74

Source: Computed based on figures from GoI (2000, 2007).

Note: ha: hectare.

Table 2.17 International Commodity Price Index* of Cotton with Base Year 1990 (US cents/pound)

Year	Price Index with base 1990
1989	91.99
1991	93.16
1993	70.28
1995	119.06
1997	95.97
1999	64.35
2001	58.14
2002	56.03
2003	76.84
2005	66.82
2007	76.64
2009	75.97
2011	187.23
2013	109.5

Source: Computed based on figures from International Monetary Fund (IMF 2006, 2014).
Note: *Liverpool Index.

decline in price of cotton and other crops in India. Despite promises to cut protection in agriculture, there has been no reduction in the protection given to farmers in rich countries. The aggregate data for Organisation for Economic Co-operation and Development (OECD) countries show that the total amount of support given to the farm sector was actually higher in 2003 as compared to the corresponding figures in 1986–87 (Pal 2005).

At the same time, the little protection that Indian farmers once enjoyed was lifted. When international prices are low and production costs are high, developed countries use subsidies or tariffs to protect their farmers. India, on the other hand, has avoided both the options. The total effective import duty on cotton (CITI, Annual Reports various years), which declined from 50 per cent in 1990–91 to 45 per cent in 1991–92, was abolished from 1995–96 to 1998–99. It was then raised to a meagre 5.5 per cent in 1999–2000. It was equal to 14 per cent in 2007–08 and is scrapped from 8 July 2008. In the absence of minimal protection, Indian farmers had to operate in a highly uncertain and volatile international environment, effectively competing against highly subsidised large producers in the developed countries. Cotton imports, which were less than 0.25 million bales during the 1980s and varied roughly between 0.03–0.6 million bales from 1990–91 to 1997–98, jumped thereafter to reach 2.2 million bales in 1999–2000 (ICMF 2002–03). The year 2000–01 recorded imports of 2.52 million bales of cotton. The dumping of these agricultural commodities resulted in a steep decline in the domestic prices after the mid-1990s, which led to a slowdown in the growth of cotton production. Thus, the fall in the international price of cotton after the mid-1990s led to a steep fall in the domestic price of cotton. The WPI of cotton (with base year 1993–94) which had been rising since the 1980s, declined from 159 in 1995–96 to 133 in 1996–97. While the price of cotton in the international market continued to decline up to 2002 (Table 2.17), the crisis in the agricultural sector led to an increase in the domestic price of cotton from 1997–98 onwards. The WPI increased to 155.4 in 1997–98 and further to 166.9 in 1998–99 (Figure 2.1).

Another factor behind the slowdown in the growth rate of yield per hectare and growth rate of cotton production after the 1990s was the drastic decline in real investment in agriculture (Chandrasekhar 2004). Though the deceleration in investment had started during the 1980s, the 1990s witnessed an intensification of that trend. Real capital formation in agriculture, which was around 2.75 per cent of GDP at the beginning of the 1980s, declined to an average of about 2 per cent by the early 1990s. It then registered a further decline to touch an average of less than 1.7 per cent by the end of the 1990s. The principal factor underlying the decline in capital formation in agriculture was the decline in public capital formation, which in constant 1993–94 prices fell by 18 per cent from around Rs 5,500 crore in 1994–95 to below Rs 4,500 crore in 1998–99. There was hardly any increase in private investment, which rose from Rs 11,000 crore in 1995–96 at 1993–94 prices to a mere Rs 11,600 crore in 1998–99. Overall, the decline in investment, along with the faulty agricultural trade policies during the period, adversely affected the growth rate of cotton production.

The production of cotton started reviving after 2003 due to increase in domestic demand as incomes grew fast during the period and exports of cotton[22] increased. The WPI of cotton was high and fluctuating after the 1990s and had reached 180.6 when there was a sudden increase in the international price of cotton in 2003. Thereafter, the prices in the international and domestic markets fluctuated before rising high in 2011. However, the world stocks of cotton increased after 2011–12 because of increase in world production of cotton. There was sharp decline in world exports of cotton after 2012–13 due to fall in demand from Chinese market. Although domestic consumption increased, these international trends affected Indian cotton markets also (Gera and Sreekumar 2015). And though not reflected in the WPIs, the annual average prices of *kapas* for important varieties like J34, S6, and BB declined in recent years.[23] Overall, cotton became less expensive vis-à-vis polyester in the recent years.

* * *

Overall, this discussion on the availability and cost of raw materials of the Indian textile industry suggests that, on the one hand, the prices of synthetic fibres declined substantially during the 1990s, leading to an increase in their demand. On the other hand, the prices of cotton continued to remain high during the period resulting in a shift in demand away from cotton textiles. However, the trend seems to be changing after 2010–11 when polyester became more expensive vis-à-vis cotton. These relative price movements of cotton and synthetic fibres provide the basis for the important inter-fibre shifts in demand for,[24] and production of,[25] the T&C industry.

---

[22] Available at www.cotcorp.gov.in (last accessed on 25 November 2015).

[23] Available at www.cotcorp.gov.in (last accessed on 25 November 2015).

[24] For details, see Chapter 1, 'Trends in Domestic Demand and their Implications'.

[25] For details, see Chapter 4, 'Structural Changes in the Indian Textile Industry'.

3

Exports

The New Driver of Growth?

The period since the 1990s has seen a tremendous increase in India's exports of textiles and clothing (T&C). India's share in the world exports of textiles, which declined from 2.4 per cent in 1980 to 2.1 per cent in 1990, started rising fast thereafter and increased to 6.2 per cent in 2013 (WTO 2014). India's share in the world exports of clothing has also been rising since the 1980s. It increased from 1.7 per cent in 1980 to 2.3 per cent in 1990 and further to 3.7 per cent in 2013 (WTO 2014). According to the Directorate General of Commercial Intelligence and Statistics (DGCIS) data, the period since the mid-1980s saw tremendous growth in exports of all kinds of textile products, including yarn, cloth, garments, and made-ups. In addition to this, there were remarkable changes in the structure of textile exports during the period. For example, the share of exports using cotton as a fibre declined due to faster growth in the exports of T&C using man-made fibres (MMFs). The pattern of exports reflected a trend towards greater value addition within the economy. In addition to this, India's exports of T&C, which were mainly in the form of woven products up to the middle of the 1980s, experienced remarkable growth in exports of knitted products.

This chapter examines the growth of India's exports of T&C and explores the factors that have contributed to this growth. The chapter provides an analysis of the changes in the structure of exports during the period and their implications. It also examines the impact of growth of India's exports of textiles on the balance of payments (BoP) of the economy. Changes in the share of exports in the overall production of India's T&C industry are also examined. The study draws heavily on the annual data from the DGCIS. In the DGCIS data, the commodities are classified according to the Indian Trade Classification, based on United Nations Standard International Trade Classification, for the period 1977–78 to 1986–87. From 1987–88 onwards, the commodities are classified according to the Indian Trade Classification based on Harmonised Commodity Description and Coding System, which is an extended version of the international classification system called 'Harmonised Commodity Description and Coding System' by World Customs Organization.

Changes in the Composition of Exports

Fall in the Share of Cotton T&C

According to the DGCIS data, almost all exports of T&C during the first half of the 1980s were cotton based. Cotton textiles continued to dominate the overall exports but there was a fall in the share of its exports because of the growing exports of synthetic textiles (Figure 3.1). The share of exports of cotton textiles in the total value of exports of the cotton and synthetic textiles fell from above 90 per cent during most of the 1980s to around 80–5 per cent during the 1990s and after. The share has been around 70–5 per cent in recent years.

Though the shift from cotton to synthetics was not apparent in the export of yarn, which remained largely cotton based, there was a substantial increase in the export of synthetic fabric since the 1990s. The export of synthetic fabric from India, which was negligible previously, grew at a high rate of about 26 per cent per annum during the first half of the 1990s (Table 3.1). As a result, though the export of cotton[1] fabric continued to dominate, its share in the quantity of fabric

---

[1] These include woven fabric of cotton containing >= 85 per cent cotton, by weight weighting not more than 200 grams (g) as well as more than 200 g per sq. m. These include also woven fabrics of cotton containing < 85 per cent cotton, mixed mainly with MMFs weighting <= 200 g as well as more than 200 g per sq. m and other woven fabrics of cotton.

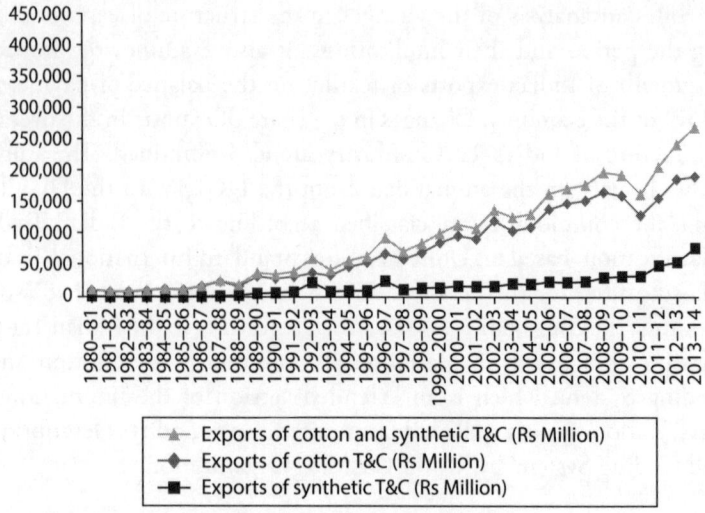

Figure 3.1   Fibre-wise Exports of T&C (Rs million)

Source: Computed based on annual figures from DGCIS, *Monthly Statistics of Foreign Trade of India,* vol. 1 March (various years).

Notes: 1. All major exports of cotton and synthetic textile industry are considered to calculate the exports.

2. Exports of cotton textiles include exports of cotton yarn, cotton cloth (woven, knitted, and crocheted), cotton garments, and cotton made-ups. Exports of synthetic textiles include exports of cloth, garments, and made-ups using MMFs.

3. The codes and the deflators used are explained later in the notes to the table of the export of relevant items:

    a. For exports of cotton yarn, refer to Notes to Figure 3.7.

    b. For exports of cotton cloth, refer to Notes to Table 3.1 (woven) and Figure 3.4 (knitted).

    c. For exports of cotton garments, refer to Notes to Figure 3.2.

    d. For exports of cotton made-ups, refer to Notes to Figure 3.3.

    e. For exports of synthetic cloth, refer to Notes to Table 3.1 (woven) and Figure 3.4 (knitted).

    f. For exports of synthetic garments, refer to Notes to Figure 3.2.

    g. For exports of synthetic made-ups, refer to Notes to Figure 3.3.

exports declined from about 95 per cent during the 1980s to around 77 per cent during the mid-1990s (Table 3.1). Further, the share of export of cotton fabric varied between 73 per cent and 80 per cent during the second half of the 1990s (TEXPROCIL, in ICMF [2001]).

Table 3.1   Export of Woven Fabric (million sq. m)

Year	Export of cotton fabric	Export of synthetic fabric	Total export of fabric	Share of export of cotton fabric (%)	Share of export of synthetic fabric (%)
1980–81	582.87	30.34	613.21	95.05	4.95
1985–86	475.88	15.09	490.97	96.93	3.07
1990–91	614.41	89.09	703.5	87.34	12.66
1995–96	936.39	286.26	1,222.65	76.59	23.41
2003–04	772.97	626.82	1,399.8	55.22	44.78
2005–06	612.7	659.71	1,272.4	48.15	51.85
2010–11	839.14	1,212.9	2,052.04	40.89	59.11
2013–14	1,202.83	1,459.16	2,661.99	45.19	54.81

Sources: Computed based on annual figures from DGCIS, *Monthly Statistics of Foreign Trade of India*, vol. 1, March 1981, March 1986, March 1991, March 1996, March 2004, March 2006, March 2011, March 2014.

Notes: 1. The DGCIS data on fabric export are not comparable from 1996–97 to 2002–03 because of change of unit from square metres to kilograms during this period. 2. For woven fabric of cotton, codes 6521 and 6522 are used for 1980–81 and 1985–86. (A very small part of fabric exported under codes 6521, 6522, 6531, and 6535 is given in metres for some years, which is converted into square metres using the calculated average unit value (rupees/sq. m) of the exports under that code for the particular year.) For the later years, codes 5208–12 are used for the woven fabric of cotton. 3. For man-made fabric, codes 6531, 6532, 6534, 6535, 6536, 6538, and 6539 are used for 1980–81 and 1985–86. For the later years, codes 5407, 5408, 5512, 5513, 5514, 5515, and 5516 are used for the same.

Overall, the share of synthetic woven fabric, in quantity terms, which was less than 10 per cent in the 1980s, increased to around 55–60 per cent in the recent years (Table 3.1).

Similar changes were observed in the composition of the exports of garments as well. Though the export of cotton garments continued to dominate, the DGCIS data point to an increase in the export of synthetic garments after the mid-1980s (Figure 3.2). As a result, the share of export of cotton garments in the total exports of garments, which was declining but was more than 90 per cent until the

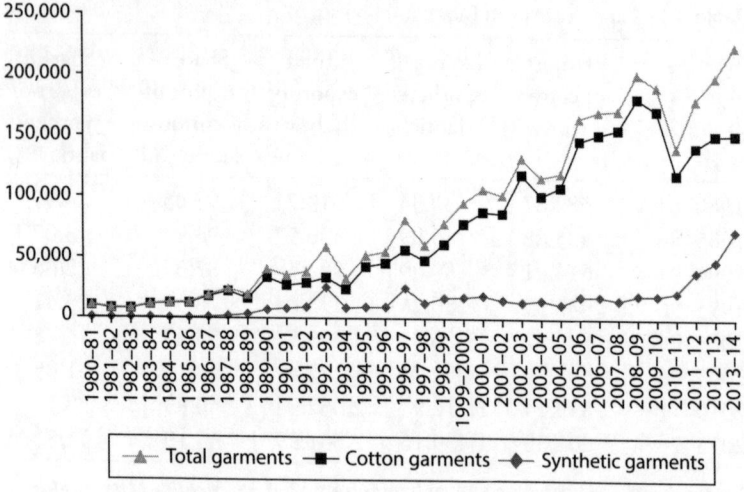

Figure 3.2   Value of Exports of Garments (Cotton and Synthetic) with Base Year 1990–91 (Rs million)

Sources: Computed based on annual figures from DGCIS, *Monthly Statistics of Foreign Trade of India,* vol. 1 March (various years). Unit value index for export of cotton yarn is computed based on figures from DGCIS and unit value index for export of textile fibres other than cotton is obtained from RBI (2006, 2014).

Notes: 1. For the exports of woven garments of cotton, figures from codes 842, 843, 844, and 847 are used for the period from 1980–81 to 1986–87. Figures from the code 62 are used for the later years. For the exports of knitted and crocheted garments of cotton, figures from codes 845 and 846 are used for the period 1978–79 to 1986–87. Figures from code 61 are used for the later years.

2. For the exports of woven synthetic garments, figures from codes 842, 843, 844, and 847 are used for the period from 1980–81 to 1986–87. Figures from the code 62 are used for the later years. For the exports of knitted and crocheted garments of synthetic fibres, figures from codes 845 and 846 are used for the period 1980–81 to 1986–87. Figures from code 61 are used for the later years.

3. The exports of cotton garments are deflated using unit value index for export of cotton yarn and the exports of synthetic garments are deflated using unit value index for export of textile fibres other than cotton.

mid-1980s, fluctuated and remained lower afterwards. The share has been around 67–76 per cent in recent years.

As far as the export of made-ups is concerned, cotton made-ups used to form almost the whole of exports of made-ups during the

1980s and the 1990s. Items like bedsheets, bedcovers, towels, and napkins, the exports of which were increasing, required cotton as a fibre in their manufacture. As a result, cotton made-ups continued to dominate the export basket, but their share in the total exports of made-ups also declined after 2002–03 to about 78–85 per cent in recent years due to faster growth of exports of synthetic made-ups (Figure 3.3).

This shift from cotton to synthetic products in the exports of India's T&C reflects the changing composition of destination countries. The DGCIS data indicate that, traditionally, India had been exporting mainly to the developed countries, such as the US and the United Kingdom (UK), that demanded cotton T&C. However, another set of countries, including the United Arab Emirates (UAE),

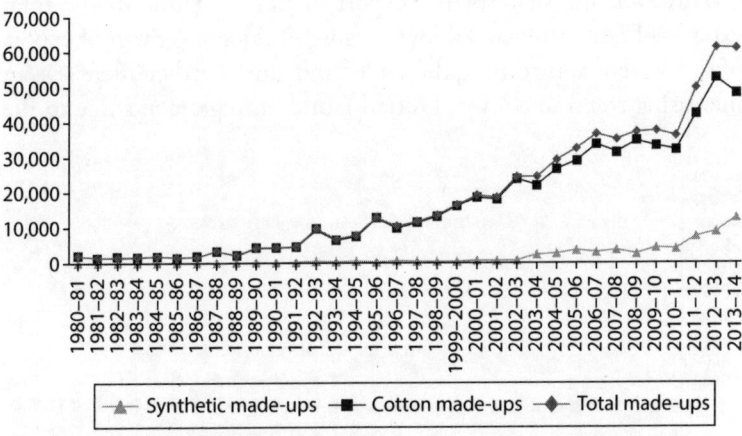

Figure 3.3   Value of Exports of Made-ups (Cotton and Synthetic) with Base Year 1990–91 (Rs million)

Sources: Computed based on annual figures from DGCIS, *Monthly Statistics of Foreign Trade of India,* vol. 1 March (various years). Unit value index for export of cotton yarn is computed based on figures from DGCIS and unit value index for export of textile fibres other than cotton is obtained from RBI (2006; 2014).

Notes: 1. For exports of made-ups (cotton and synthetic), figures from code 658 are used for the period 1980–81 to 1986–87. Figures from code 63 are used for the later years.

2. The exports of cotton made-ups are deflated using unit value index for export of cotton yarn and the export of synthetic made-ups are deflated using unit value index for export of textile fibres other than cotton.

Singapore, Indonesia, and Malaysia, has emerged as the major importer of India's synthetic textiles, which have turned cheaper than the cotton textiles roughly since the mid-1990s.[2]

Increasing Exports of Hosiery Sector

Another important change in the composition of exports from India has been the rapid growth of exports of knitted products. According to the DGCIS data, export of fabrics was mainly in the form of woven fabric up to the mid-1980s. Though the export of knitted fabric of synthetic fibres remained insignificant, the exports of knitted fabrics of cotton did increase considerably, recording very high levels in the mid-1990s. The exports declined during the second half of the 1990s, but have been increasing fast ever since (Figure 3.4).

However, the share of the export of knitted fabric in the total exports of fabrics remained low because of the fast growth of export of the woven fabric during the 1990s and after. Further, there was an increasing trend to convert knitted fabrics into garments due to the

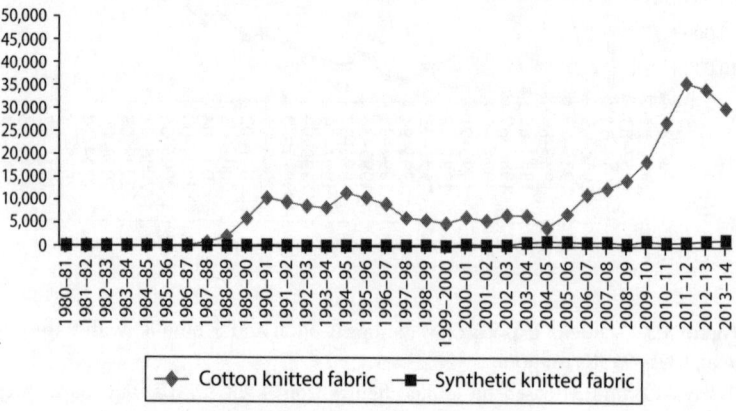

Figure 3.4   Export of Knitted Fabric (thousand kilograms)
Source: Computed based on annual figures from DGCIS, *Monthly Statistics of Foreign Trade of India*, vol. 1 March (various years).
Note: For export of knitted fabric of cotton and MMFs, figures from code 655 are used for the period 1980–81 to 1986–87. The figures from code 600 are used for the later years.

[2] For details, see Chapter 2, 'Availability and Cost of Raw Materials'.

increase in demand for export of knitted garments since the 1980s. The share of export of knitted garments in the exports of total garments (woven and knitted), which was less than 15 per cent in the first half of the 1980s, increased after the mid-1980s, and varied between 20 and 30 per cent in the 1990s. It increased further and varied between 30 and 47 per cent after the 1990s (Figure 3.5). Overall, the share of knitted exports either in the form of fabric or garments in the total exports of fabric and garments, which was between 6–10 per cent during the first half of 1980s, increased thereafter, and crossed 25 per cent by the end of the 1990s. It kept rising further and was around 32–34 per cent in the recent years (Table 3.2).

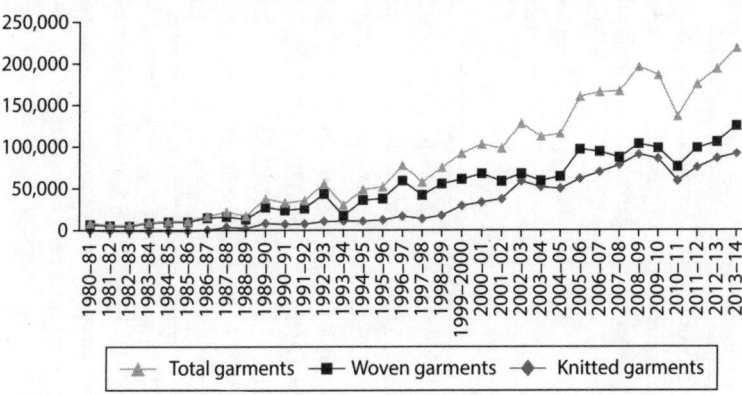

Figure 3.5   Value of Export of Garments (Woven and Knitted) with Base Year 1990–91 (Rs million)

Sources: Computed based on annual figures from DGCIS, *Monthly Statistics of Foreign Trade of India,* vol. 1 March (various years). Unit value index for export of cotton yarn is computed based on figures from DGCIS and unit value index for export of textile fibres other than cotton is obtained from RBI (2006, 2014).

Notes: 1. For calculating the value of export of woven garments of cotton and MMFs, figures from codes 842, 843, 844, and 847 are used for the period 1980–81 to 1986–87. Figures are used from code 62 for the later years.

2. For calculating the value of export of knitted garments of cotton and synthetic fibres, codes 845 and 846 are used for the period 1980–81 to 1986–87. Appropriate figures from code 61 provide the required data for the later years.

3. The exports of cotton garments are deflated using unit value index for export of cotton yarn and the export of synthetic garments are deflated using unit value index for export of textile fibres other than cotton.

Table 3.2 Exports of Fabrics and Garments with Base Year 1990–91: Values (Rs million) and Shares (%)

Year	Exports of knitted fabric	Exports of woven fabric	Exports of knitted garments	Exports of woven garments	Share of export of knitted fabric in the total export of fabric	Share of export of knitted garments in the total export of garments	Share of export of knitted fabric and knitted garments in the total export of fabric and garments
1980–81	5.12	6,614.70	1,659.92	8,505.64	0.08	16.33	9.92
1985–86	1.46	4,423.07	1,015.05	11,382.02	0.03	8.19	6.04
1990–91	1,217.95	13,117.93	8,738.87	24,831.91	8.50	26.03	20.78
1995–96	1,031.02	21,700.23	13,535.74	38,267.04	4.54	26.13	19.54
2000–01	648.57	29,931.81	34,105.25	66,872.92	2.12	33.77	26.42
2005–06	766.04	35,272.45	61,217.91	95,142.65	2.13	39.15	32.22
2010–11	2,082.53	43,018.43	58,738.79	74,829.59	4.62	43.98	34.04
2013–14	2,956.11	68,772.78	89,805.57	12,2519.4	4.12	42.30	32.66

Sources: Computed based on annual figures from DGCIS, *Monthly Statistics of Foreign Trade of India*, vol. 1, March 1981, March 1986, March 1991, March 1996, March 2001, March 2006, March 2011, March 2014. Unit value index for export of cotton yarn is computed based on figures from DGCIS and unit value index for export of textile fibres other than cotton is obtained from RBI (2006, 2014).

Notes: 1. Woven fabric exports include the exports of woven fabrics using cotton or synthetic fibres. Codes 6521 and 6522 are used for calculating the exports of woven fabric of cotton for 1980–81 and 1985–86. Codes 5208–12 are used for the later years. For calculating the exports of man-made woven fabric, codes 6531, 6532, 6534, 6535, 6536, 6538, and 6539 are used for 1980–81 and 1985–86. Codes 5407, 5408, and 5412–16 are used for the same for the later years.

2. Exports of knitted fabrics include the exports of knitted fabrics using cotton or synthetic fibres. For export of knitted fabric (using cotton or MMFs), figures from code 655 are used for 1980–81 and 1985–86. The figures from code 600 are used for the later years.

3. The export of woven garments includes the exports of woven garments using cotton or synthetic fibres. For calculating the value of export of woven garments (using cotton or MMFs), figures from codes 842, 843, 844, and 847 are used for 1980–81 and 1985–86. Figures are used from code 62 for the required data for the later years.

4. The exports of knitted garments include garment exports of cotton or synthetic fibres. For calculating the value of export of knitted garments (of cotton and synthetic fibres), codes 845 and 846 are used for 1980–81 and 1985–86. Appropriate figures from code 61 provide the required data for the later years.

5. The exports of fabrics and garments of cotton are deflated using unit value index for export of cotton yarn and the exports of fabrics and garments using MMFs are deflated using unit value index for export of textile fibres other than cotton.

This rapid growth of exports of hosiery products since the 1990s reflects changing structure of demand worldwide. The shift was driven by the inherent qualities of knitted fabrics, like softness, coolness, easy maintenance, and durability, which made these products more attractive than the woven products.

Shift towards High-value Products

The growth of exports since the mid-1990s was accompanied by a clear shift in the pattern of exports of the textile industry. The pattern was prominent in the cotton textile industry and has become evident in recent years (Table 3.3). The shift involved a fall in the share of exports of fabric and a rise in the share of finished products, including garments and made-ups.

The share of exports of cotton fabric in the total exports of the cotton products declined from about 30 per cent in the first half of the 1980s to about 18 per cent in the mid-1990s, and further to 8–9 per cent by 2005–06. This was mainly because of a much faster growth in the exports of other categories of cotton goods (including cotton yarn, cotton garments, and cotton made-ups). For example, while the value index of export of cotton fabrics increased (with base year 1990–91) to 163, it crossed 540 for cotton garments by the year 2005–06. The highest increase was seen in the export of cotton made-ups for which the value index increased to 679. Overall, the share of finished products in the total exports of cotton products, which fluctuated around 65 per cent during the 1990s, increased consistently thereafter to reach approximately 77 per cent in the year 2005–06 (Table 3.3). Clearly, the acceleration in the growth of the exports of the cotton textile industry during the mid-1990s to 2005–06 was accompanied by a much faster increase in the exports of the high-value products in the textile chain. The industry was converting more and more of cotton fabric into home furnishing and garments and exporting these final products of the textile chain during the period.

However, the share of the cotton yarn in the overall exports of the cotton products continued to increase from about 3 per cent in the mid-1980s to 19.4 per cent during the year 2000–01. The share declined thereafter, but continued to be higher than what it was up

Table 3.3 Structure of Exports of Cotton T&C Industry with Base Year 1990–91: Values (Rs million) and Shares (%)

Year	Cotton yarn	Cotton fabric	Cotton garments	Cotton made-ups	Overall exports of cotton	Share of cotton yarn	Share of cotton fabric	Share of finished products
1980–81	570	5,572	9,622	1,935	17,699	3.2	31.5	65.3
1985–86	610	4,068	11,829	1,521	18,027	3.4	22.6	74.1
1990–91	4,973	11,488	25,709	4,272	46,441	10.7	24.7	64.6
1995–96	14,983	15,662	42,995	12,578	86,218	17.4	18.2	64.5
2000–01	29,520	21,420	82,952	18,593	152,485	19.4	14.0	66.6
2005–06	31,721	18,747	138,787	29,046	218,301	14.5	8.6	76.9
2010–11	40,041	17,953	112,538	32,273	202,804	19.7	8.9	71.4
2013–14	75,536	31,098	143,572	48,274	298,480	25.3	10.4	64.3

Source: Computed based on annual figures from DGCIS, *Monthly Statistics of Foreign Trade of India*, vol. 1, March 1981, March 1986, March 1991, March 1996, March 2001, March 2006, March 2011, March 2014.

Note: The codes used and the conversion of export values at base year prices is explained in the Notes to Table 3.1 and Figures 3.2, 3.3, 3.4, and 3.7.

to the early 1990s. The share of yarn has been increasing since then and crossed 25 per cent in 2013–14 (Table 3.3). The rapid growth of exports of cotton yarn was driven by the increase in the price of yarn in the international market (discussed later in detail). Overall, it indicates that much is still left to be attained as far as converting yarn into fabric is concerned. The ideal situation for the economy would be one in which the industry handles the entire value addition from fibre to fashion internally and exports only the final product.

Further, the scenario seems to have changed after the financial crisis in the developed economies, which adversely affected their demand for finished products, mainly cotton garments. The decline in demand for cotton garments in the developed economies led to fall in the share of exports of finished products to 71.4 per cent during 2010–11 (Table 3.3). A substantial increase in the export of cotton yarn during 2013–14, coupled with slower growth of export of garments, resulted in a further decline in the share of exports of finished products.

Further, this shift in the exports from fabric to the finished products, which is apparent in cotton textiles, is not visible when the exports of the synthetic products are considered (Table 3.4). This is because a major part of the exports of synthetic products continued to be in the form of synthetic fabric. The share of synthetic fabric, which increased in the first half of the 1990s from 26 to 44 per cent, continued to remain high, varying between 32 and 52 per cent.

One possible explanation for this trend peculiar to the exports of synthetic products seems to be the composition of the destination countries. As mentioned earlier, the DGCIS data indicate that while the external demand for cotton fabric during the 1990s increased in the developed countries such as the US and the UK, the demand for synthetic cloth increased in a different set of countries, including the UAE, Indonesia, Malaysia, Singapore, and Saudi Arabia (Table 3.5). The UAE emerged as the major destination for synthetic fabric exports. As incomes grew fast in these developing economies in Asia, they demanded more of synthetic textiles, which were cheaper and had additional properties of durability and wash and wear. Further, the exports of synthetic made-ups remained negligible because the manufacture of made-ups like towels, napkins, and bedsheets essentially requires the use of cotton as a fibre.

Table 3.4 Structure of Exports of Synthetic T&C with Base Year 1990–91: Values (Rs million) and Shares (%)

Year	Synthetic fabric	Synthetic garments	Synthetic made-ups	Total	Share of synthetic fabric	Share of synthetic finished products
1980–81	1,048.27	543.42	6.37	1,598.06	65.6	34.40
1985–86	356.65	5,68.31	4.08	929.04	38.39	61.61
1990–91	2,848.06	7,862.2	55.55	10,765.81	26.45	73.55
1995–96	7,069.7	8,807.94	169.06	16,046.71	44.06	55.94
2000–01	9,160.67	18,026.2	609.49	27,796.36	32.96	67.04
2005–06	17,291.27	17,573.3	3,526.11	38,390.68	45.04	54.96
2010–11	27,147.98	21,030.69	3,957.94	52,136.61	52.07	47.93
2013–14	40,630.63	68,753.14	12,870.77	122,254.5	33.23	66.77

Source: Computed based on annual figures from DGCIS, *Monthly Statistics of Foreign Trade of India*, vol. 1 March 1981, March 1986, March 1991, March 1996, March 2001, March 2006, March 2011, March 2014.

Notes: 1. The codes and deflators used are explained in the Notes to Table 3.1 and Figures 3.2, 3.3, and 3.4.

2. Exports of synthetic fabric, synthetic garments, and synthetic made-ups include exports of woven and knitted garments and made-ups using synthetic fibers.

Table 3.5   Export of Synthetic Cloth (woven) from India (million sq. m)

Year	UAE	Singapore	Indonesia	Malaysia	Saudi Arabia
1980–81	1.89	1.59	0.00	0.46	6.68
1985–86	10.58	0.68	0.00	0.88	3.49
1989–90	17.06	2.49	0.02	1.30	3.26
1995–96	105.76	18.80	0.58	3.19	17.04
2004–05	210.83	40.67	22.02	23.06	47.79
2010–11	260.43	18.40	15.18	41.96	49.59
2013–14	285.24	20.81	17.09	46.60	17.66

Sources: Computed based on annual figures from DGCIS, *Statistics of Foreign Trade of India*, vol. 1, March 1981, March 1986, March 1990, March 1996, March 2005, March 2011, March 2014.
Notes: 1. Codes 6531, 6532, 6534–6, 6538, and 6539 are used for the export of woven fabric for 1980–81 and 1985–86. Codes 5407, 5408, and 5512–16 are used for 1989–90, 1995–96, 2004–05, 2010–11, and 2013–14.
2. The DGCIS data on export of fabric are not comparable from 1996–97 to 2002–03 because of change of unit from sq. m to kg during this period.

The overall textiles (synthetic and cotton) reflect a shift in exports from fabric to the finished products (Table 3.6). The share of exports of finished products, which varied between 63 and 66 per cent during the first half of the 1990s, increased thereafter and varied between 65 and 74 per cent. The share of fabric, which was more than 20 per cent up to the middle of the 1990s, declined thereafter. The share of yarn, however, rose during the period.[3]

Overall, there was a much faster increase in the exports of high-value products in the period since the 1990s. This is a good sign as it indicates that much of the value addition was taking place within the economy.

Analysis of Growth of Exports

The consistent growth of the exports of T&C roughly after the middle of the 1980s can partly be seen as the result of changes in economic policies. The NTP of 1985 initiated the process of deregulation of

[3] Exception was 2005–06.

Table 3.6 Structure of Exports of T&C Industry: Values (Rs million) and Shares (%)

Year	Cotton yarn	Cotton and synthetic fabric	Cotton and synthetic garments	Cotton and synthetic made-ups	Total cotton and synthetic exports	Share of cotton yarn exports	Share of total fabric exports	Share of finished products
1980–81	570	6,620	10,166	1,941	19,297	3	34	63
1985–86	610	4,425	12,397	1,525	18,956	3	23	73
1990–91	4,973	14,336	33,571	4,327	57,207	9	25	66
1995–96	14,983	22,731	51,803	12,747	102,264	15	22	63
2000–01	29,520	30,580	100,978	19,203	180,281	16	17	67
2005–06	31,721	36,038	156,361	32,572	256,692	12	14	74
2010–11	40,041	45,101	133,568	36,231	254,941	16	18	67
2013–14	75,536	71,729	212,325	61,145	420,735	18	17	65

Source: Computed based on annual figures from DGCIS, *Monthly Statistics of Foreign Trade of India*, vol. 1, March 1981, March 1986, March 1991, March 1996, March 2001, March 2006, March 2011, March 2014.

Note: The codes used and the conversion of export values at base year prices are explained in the Notes to Table 3.1 and Figures 3.2, 3.3, 3.4, and 3.7.

the industry. The changed scenario when the ceiling on the exports of cotton yarn of counts 41s and above was removed, and that for count group 1–40s raised, seems to have led to a fast growth in the export of cotton yarn from the mid-1980s. The exporters could import duty-free machinery and equipment (Gangopadhyay and Krishnan 2005, cited in Tewari 2005: 22). The government used generous subsidies and duty drawback programmes to encourage firms to establish export-oriented units (EOUs) and absorb new technology. However, the more important development that led to the fast growth of external demand for textile products during the 1990s was with respect to the determination of the exchange rate of the Indian currency.

Depreciation of the Indian Currency

The fixed administered exchange rate system adopted up to 1991 was subsequently replaced by a dual exchange rate mechanism (involving 60 per cent conversion at market rate and 40 per cent conversion at RBI rate). In March 1993, India moved from the dual exchange rate system to a single, market-determined exchange rate system. All foreign exchange receipts and payments by the government and private sector, after that, were made at this market-determined rate. The market forces determined the movements in the exchange rate, though the RBI intervenes periodically. In 1991–92, the rupee was devalued significantly. But the devaluation was accompanied by withdrawal of export subsidies. The Cash Compensatory Support Scheme, which provided compensation for unrebated indirect taxes on both final and intermediate stages of production of export industries but is not refunded through the duty drawback system, was discontinued after the introduction of the economic reforms (Dikshit 2002). This reduced the effectiveness of the devaluation of the exchange rate from the point of view of exporters.

However, the depreciation of the Indian rupee occurred at a rate that was higher than the rate at which the currencies of the other competitive countries depreciated. This led to the fast growth of external demand for textile products during the 1990s. As the currency of a country depreciates, the exports become more competitive in the world market. This did not happen in India's case during the 1980s because of a lower depreciation in relative terms. India's market

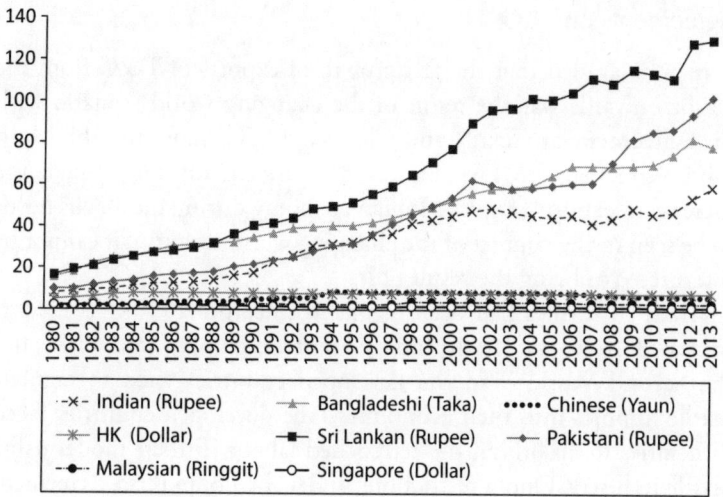

Figure 3.6 Market Exchange Rate of National Currencies per US Dollar
Source: IMF, International Financial Statistics (2001, 2013).

exchange rate per US dollar, which was equal to 7.9 in the year 1980, increased to 16.2 towards the end of the 1980s (Figure 3.6). This implies a depreciation of the Indian rupee of about 105 per cent during the 1980s. However, the currencies of other competing countries depreciated more sharply during this period. For example, the Chinese yuan depreciated by 153.3 per cent, the Sri Lankan rupee depreciated by 188.8 per cent, the Pakistani rupee depreciated by 107.1 per cent, and the Bangladeshi taka depreciated by 108.4 per cent. As a result, India's manufactured exports did not become relatively cheaper in comparison to the exports of the other competing countries. However, the scenario was different during the 1990s when the increase in the market exchange rate of the Chinese yuan, the Sri Lankan rupee, the Pakistani rupee, and the Bangladeshi taka slowed down and the Indian rupee depreciated more sharply. The Chinese yuan depreciated by 73 per cent, the Sri Lankan rupee by 76.5 per cent, the Pakistani rupee by 129 per cent, and the Bangladeshi taka by 42 per cent during the 1990s. The Indian rupee depreciated by a higher 146 per cent during this period. This affected the demand for India's manufactured exports favourably as they became relatively cheaper in comparison to the exports of the other competing countries.

Agreements on T&C

It may be argued that the fast growth of exports of T&C from the 1990s onwards was the result of the changing world scenario with the Agreement on Textile and Clothing (ATC) replacing the Multi Fibre Agreement (MFA). However, as argued further, though the increase in exports from the Indian economy during the 1990s needs to be seen in the context of the changing world scenario, it cannot be interpreted as being the result of it.

Trade in textiles had been regulated since the 1950s. As exports increased from the newly independent developing countries after the Second World War, the developed countries tried to regulate textile imports into their economies. The developed countries faced difficulties in absorbing the retrenched labour in their modernising textile industry. Quota restrictions under the Long-Term Agreement (LTA) (1962) and MFA (1974) became characteristic features of world trade. The LTA facilitated the protectionist moves of the richer nations against the increasing exports of cotton textiles from developing countries. The MFA enlarged the scope of the LTA to include fibres other than cotton and restricted the imports of synthetic garments and made-up articles. These arrangements exempted the textile and garment trade from the discipline of the General Agreement on Trade and Tariffs (GATT) and allowed industrial countries to impose bilateral quotas on imports of various textiles and garment product categories. It protected producers in the developed countries and allowed them time to adapt to competition from cheaper imports from the developing countries (Uchikawa 1998).

The MFA was phased out in steps through the implementation of the ATC (1995). The agreement led to dismantling of the discriminatory quota regime practised under the MFA within a definite time span of 10 years from 1995 to 2004. This was carried out progressively in three stages (3 years, 4 years, and 3 years), with all products standing integrated at the end of the 10-year period. The first stage that started on 1 January 1995, led to the integration of products representing not less than 16 per cent of the members' total 1990 imports of all the products in the Annexure. In stage 2, started on 1 January 1998, not less than a further 17 per cent was integrated. In stage 3, on 1 January 2002, not less than a further 18 per cent was integrated. Finally, at the end, on 1 January 2005, all remaining products (amounting up to 49 per cent of 1990 imports into a member) were integrated and the agreement was terminated. However, the decision regarding which products a country would integrate at each stage to reach these thresholds was left to be decided by the each importing member. The only constraint was that the integration list must encompass products from each of the four groupings: tops and yarn; fabrics; made-up textile products; and clothing (Uchikawa 1998).

Thus, the ATC acted as a transitory regime between the MFA and the full integration of T&C into the multilateral trading system. As mentioned earlier, the products to be included in the agreement were listed in the Annexure to the ATC, which included, however, items that were not restricted under the MFA, and the list served as the basis on which the extent of liberalisation was calculated. It was observed by the Textile Monitoring Body that the unrestricted products were integrated first during stages one and two. When the third stage was reached, the opportunity to integrate products that previously had not been restricted under the MFA had been exhausted. However, it was observed that there was a tendency to integrate products where quota utilisation was particularly low. The removal of a large number of barriers was left to the fourth stage and the share of clothing in the volume of integrated products remained low during the initial stages. All this suggested that the products with the highest value addition were left to the final stage of integration (Basu and Shanmugasundaram 2002). Thus, the developed countries largely used all opportunities available to retain restrictions in the most sensitive areas. They inflated the basis from which liberalisation was to be measured. They first liberalised the restrictions that appeared not to be binding. The ATC started in 1995, but was not effective until 2002, and its full impact became apparent only as recently as 2005.

Kar and Kar (2015) show that the number of India's textile and apparel manufacturing firms engaged exclusively in exports was fairly small[4] in the early 1990s. This number grew fast thereafter, with minor fluctuations, to reach up to 30 by 1998. The number almost stabilised thereafter up to 2004, but was followed by a steep decline towards the end of MFA regime. The number stabilised around 20 until 2011. It declined fast thereafter and reached five by 2013. Clearly, much of the

---

[4] Only two to three firms were engaged exclusively in exports.

growth occurred during the phase when the ATC was not effective. Many such firms in India found it difficult to cope with the increased competition from the exports of the competing countries after the expiry of the quota regime and this resulted in industrial concentration in a few firms. Further, an analysis of the growth of exports of multi-market firms[5] also suggests that the exports as percentage of total sales increased fast from about 20 per cent in the early 1990s to about 38 per cent by 1998–99. It then stabilised around 35 per cent up to 2007–08. During the years following the crisis, the share declined and almost stabilised around 32 per cent (Kar and Kar 2015).

Clearly, the fast growth of India's exports of T&C since the 1990s cannot be attributed to the ATC. Overall, it helped only indirectly by providing incentives for capacity expansion and modernisation during a period when domestic demand had started rising and the competition among the exporting countries was expected to increase after the expiry of the ATC. However, there were changes in the structure of the world's industry that led to the fast growth of India's textile exports.

Changes in the Structure of World's Industry

Shift of Highly Developed Asian Economies from Textile Industry to High-tech Industries

Changes in the structure of the world's industry around this period proved beneficial for the growth of India's textile exports. One such change was the shift of highly developed Asian economies like Japan, Hong Kong, Korea, and Taiwan to high-tech areas, and the consequent shift of cotton yarn manufacturing from these Asian countries to lower-cost economies like India and China. The high-tech industries generate new products and processes, stimulate other business activity, increase productivity, and create high-wage jobs. These include aerospace, pharmaceuticals, computers and office machinery, communication equipment, and scientific instruments. High-tech manufactures accounted for 8.2 per cent of Taiwan's total manufacturing output in 1980 (National Science Foundation 2006). This proportion jumped to 12.4 per cent in

---

[5] Firms that operate in the domestic as well as the foreign markets.

1989 and reached 29.2 per cent in 2001. The transformation of South Korea's manufacturing base is even more striking. High-tech manufactures in South Korea accounted for 6.1 per cent of total output in 1980, 10 per cent in 1989, and 31 per cent in 2001. Japan, which had already shifted to high-tech areas, observed little slowdown in the growth of high-tech industries during the 1990s, though some fall was also recorded afterwards. The shift of these economies away from the labour-intensive to technology-intensive areas is reflected in the nature of export of these economies which became more technology intensive. While the export of textiles from Japan, South Korea, Taiwan, and Hong Kong recorded a fall after the mid-1990s,[6] there was a rapid increase in the export of high-tech manufacturing industries. The share of these economies in the world exports of high-tech industries grew fast. For example, the share of South Korea and Taiwan, which accounted for 2.5 per cent of world export of high-tech manufactures in 1990, nearly doubled by 2001 (National Science Foundation 2006).

Although the share of these Asian economies in the world textile exports fell after 2000, there was a fall in the share of textile exports in the merchandise exports of these economies during the 1990s itself. According to the figures published in WTO's *International Trade Statistics* (2007 and 2014), the share of Hong Kong in the world textiles exports increased from 3.2 per cent in 1980 to 7.9 per cent in 1990, and continued to increase further to 8.5 per cent in 2000. It declined thereafter to 6.4 per cent by 2006. The share of Korea increased from 4 per cent in 1980 to 5.8 per cent in 1990, and further to 8 per cent in 2000. It reduced to 4.6 per cent by 2006, and further to 3.9 per cent by 2013. The share of Taiwan, which grew from 3.2 per cent in 1980 to 5.9 per cent in 1990, and further to 7.7 per cent in 2000, came down to 4.5 per cent in 2006 and to 3.3 per cent by 2013. Japan's share in the world export of textiles started falling much earlier. Its share declined from 9.3 per cent in 1980 to 5.6 per cent in 1990 and 4.5 per cent in 2000. It further declined to 3.2 per cent in 2006 and to 2.2 per cent by 2013.

The share of textile exports in the overall merchandise exports of these Asian economies started falling much earlier. The WTO

[6] As indicated by WTO (2007, 2014).

(*International Trade Statistics* 2001 and 2014) figures indicate that share of textiles exports in the overall merchandise exports of South Korea declined from 9.3 per cent in 1990 to 7.4 per cent by 2000. It declined further to 3.7 per cent by 2005 and to 2.2 per cent by 2013. Taiwan's share fell from 9.1 per cent in 1990 to 7.9 per cent in 2000, and further to 4.9 per cent in 2005, and 3.4 per cent in 2013. Hong Kong recorded a decline from 10 per cent in 1990 to 6.6 per cent by 2000 and 4.7 per cent in 2005. It declined further to 2 per cent by 2013. Japan, which had already shifted away from textiles to high-tech areas, continued to record a fall in its share of exports of textiles in its overall merchandise exports. Its share fell from 2 per cent in 1990 to 1.5 per cent in 2000, which declined then to 1.2 per cent in 2005 and further to 1 per cent in 2013.

As these highly developed Asian economies moved on to high-tech, high-value, and more sophisticated products, their dependence on the developing economies to meet their requirements of textiles increased. This led to the fast growth of export of cotton yarn from the least-cost economies like India to these countries. According to the DGCIS data, India's export of cotton yarn to these economies, which was negligible during the 1980s, increased from the mid-1990s (Table 3.7). The exports to these economies were adversely affected by the East Asian crisis (1997), but they seem to have improved subsequently.

An analysis of the data on the export of cotton textiles from the TEXPROCIL (Office of Textile Commissioner various years) also points to an increase in the exports of textiles from India to these countries. The share of Taiwan in the export of cotton textiles from India, which was less than 1 per cent in the second half of the 1980s, increased to more than 2 per cent during the mid-1990s. Hong Kong's share was around 2 per cent during the second half of the 1980s, which increased to about 8–9 per cent after the mid-1990s.[7] The share of Korea increased from around 1–3 per cent during the second half of the 1980s to over 6 per cent during the late 1990s. Japan's share, which was very low (generally less than 1 per cent) during the second half of the 1980s, increased to 2–3 per cent after the mid-1990s.

[7] It declined to about 6 per cent during the late 1990s.

Economic development in Korea, Taiwan, and Hong Kong led to substantial increase in domestic wages, and thus affected the cost of production of the labour-intensive exports of textiles. However, these newly industrialising countries were protected by the discriminatory quota regime practised under the MFA. But when the MFA was dismantled, these economies became non-competitive and China emerged as the leading exporter of T&C due to its low-cost advantage. According to the WTO figures published in the *International Trade Statistics* (2014), China's share in world exports of textiles increased from 4.6 per cent in 1980 to 6.9 per cent in 1990 and 10.4 per cent in 2000. It increased further to 34.8 per cent in 2013. China's share in world exports of clothing increased from 4 per cent in 1980 to 8.9 per cent in 1990 and 18.2 per cent in 2000, which increased further to 38.5 per cent in 2013. In order to continue its exports of T&C, China started importing yarn from the other low-cost economies. China's share in world imports of textiles increased from 1.9 per cent in 1980 to 4.9 per cent in 1990 and 7.8 per cent in 2000. Its share declined recently to 6.7 per cent in 2013. The DGCIS data indicate a fast increase in the exports of India's cotton yarn to China after the mid-1990s (Table 3.7).

Table 3.7   Export of Cotton Yarn from India (million kg)

Year	Hong Kong	Korea Republic	Taiwan	Japan	China	Bangladesh
1980–81	0	0	0	0	0	0.29
1985–86	0	0	0	0.7	0	3.75
1989–90	3.55	4.19	0.78	2.62	0.03	9.02
1995–96	30.27	0.91	7.77	0.08	5.59	53.99
2000–01	70.32	22.01	14.70	13.44	21.14	59.60
2005–06	28.56	79.91	12.26	12.65	44.72	74.44
2010–11	25.06	66.39	1.67	10.29	83.53	133.92
2013–14	40.89	48.43	9.65	9.49	144.95	602.67

Source: Computed based on annual figures from DGCIS, *Statistics of Foreign Trade of India*, vol. 1, March 1981, March 1986, March 1990, March 1996, March 2001, March 2006, March 2011, March 2014.

Note: Code 6513 is used for 1980–81 and 1985–86. Codes 5205–7 are used for the later years.

Similarly, the exports of clothing increased fast from a low-cost economy like Bangladesh after the MFA, which led to an increase in its requirements of imports of cotton yarn. Its share in world exports of clothing increased from 0.6 per cent in 1990 to 2.6 per cent in 2000, and further to 5.1 per cent by 2013. This provided an opportunity for India to meet its growing demands for cotton yarn. This is reflected in the DGCIS data as an increase in the export of yarn from India to Bangladesh (Table 3.7). Clearly, the low-cost developing Asian economies like China and Bangladesh are meeting part of their increased demand for yarn from other Asian economies like India and are converting yarn into cloth and garments, which are then exported to the developed economies.

The impact of the substantial increase in the demand for cotton yarn in the international market was that the price of cotton yarn started increasing. The rising prices of cotton yarn in the international market made yarn exports more lucrative. The unit value of the cotton yarn exported from India, which was less than Rs 42 per kg during most of the 1980s, started rising thereafter (Figure 3.7). It increased from Rs 57.5 per kg in 1990–91 to Rs 125 per kg in

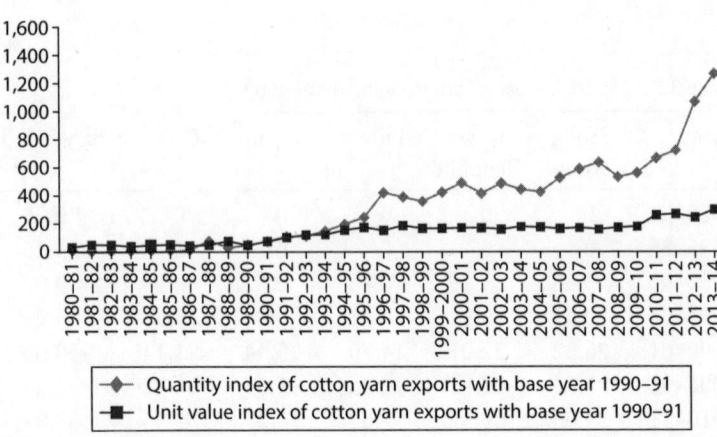

—◆— Quantity index of cotton yarn exports with base year 1990–91
—■— Unit value index of cotton yarn exports with base year 1990–91

Figure 3.7   Quantity Index and Unit Value Index of Cotton Yarn Exports with Base Year 1990–91

Source: Computed based on annual figures from DGCIS, *Monthly Statistics of Foreign Trade of India*, vol. 1 March (various years).

Note: Figures are calculated using code 6513 for 1980–81 to 1986–87 and codes 5205–7 for later years.

1995–96. Since then, it has fluctuated roughly around that level. The unit value index of cotton yarn export (using 1990–91 as base year), which was less than 75 during most of the 1980s, increased to more than 200 by the mid-1990s. It fluctuated around that level before rising fast in recent years. The increase in the price of yarn in the international market encouraged its exports from India.

Shift of Cloth Production from the Highly Developed Economies to the Labour-abundant Economies

Another important change in the structure of world's textile industry, which helped the growth of India's textile exports, was the shift of cloth production from the highly developed economies like the UK, the US, and Italy, to the labour-abundant economies like India and China (Table 3.8). The shift was mainly due to the differences in the labour costs of these economies. As weaving is labour intensive and labour was more expensive in these developed economies, cloth production was relocated to the least-cost countries of the world. According to the DGCIS data, exports of cotton cloth from India to these economies, which were low up to the mid-1980s, picked up afterwards. For example, the quantity of export of cotton cloth to the UK grew at 11.7 per cent per annum from 1985–86 to 1995–96.

Table 3.8   Exports of Woven Cloth of Cotton from India (million sq. m)

Year	UK	US	Italy	Bangladesh	Sri Lanka
1980–81	171.49	40.73	10.01	0.67	2.5
1985–86	40.94	45.45	22.76	7.88	10.92
1989–90	63.8	74.47	23.89	43.14	8.66
1995–96	123.74	151.88	33.41	55.61	30.75
2004–05	26.37	64.11	28.99	55.92	38.59
2010–11	13.45	31.59	32.65	40.7	86.47
2013–14	14.93	41.77	33.45	147.51	105.74

Source: Computed based on annual figures from DGCIS, *Statistics of Foreign Trade of India*, vol. 1, March 1981, March 1986, March 1990, March 1996, March 2005, March 2011, March 2014.
Note: Codes 6521 and 6522 are used for exports of woven cloth of cotton for 1980–81 and 1985–86. Codes 5208–12 are used for the same for later years.

The exports to the US grew at a higher rate of 12.82 per cent per annum and the export of cotton cloth to Italy grew at 3.91 per cent per annum during the same period. However, the cotton cloth exports to these developed economies started declining thereafter. This decline in cotton cloth export, roughly after the 1990s, can be seen in the context of the sharp increase in the exports of ready-made garments from India during this period. The data indicate that while cloth exports declined to the US, the UK, and Italy, the exports of cotton garments continued to grow (Table 3.9). Since garment manufacturing is more labour intensive when compared with weaving, the increase in the exports of garments to these developed countries reflects the increasing preference of these developed economies for direct imports of ready-made garments. Instead of importing cloth and then converting it into garments, the developed countries are shifting to imports of the garments.

Table 3.9 Value of Export of Cotton Garments with Base Year 1990–91 (Rs million)

Year	US	UK	France	Germany
1980–81	19.99	10.95	7.07	17.55
1985–86	37.22	11.48	6.77	15.78
1989–90	83.62	25.86	21.91	41.90
1995–96	115.72	40.81	31.27	51.01
2000–01	234.09	57.93	52.26	53.75
2004–05	222.22	75.07	67.38	84.50
2010–11	298.61	111.53	66.24	111.18
2013–14	344.00	172.95	80.98	136.40

Sources: Computed based on annual figures from DGCIS, *Statistics of Foreign Trade of India*, vol. 1, March 1981, March 1986, March 1990, March 1996, March 2001, March 2005, March 2011, March 2014. Unit value index for export of cotton yarn is computed based on figures from DGCIS, *Monthly Statistics of Foreign Trade of India*, vol. 1 (various years).

Notes: 1. The garment exports to all the countries include exports of woven, knitted, and crocheted garments of cotton. For 1980–81 and 1985–86, figures are obtained using codes 842–7. Codes 61 and 62 are used for the later years.

2. Garment exports are deflated using unit value index for export of cotton yarn from India.

According to the DGCIS data, India's garments exports remained low to these economies up to the 1980s and picked up thereafter. The compound annual average growth rate of exports of garments (at constant prices) from the mid-1990s to 2013–14 was 6.24 per cent and 8.35 per cent for the US and the UK respectively. The exports of cotton garments also increased from India to France and Germany during the same period, but at a lower rate of 5.43 and 5.62 per cent per annum respectively. The abundance of skilled workforce and small scales of operation are additional advantages that India's garment exporters enjoy over Hong Kong, Taiwan, South Korea, and China (Tewari 2005). In addition to this, the Indian garment export industry has developed an export-oriented industrial structure. Most exporters exclusively concentrate on export without supplying to the domestic market.

During the MFA regime, India was exporting cotton fabric mainly to the developed economies, which are its traditional trading partners; after the end of post-MFA regime, the demand for export of cotton fabric from India increased in the low-cost developing economies like Bangladesh and Sri Lanka, which experienced substantial increase in their exports of garments. Bangladesh, in fact, has emerged as the leading world exporter of T&C. Bangladesh's share in world exports of clothing, which was negligible in 1980, increased to 5.1 per cent in 2013. Sri Lanka's share in world exports of clothing increased from 0.6 per cent in 1990 to 1.4 per cent in 2000 (WTO 2014). The share declined to 1 per cent in 2013. The labour costs are even lower in these economies (as discussed further). The increasing imports of fabric from countries like India have helped these economies to maintain the growth in their exports of garments to the developed economies. This has led to the fast growth of India's exports of fabric to these economies (Table 3.8).

Costs of Production

Overall, the evidence suggests that there were changes in the structure of the world textile industry that proved favourable for the growth of India's exports. In the context of these changes, the costs of production became the prime determinant of trade in T&C. Costs continued to play a very important role in deciding the direction of trade in the years after the expiry of the ATC. International cost comparisons of the textile industry in Brazil, China, India, Italy, Korea, Turkey, and the US, by the International Textile Manufacturers Federation (ITMF 2006), suggest that the wage rate is much lower in India in spinning, weaving, and knitting. The wage rate is lowest in India for spinning. In weaving also, the wage rate is low (next to the least-wage rate country, China). In knitting, it is lowest in India for skilled personnel and only next to China for unskilled personnel.

The raw material costs in spinning and weaving are also found to be the lowest in India. A comparison of the total manufacturing costs by the ITMF (2006) indicates that though costs for power and interest are higher in India in comparison to other countries, the total manufacturing costs are low in spinning, weaving, and knitting. The ITMF's comparison of the total cost, which includes the manufacturing costs and the cost of raw materials (cotton/polyester), indicates that India is the least-cost producer of ring and open-end yarn and fabric (except for textured yarn and fabric where India is next to China, which is the least-cost producer of these products).

A WTO (2001) study, 'The Global Textile and Clothing Industry Post the Agreement on Textiles and Clothing', which compares the cost structure of the T&C sector, given as percentages of gross value of the sector's production in selected countries, indicates a higher unskilled labour intensity of the clothing sector in comparison to the textile sector. This suggests that the countries with low labour costs are at a greater advantage in the exports of clothing. Since the labour costs in the garment industry in India are much lower than the US, Korea, Mexico, Hong Kong, and even China (Table 3.10), as indicated by a study on comparative labour costs in the apparel industry (United Nations Conference on Trade and Development [UNCTAD] 2002), this indicates that one of the important reasons for the fast growth of garment exports from India lies in its cheap labour. But this also points to the tough competition that India faces from Indonesia and Bangladesh, which have even lower average hourly wages.

In an overall scenario, where costs had become the main determinant of the direction of trade, this played an important role in the growth of exports of T&C.

Table 3.10 Hourly Labour Cost in Clothing Industry in Selected Countries in 1998 (US dollar)

United States	9.93
Costa Rica	5.25
Hong Kong	5.20
Republic of Korea	2.71
Mexico	1.51
Guatemala	1.29
India	0.39
Bangladesh	0.30
Indonesia	0.17
China	0.43

Source: UNCTAD (2002: 159).

Impact on BoP

The growth of exports of T&C industry affected the BoP of the economy favourably because the extent of dependence of this industry on imported inputs continued to be low. The WTO study on the cost structure of the clothing sector of selected countries for 2001 revealed that the cost of imported inputs as a percentage of gross output was in the 10–15 per cent range in the US, Italy, Hong Kong, and Taiwan. It varied between 15 and 20 per cent in Canada and Republic of Korea. The share was much higher for France (24.3 per cent), Vietnam (40.4 per cent), and Morocco (37.9 per cent). However, it was 5.7 per cent in China and 1.8 per cent in India. The low dependence on imports helped in maintaining the growth of garment exports, as it is difficult to use imported fabrics in the manufacture of garments because the limited time available to cater to seasonal fashions and designs does not permit their import on an appreciable scale (GoI 1985, cited in Uchikawa 1998: 38). Similarly, the cost of imported inputs as a percentage of gross output for the textile sector in the year 2001 was the least (4 per cent) for India. The share was between 20 and 25 per cent for Canada, France, and Republic of Korea. It was between 8 and 12 per cent for the US, Japan, Taiwan, and China. Italy, Vietnam, and Morocco had shares in the 35–45 per cent range (WTO 2001).

While the growth in exports was a consequence of global market development, depreciation of the rupee, and availability of cheaper inputs, the low import shares were due to the restrictive import policy followed since the 1950s. India justified the use of QRs under the GATT BoP provision. While QRs were removed on most capital goods and manufactured intermediate products after the reforms that began in 1991, the import of consumer goods, including T&C, remained practically banned. However, India's position was challenged by the US, the EU, and other developed countries after the Uruguay Round Agreement. Large foreign exchange reserves, a strong current account, and substantial capital inflows characterised India's BoP account (Goldar 2005). Failing to justify QRs on grounds of BoP, India agreed to eliminate QRs in a phased manner by March 2003.

Further, international pressures for liberalising textile imports increased after December 1994 when India held market access negotiations and signed memoranda of understanding (MoUs) with the US and the EU. India agreed to remove restrictions on import of a large number of textile products and to reduce tariffs on imports of textiles products as a quid pro quo for the ATC and in exchange for increased MFA quotas in the US and the EU markets. As a result of the market access MoUs and the BoP negotiations, India was compelled to fully open up its textile market, leading to an increase in imports (Table 3.11). The process began in early 1995 with the removal of QRs on imports of wool tops, synthetic fibres, textile yarn, and some industrial fabrics. Some selected textile fabrics, made-ups, and apparel items could also be imported against special import licence by the exporters. It was agreed that these products would be free from import licensing at specified future dates (1998, 2000, and 2002). The tariff rates would also be lowered on these products (Goldar 2005).

The opening up of the domestic market led to an increase in imports into this industry. According to WTO data published in the *International Trade Statistics* (2014), India's textile imports increased from 240 million dollars in 1990 to 575 million dollars in 2000. The imports increased fast thereafter to 3,579 million dollars by 2013. In other words, imports grew at a rate of 15.10 per cent per annum between 2000 and 2013. Though the share of India's textile imports

Table 3.11 Value of Imports of India's T&C Industry with Base Year 1990–91 (Rs million)

	1980–81	1985–86	1990–91	1995–96	2000–01	2005–06	2010–11	2013–14
Textile fibres & their waste	4,680.51	5,997.00	4,038.41	10,852.80	15,588.12	12,568.83	30,207.93	27,489.77
Textile yarn	1,239.49	1,603.85	2,546.19	2,239.71	4,458.90	11,247.62	14,326.33	16,489.03
Fabrics	19.68	501.82	1,847.83	3,353.29	7,000.96	35,936.78	27,674.21	30,361.85
Garments and made-ups	18.11	196.17	631.80	733.68	2,374.49	4,039.66	7,971.86	12,863.33
Carpets and floor coverings	0.00	0.00	91.46	14.60	220.48	863.37	1,153.81	1,200.87
Wadding	181.55	282.94	180.49	447.49	636.18	2,077.01	2,393.04	3,012.97
Total	6,139.35	8,581.79	9,336.19	17,641.57	30,279.13	66,733.26	83,727.18	91,417.83

Sources: Computed based on annual figures from DGCIS, *Monthly Statistics of Foreign Trade of India*, vol. 1, March 1981, March 1986, March 1991, March 1996, March 2001, March 2006, March 2011, March 2014 and RBI (2006, 2014).

Notes: 1. For 1980–81 and 1985–86:

a. Import of textile fibres is calculated using DGCIS code 26.

b. Import of textile yarn is calculated using code 651.

c. Codes 653–7 are used for import of fabrics.

d. Codes 84 and 658 are used for calculating imports of garments and made-ups.

2. For 1990–91, 1995–96, 2000–01, 2005–06, 2010–11, and 2013–14:

a. Figures for import of textile fibres and their wastes are calculated using DGCIS codes 5001–3, 5101–5, 5201–3, 5301–5, and 5501–7.

b. Import of textile yarn is calculated using DGCIS codes 5004–6, 5106–9, 5204–7, 5306–8, 5401–6, and 5508–11.

c. Import of fabrics is calculated using 5007, 5110–13, 5208–12, 5309–11, 5407–8, 5512–16, 58, and 60.

d. Imports of garments and made-ups are calculated using DGCIS codes 61, 62, and 63.

e. Import of carpets, etc., is based on code 57.

f. Import of wadding, felt, etc., is based on code 56.

3. Deflators used:

a. The figures for import of textile fibres are deflated using unit value index for import of fibres and their waste.

b. The imports in other categories are deflated using unit value index for import of textile yarn.

in the economy's total merchandise imports declined from 1.1 per cent in 2000 to 0.8 per cent in 2013, India's share in world imports of textiles increased from 0.4 per cent of world textile imports in 2000 to 1.1 per cent by 2013.

The DGCIS data also indicate substantial increase in India's textile imports. The removal of restrictions on imports of a large number of textile products and reductions in import tariffs on several others resulted in an increase in all types of T&C imports, including textile fibres, yarn, garments and made-ups, carpets, and floor coverings (Table 3.11). The value index of overall imports of T&C industry (with base 1990–91) increased to 715 by 2005–06. However, the sharp decline in exports of garments to the developed economies after the crisis in September 2008 seems to have reduced the demand for imports of fabric in the following years, affecting the growth of overall imports of the industry in the recent years.

Previously, heavy tariffs were imposed on the import of synthetic fibres/filament yarn. The reductions in customs duties during the course of liberalisation resulted in an increase in their imports.[8] The import of textile fibres grew at 5.3 per cent per annum from 1995–96 to 2013–14 (Figure 3.8). The value index of import of textile fibres increased (with base 1990–91) to 680.70 during 2013–14.

The import of textile yarn also grew fast at 11.73 per cent per annum from 1995–96 to 2013–14 (Figure 3.8). The value index of import of textile yarn (with base 1990–91) increased to 647.60 by 2013–14. China emerged as the important source of import of yarn for India. India's import of cotton yarn from China grew at a high average annual rate of 37.32 per cent since the middle of the 1990s.[9] India's import of yarn from Pakistan also expanded in the same period. However, this increase in the imports of synthetic fibre/filament yarns needs to be seen in the overall context of changing scenario after the mid-1990s, when reductions in customs duties reduced the domestic prices of synthetic fibres/filament yarns lead-ing to increase in their demand for producing fabric.[10] As a result,

[8] For details, see Chapter 2, 'Availability and Cost of Raw Materials'.

[9] Computed based on figures from DGCIS, *Statistics of Foreign Trade of India by countries,* vol. 2 (various years).

[10] For details, see Chapter 2, 'Availability and Cost of Raw Materials'.

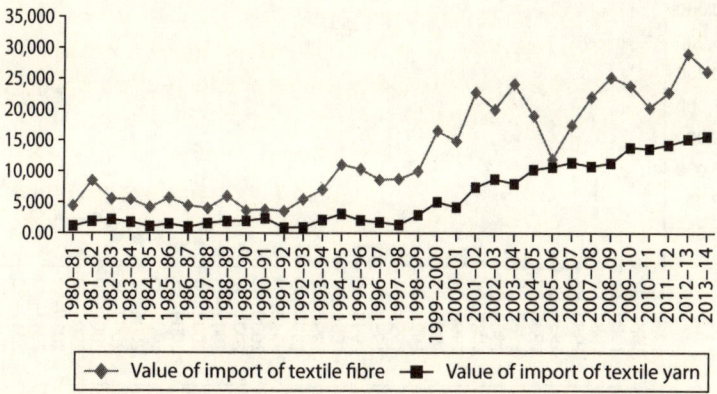

Figure 3.8 Value of Imports of Textile Fibre and Textile Yarn with Base Year 1990–91 (Rs million)

Sources: Computed based on annual figures from DGCIS, *Monthly Statistics of Foreign Trade of India*, vol. 2 March (various years) for imports; and RBI (2006, 2014) for deflators.

Note: The codes used are mentioned in Notes to Table 3.11. The unit value index for import of textile fibre and their waste is used as deflator for import of textile fibre and the unit value index for import of textile yarn is used as deflator for import of textile yarn.

synthetic fabrics, which were far more expensive and were considered as items of luxury roughly up to the mid-1990s, became cheaper in comparison with cotton fabrics, thereby becoming items of mass consumption. This led to further increase in the demand for polyester, which encouraged expansion in its domestic capacity and greater capacity utilisation. This resulted in a substantial growth in domestic production of polyester, which was made widely available at lower prices after the mid-1990s. In this overall context of falling domestic prices, growing demand, growing production, and growing imports of synthetic fibres/filament yarns, it is important to highlight that though the imports were rising, the share of imports in domestic consumption of PSF and PFY declined considerably after the 1990s, signifying reduction in the country's dependence on imports.[11]

The import of fabric was minimal during the 1970s and 1980s. The removal of QRs and reductions in tariffs on a large number of

[11] For details, see Chapter 2, 'Availability and Cost of Raw Materials'.

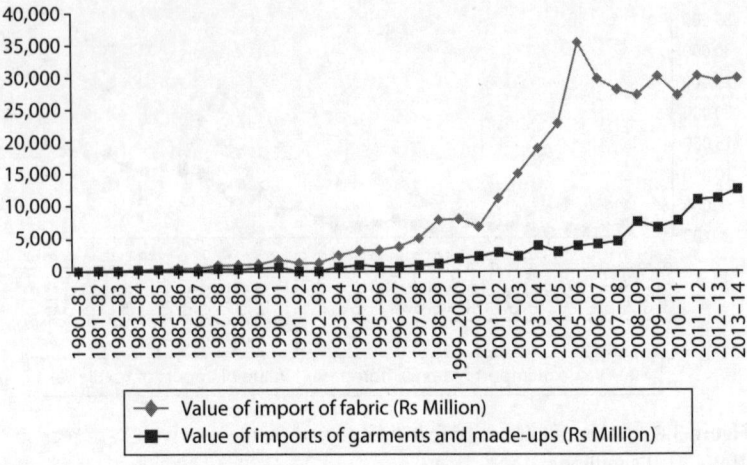

Figure 3.9   Value of Imports of Fabric and Garments and Made-ups with Base Year 1990–91 (Rs million)

Sources: Computed based on annual figures from DGCIS, *Monthly Statistics of Foreign Trade of India,* vol. 2 March (various years) for imports; and RBI (2006, 2014) for the deflator.

Note: The codes used are mentioned in Notes to Table 3.11. The unit value index of import of textile yarn is used as deflator.

textile products resulted in a sharp increase in the import of fabrics after the mid-1990s (Figure 3.9). In value terms, the import of fabric (with base year 1990–91) increased at a high rate of 13.02 per cent per annum from 1995–96 to 2013–14. China emerged as the important source of import of fabric for India. India imported 1.71 million sq. m of woven fabric of cotton from China during 1995–96, which increased to 123.63 million sq. m during 2005–06.[12] India's import of fabric increased recently from Pakistan too. It may be argued that the increase in imports of fabrics after the mid-1990s reflects the low quality and poor standards of the domestically produced fabric, which has almost entirely shifted to the unorganised sector where power looms, handlooms, and hosiery units produce about 96 per cent of the total fabric production. However, the figures from the Office of the Textile Commissioner indicate that power looms, which

[12] Computed based on annual figures from DGCIS, *Statistics of Foreign Trade of India by Countries,* vol. 2 March (various years).

have increased their share in fabric production and account for about 65 per cent of total fabric produced in the unorganised sector, have become the leading suppliers of fabric in the world market as well.[13]

The imports of garments and made-ups were practically banned up to the mid-1990s. The removal of QRs and reductions in tariffs on a large number of garments and made-ups after the mid-1990s led to a consistent increase in the imports of garments and made-ups at a rate of 17.25 per cent per annum during 1995–96 to 2013–14 (Figure 3.9). The value index of imports of garments and made-ups with base 1990–91 increased to 2035.98 during 2013–14. China also emerged as the important source of imports of garments after the 1990s. Nepal, Bangladesh, Hong Kong, and Thailand are the other countries which export garments to India.

The sudden increase in imports of fabrics and garments and made-ups after the mid-1990s resulted in a structural change in the imports of the industry. The imports of the industry mainly consisted of textile fibres and textile yarn during the 1980s. Textile fibres alone accounted for about 76 per cent of the overall imports of the industry during 1980–81 (Table 3.11). The share of textile fibres in the overall T&C imports declined from about 62 per cent during the mid-1990s to about 19 per cent in 2005–06. The share increased after 2009–10 when the import of fabric, which increased substantially after the 1990s, declined suddenly.

The share of import of textile fabrics was low (about 4 per cent) during 1980–81. It increased to 54 per cent by 2005–06 and then declined to about 33 per cent after 2009–10. The substantial decline in exports of garments from India after the financial crisis in the developed economies seems to have affected India's demand for fabric imports. The share of imports of garments and made-ups, which was low up to the mid-1990s, increased to about 14 per cent by 2013–14.

Overall, though imports increased, they continued to be small in relation to exports,[14] which included exports of textiles using cotton,

[13] For details, see Chapter 4, 'Structural Changes in the Indian Textile Industry'.

[14] Similar results are suggested by Goldar (2005) while analysing the impact of tariff reductions and lowering of QRs for the period 1990–91 to 2003–04.

silk, jute, wool, and synthetic and vegetable fibre; exports of carpets and other textile floor coverings; wadding, felts, and special yarns, like ropes and cables; special woven fabrics like lace and embroidery; textile articles for industrial use; knitted and crocheted fabrics; articles of apparel and clothing; and other made-up textile articles. All kinds of exports grew substantially during this period. As a result, the net exports of T&C increased from USD 1,584.63 million in 1985–86 to USD 26,025.90 million in 2013–14, experiencing a growth of 10.51 per cent per annum during the period. The increase in net exports of the industry affected the BoP of the economy favourably (Table 3.12).

Further, the import intensity of T&C exports (measured as the proportion of total imports to total exports of the T&C industry)

Table 3.12   Net Exports (million dollar) and Import Intensity (%) of India's T&C Industry

Year	Exports	Imports	Net exports	Import intensity
1980–81	2,000.00	283.19	1,716.81	14.16
1985–86	1,929.68	345.05	1,584.63	17.88
1990–91	4,396.68	520.62	3,876.06	11.84
1995–96	7,837.06	974.59	6,862.47	12.44
2000–01	11,121.00	1,170.53	9,950.46	10.53
2005–06	16,531.48	2,674.05	13,857.43	16.18
2010–11	23,249.56	4,086.21	19,163.35	17.58
2013–14	31,331.40	5,305.50	26,025.90	16.93

Sources: Computed based on annual figures from DGCIS, *Monthly Statistics of Foreign Trade of India*, vols 1 and 2, March 1981, March 1986, March 1991, March 1996, March 2001, March 2006, March 2011, March 2014 for exports and imports; and RBI (2006, 2014) for exchange rate.

Notes: 1. The figures on exports are calculated using DGCIS codes 65 and 84 for 1980–81 and 1985–86. For the later years, the codes used are 5004–7, 5107–13, 5204–12, 5306–11, 5407–8, 550941, 550942, 55095300, 55096200, 55099200, 55101101, 55101102, 55101201, 55101202, 55102001, 55102002, 55103001, 55103002, 55109001, 55109002, 5512–16, and 56–63.

2. The import figures are calculated using DGCIS codes 26, 65, and 84 for 1980–81 and 1985–86. For the later years, codes 50–63 are used.

3. Rupee figures are converted into dollars using exchange rate.

from India declined considerably after the mid-1980s (Table 3.12). The decline was from 17.88 per cent in 1985–86 to 10.53 per cent by 2000–01. However, the import intensity has been increasing thereafter. It increased to 16.18 in 2005–06 and further to 17.58 in 2010–11. Though there was a slight decline in the year 2013–14, it continued to be higher than what it was before 2010–11, reflecting fast growth of India's imports of T&C after the opening up of the economy.

Overall, the net exports of the industry continued to increase and the industry continued to perform as a net foreign exchange earner, affecting the BoP favourably. However, in the current scenario when India is finding it challenging to increase its exports in view of the crisis in the developed economies, this increase in import intensity of textile exports is worrisome and needs to be explored further.

Proportion of Exports in the Production of T&C Industry

The DGCIS data indicate tremendous increase in the exports of T&C industry since the 1990s. The exports of all types of textile products and clothing like yarn, cloth, garments, and made-ups have grown substantially. However, as has already been explained in Chapter 1, this period was also characterised by growth in the home demand for T&C. According to the NSSO (1996, 2006) figures on consumer expenditure, the overall real monthly consumption expenditure (with base 1983) on clothing grew at a compound annual average rate of 4.62 per cent from 1993–94 to 2004–05. The growth rate for the rural areas (4.05 per cent per annum) was lower than that observed for the urban areas (5.73 per cent per annum).

Overall, this indicates that it was a combination of growth in exports as well as growth in home demand that led to the growth of the T&C industry since the 1990s. In order to examine which of these has been crucial for the growth of the industry during the period, this section examines changes in the proportion of overall exports of this industry to the total value of output produced by this industry at current prices.

Since the production of T&C industry takes place in both the registered and the unregistered sectors, the total value of output produced in this industry is calculated as the value of output produced in the registered and the unregistered T&C sectors combined (Table 3.13). This includes the production of textiles and the production of garments and made-ups (using cotton, silk, wool, jute, and vegetable as fibres).

Table 3.13 Value of Output of T&C Industry at Current Prices (Rs million)

Year	Registered sector	Unregistered sector	Total
1978–79	71,260	23,050	94,310
1984–85	140,610	69,710	210,320
1989–90	281,520	105,080	386,600
1994–95	624,740	128,320	753,050
1999–2000	1,059,010	392,090	1,451,100
2000–01	1,177,280	442,270	1,619,550
2002–03	1,244,230	465,440	1,709,670
2004–05	1,518,960	570,780	2,089,740
2006–07	1,797,690	680,550	2,478,240
2008–09	2,404,320	1,274,870	3,679,190
2010–11	4,079,330	1,635,570	5,714,900
2012–13	4,711,970	1,859,630	6,571,600

Sources: For the registered sector–computed based on figures from Central Statistical Organisation (CSO 2007, 2014). For the unregistered sector–computed based on figures from NSSO (1987, 1989, 1995, 1998); CSO (1985, 1989, 1995); and CSO (2014) for 1999–2000 to 2012–13.

Notes: 1. Figures for the unregistered sector, up to 1994–95, are obtained as the value of output produced per enterprise (Own Account Enterprises [OAEs], Non-directory Establishments [NDEs], and Directory Manufacturing Establishments [DMEs]) engaged in manufacturing of T&C, multiplied by the number of such enterprises (that is, adding for codes 23, 24, 25, and 26 and then adjusting by subtracting code 230 [following NIC-1970 for 1978–79 and 1984–85 and NIC-1987 for 1989–90 and 1994–95] for both rural and urban areas as code 230 [cotton ginning, cleaning, and baling] is not included in the data from 1999–2000 onwards following NIC-1998).

2. For the unregistered sector, for the year 1984–85, the estimates also include the value of output produced in code 230, cotton ginning, cleaning, and baling, in the OAEs and NDEs as they are not available at 3-digit codes and therefore could not be adjusted.

3. Figures for the registered sector from 1978–79 to 1994–95 are adjusted for code 230 (cotton ginning, baling) using ASI data as code 230 is not included in the data from 1999–2000 onwards (following NIC-1998).

For the registered sector, the value of output produced[15] at current prices is obtained from the NAS. These figures are available on annual basis since 1950–51. For the unregistered T&C sector, the required data on the value of output produced at current prices are provided in the NAS, but only from 1999–2000 onwards. For the period prior to 1999–2000, the study relies on the NSS surveys on unorganised manufacturing (NSSO 1987, 1989, 1995, 1998).

The data on the exports of T&C industry are obtained from the *Monthly Statistics of Foreign Trade of India* (various years), published by DGCIS and include exports of textiles using a wide variety of fibres, exports of carpets and other textile floor coverings, wadding, felts and special yarns, special woven fabrics, textile articles for industrial use, knitted and crocheted fabrics, articles of apparel and clothing, and other made-up textile articles.

The export intensity is measured as the proportion of exports of textile industry to the overall value of output produced in the T&C industry at current prices. It is observed that the export intensity was very low up to the mid-1980s (around 11–12 per cent), but it increased sharply from 11 per cent during the mid-1980s to 29 per cent during the mid-1990s. However, it almost stabilised thereafter (Table 3.14), varying in the range of 28–33 per cent, except for the period after the financial crisis, when it declined sharply to 18.86 per cent.

Similar results are obtained from a detailed analysis of export performance of India's textile and apparel manufacturing firms using Centre for Monitoring Indian Economy (CMIE) data from 1991 to 2013 (Kar 2015). For 415 firms that operated in domestic as well as export markets, the exports as percentage of total sales increased fast from the early 1990s to 1998–99. It then declined and stabilised up to 2007–08. The share declined further during the years after the financial crisis. Also, the number of firms that cater exclusively to the

[15] Central Statistical Organisation (2007) provides estimates for the value of output at current prices produced in the registered sector for textile products (including wearing apparel) from 1970–71 to 1999–2000. Central Statistical Organisation (2014) provides the value of output at current prices produced in the registered sector in textile sector and garment sector separately from 1999–2000 onwards.

Table 3.14   Proportion of Exports to the Value of Output of India's T&C Industry

Year	Value of output (registered and unregistered) at current prices (Rs million)	Value of exports of textile and clothing at current prices (Rs million)	Proportion of exports to value of output (%)
	2	3	4
1978–79	94,310	11,410	12.10
1984–85	210,320	23,740	11.29
1989–90	386,600	62140	16.07
1994–95	753,050	218,380	29.00
2000–01	1,619,550	508,000	31.37
2002–03	1,709,670	551,760	32.27
2004–05	2,089,740	577,640	27.64
2006–07	2,478,240	776,940	31.35
2008–09	3,679,190	910,750	24.75
2010–11	5,714,900	1,077,620	18.86
2012–13	6,571,600	1,977,885	30.10

Sources: Table 3.13 for column 2; and computed based on annual figures from DGCIS, *Monthly Statistics of Foreign Trade of India*, vol. 1, March 1979, March 1985, March 1990, March 1995, March 2001, March 2003, March 2005, March 2007, March 2009, March 2011, and March 2013 for column 3.

Notes: 1. The figures in column 2 are obtained from Table 3.13.
2. The figures in column 3 are calculated using DGCIS codes 65 and 84 for 1978–79 and 1984–85. For the later years, the codes used are 5004–7, 5107–13, 5204–12, 5306–11, 5407–8, 550941, 550942, 55095300, 55096200, 55099200, 55101101, 55101102, 55101201, 55101202, 55102001, 55102002, 55103001, 55103002, 55109001, 55109002, 5512–16, and 56–63.

export market increased (with some minor fluctuations) fast from the early 1990s to the year 1998 and stabilised around that level up to 2003. The numbers have been much lower thereafter. This suggests a greater focus on the domestic market for Indian firms after the withdrawal of quota since 2005.

Overall, it seems that roughly about 70 per cent of the total output produced by the T&C industry was consumed within the economy after the mid-1990s. Clearly, exports grew faster than the domestic demand up to the mid-1990s, but thereafter the two increased at almost the same rate. The exports of the industry grew at a rate of 13.02 per cent per annum, while the value of output grew at 12.8 per cent per annum. Thus, there was tremendous growth in the exports of the industry, which contributed to its growth, but this seems to have been matched by the growth of the domestic demand during this period. It seems that though the growth of the industry was led by a combination of growth of exports and growth of domestic demand since the mid-1990s, the home demand continued to be the main driving force behind its growth.

* * *

Thus, the overall analysis of growth of exports of the Indian textile industry suggests that there was a tremendous growth in exports of yarn, fabrics, garments, and made-ups since the early 1990s. Several structural changes accompanied the increase in exports from the industry. The share of the cotton T&C in India's exports of overall T&C fell with faster growth in the exports of synthetic textiles. India's textile industry showed a trend towards greater value addition within the economy. This was reflected in a fall in the share of exports of fabric and a rise in the share of finished products, including garments and made-ups. The worldwide shift in demand induced by comfort and leisure considerations favoured the exports of knitted garments of cotton.

The deregulation of the industry after the NTP (1985) provided incentives to increase the export of yarn. The full convertibility of the rupee on the current account stimulated the growth of exports. The depreciation of the Indian rupee, which was much sharper in comparison to the other exporting countries, made exports from India more competitive. The ATC was not effective till 2002, and its full impact became apparent only from 2005 onwards. Its contribution towards the growth of India's exports can be seen only indirectly in the form of providing incentives for modernisation and capacity expansion in view of the increased competition among the exporters of T&C after 2004. However, some cost-driven shifts, which occurred in the structure of the world textile industry during the 1990s, favourably affected the growth of India's textile and garment exports. Cotton yarn manufacturing shifted from highly developed Asian economies to low-cost economies like India as these Asian economies shifted to the high-tech areas. Cloth and garment production shifted from highly developed economies like the US, the EU, and Italy to the low-cost, labour-abundant economies like India and China. Further, the emergence of cost of production as the main determinant of growth of exports proved favourable for the growth of India's exports.

Thus, global market developments, depreciation of the rupee, and availability of cheaper inputs were the main factors that helped India to increase its share in world markets and expand its exports of T&C. However, the main thrust for the fast expansion of the industry continued to be provided by domestic demand, which continued to account for about 70 per cent of the total production in the textile industry. Further, though the opening up of the domestic market led to an increase in imports, the net exports of the India's T&C industry continued to increase. Thus, India's T&C industry continued to perform as a net foreign exchange earner.

4

Structural Changes in the Indian Textile Industry

The recession that hit the Indian industry roughly after the mid-1960s affected the textile industry as well, which experienced stagnation in demand and, consequently, in the production of textiles. However, a resurgence of textile demand from 1993–94 led to the revival of the industry, which was accompanied by several important changes in the structure of the industry. Until the 1980s, the Indian textile industry was broadly classified into two categories: the organised mill sector and the unorganised decentralised sector. The mills could be spinning mills or composite mills. Spinning mills carried out spinning of cotton yarn, while composite mills were engaged in spinning, weaving, and processing activities. The decentralised sector, on the other hand, was engaged mainly in the weaving of cotton cloth,[1] which made it heavily dependent on the organised sector for its cotton yarn requirements. The decentralised sector was divided into two major segments—power looms and handlooms. However, there were several structural changes during the period of its revival,

---

[1] This formed about 80 per cent of their total cloth production in the early 1970s and about 70 per cent from the late 1970s to the late 1980s (Office of the Textile Commissioner, in ICMF, *Handbook of Statistics on Cotton Textile Industry* [2004: 32]).

which included changes in sectoral composition as well as shifts in the pattern of fibre use. Further, the industry was characterised by the expansion and modernisation of capacity in the spinning sector and a rapid growth of the garment sector. This chapter examines and analyses the structural changes that have characterised the Indian textile industry during the period of its revival.

Inter-fibre Changes

Steep Fall in the Share of Cotton in Weaving

One important structural change that characterised the industry was the shift in the pattern of fibre use. The data indicate that cotton fabrics, which dominated cloth production until the late 1980s, no longer do so. The share of cotton fell from above 70 per cent in the middle of the 1980s to about 67 per cent in 1989 (Figure 4.1). This trend continued during the 1990s and thereafter, taking it to a much smaller, even if absolutely high, 42.6 per cent in 2003–04. Thereafter, this declining trend in the share of cotton seems to have reversed itself, with the share rising to 56.71 per cent in 2013–14. However, it continued to be lower than what it was up to the middle of the 1990s.

The period 1990–91 to 2009–10 was characterised by an increase in the absolute level of production of fabrics using all types of fibres (Figure 4.1). However, the increase was much sharper in the production of blended and 100 per cent non-cotton fabrics (7.18 per cent per annum) compared with cotton (3.67 per cent per annum), which resulted in a fall in the share of cotton fabric. The falling share of cotton can be explained as being the response of the sector to a change in the pattern of demand in favour of synthetic and blended textiles during the period. Although per capita household demand for synthetic textiles was increasing since the 1970s, it remained insignificant, being limited largely to the rich. Cotton continued to dominate consumption since imported synthetic fabrics were expensive and subject to very high customs duties, and therefore considered as items of luxury. The reductions in customs duty on the raw materials and intermediates required for the production of synthetic fabric during the 1990s lowered the price of polyester staple fibre (PSF) and polyester filament

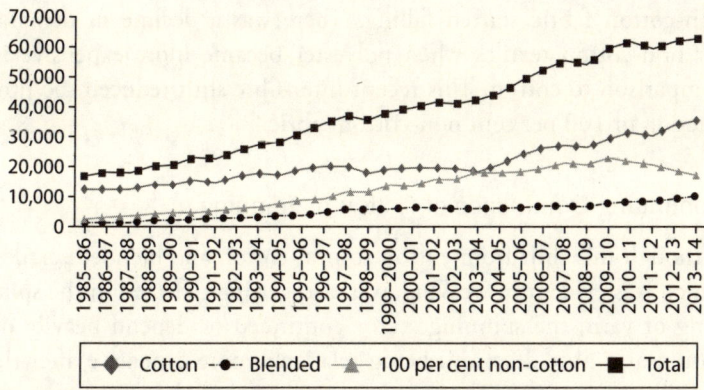

Figure 4.1 Fibre-wise Production of Cloth (million sq. m)
Sources: Office of the Textile Commissioner, in ICMF, *Handbook of Statistics on Cotton Textile Industry* (1998) up to 1989–90; CITI, *Handbook of Statistics on Textile Industry* (2008); CITI, *Annual Reports* (2006, 2007, and 2008) for 2005–06 to 2007–08; for and www.txcindia.gov.in (last accessed on 15 February 2016) for recent years.

yarn (PFY) in the domestic market, which ultimately affected the prices of synthetic textiles.[2] These products became much cheaper after the middle of the 1990s and much of the increase in their demand came from the low and lower middle income groups, which recorded a substantial increase in their monthly per capita purchases (MPCP) of non-cotton and blended textiles.[3]

However, this fall in the share of cotton fabric reversed after 2003–04. The revival of cotton was due to the fast growth of exports of and domestic demand for cotton textiles and clothing (T&C). The availability of cheaper inputs and global market developments during the period led to an expansion of cotton-based exports. The growth of national income at a higher rate combined with rising inequalities during this period increased the domestic demand for cotton-based products. The rise in the share of cotton fabric was faster after 2009–10, when the production of 100 per cent

[2] For details, see Chapter 2, 'Availability and Cost of Raw Materials'.

[3] For details, see Chapter 1, 'Trends in Domestic Demand and their Implications'.

non-cotton fabric started falling. There was a decline in demand for non-cotton textiles when polyester became more expensive in comparison to cotton. This recent inter-fibre shift reduced the production of 100 per cent non-cotton fabric.

Continuing Dominance of Cotton in Spinning

Although this shift from cotton to non-cotton and blended textiles, which was evident in weaving, was also getting reflected in the spinning of yarn, the spinning sector continued to depend heavily on cotton as a fibre despite it being relatively more expensive after the middle of the 1990s. The share of cotton yarn in the total spun yarn declined from about 82–6 per cent in the first half of the 1980s to about 70–4 per cent after the middle of the 1990s, but it continued to dominate spun yarn production (Figure 4.2). The more expensive cotton continued to be preferred by those who could afford it at home or abroad because of the comfort associated with the fabric, its tactile properties, and its moisture and heat transport properties. Studies have indicated that T-shirts containing 50 per cent polyester were not significantly different in comfort preference from those of 100 per cent non-cotton. T-shirts made entirely of polyester were considered definitely to be uncomfortable. In addition, studies have

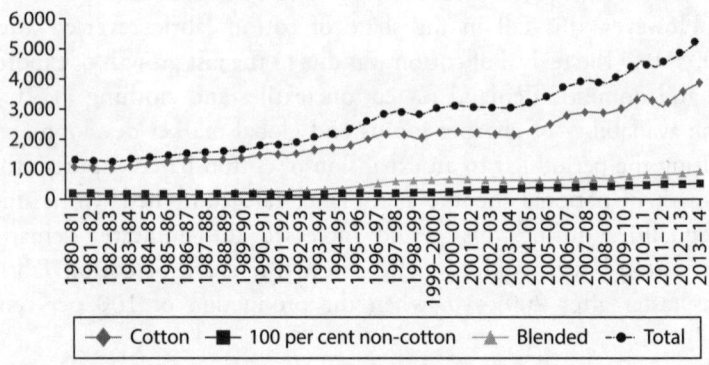

Figure 4.2   Fibre-wise Production of Spun Yarn (million kg)
Sources: CITI, *Handbook of Statistics on Textile Industry* (2008) and www.txcindia. gov.in (last accessed on 15 February 2016) for recent years.

indicated that the comfort of cotton and the discomfort of polyester involved factors other than just the transfer of heat or water vapour. For example, tests show that when cotton T-shirts were replaced with polyester T-shirts, skin temperatures under the polyester T-shirts were 1.5–2°F higher than that under the cotton T-shirts. This increase in skin temperature could be the discomfort felt when the 100 per cent polyester T-shirts were worn.[4]

The increase in the share of polyester in spinning during the 1990s was reflected in the changing composition of non-cotton and blended spun yarn. For example, within blended spun yarn, cotton/viscose, which dominated during the early 1980s, was replaced by polyester/ viscose during the 1990s (CITI, *Handbook of Statistics on Textile Industry* 2008: 18). Within the 100 per cent non-cotton spun yarn category, the 1980s observed growth of acrylic staple yarn (ASY); the trend seems to have changed since the 1990s when the production of PSY grew at a very high rate. However, the share of non-cotton and blended spun yarn (including polyester) in the total spun yarn production remained low as cotton continued to dominate.

Increasing Dependence of Weaving on Filament Yarn

Modern technological innovations have made it possible to produce continuous filaments (or filament yarn), which have the desirable qualities of synthetic staple spun yarn, without resorting to the staple spinning systems, as explained further. This has led to the increased dependence of the weaving sector on the filaments, which, as products of the chemical industry, do not require spinning and can be used for weaving directly.

Usually, polyester is produced as continuous filaments.[5] These continuous filament yarns are strong primarily due to the absence of loose ends that transmit imposed stresses. They are uniform and lack discontinuity. As a result, the filaments/strands of filament yarn lie close together in the yarn/fabric, thereby reducing the insulating

---

[4] Cotton is a good conductor of heat. It keeps heat away from skin to keep it cool, making it very comfortable to wear.
[5] All artificial fibres are normally produced most easily as continuous filaments.

air space present and creating compact filament fabric. This affects its lightness and reduces covering effectiveness and warmth-giving bulk. Before recent innovations in the technology of filament yarn production, it was a usual practice to cut a large amount of the total continuous polyester filaments into short lengths for spinning to restore these useful characteristics (Breen et al. 1957). However, the production of yarn from short staple polyester fibre was a time-consuming process requiring a complex series of operations. Initial efforts to produce continuous filaments of desirable qualities of staple spun yarn were unsuccessful. Subsequent technological innovations in the textile industry have provided useful routes for improving the bulk and covering power of continuous filament yarns without making use of the staple spinning systems.

The direct use of filament yarn in weaving, without resorting to spinning, explains the shift away from cotton in weaving even when spinning continued to remain dominated by cotton during and after the 1990s. It is the increased availability of reasonably priced filament yarn, along with its improved characteristics, during this period which underlies the growth of synthetic fabric production. The faster growth of filament yarn production compared to spun yarn (Figure 4.3) is reflected in a continuously declining ratio of spun yarn to filament yarn production from 17.84 in 1980–81 to 6.76 towards the end of the 1980s, and further to less than 3 from 2002–03 to 2009–10.[6] The share of non-cotton and blended spun yarn in the total yarn (spun and filament) production improved somewhat but continued to be low (around 20–2 per cent) since the mid-1990s. Cotton continued to dominate spinning, but its share in the overall yarn (spun and filament) available for weaving declined substantially from 78 per cent in 1980–81 to 65 per cent in the mid-1990s, and further to less than 55 per cent from 2001–02 to 2009–10 (Figures 4.2 and 4.3).[7] Clearly, it is the growth of filament yarn during the period from 1990–91 to 2009–10 that led to a shift

[6] The ratio has increased slightly in recent years as production of filament yarn has declined.

[7] The share of cotton has increased to 57 and 59 per cent in the years 2012–13 and 2013–14 respectively due to decline in the production of filament yarn.

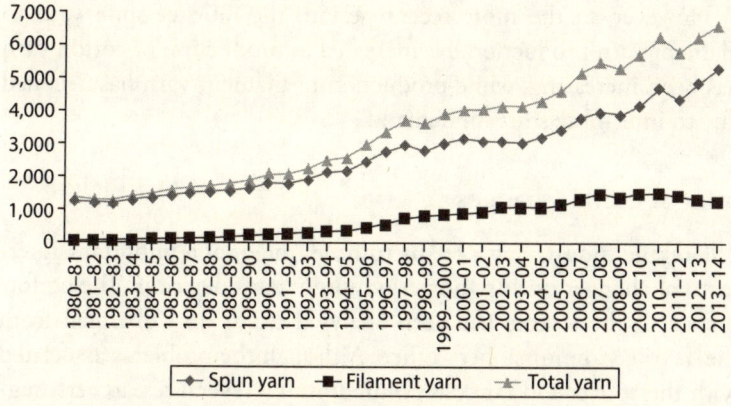

Figure 4.3   Production of Yarn (million kg)
Sources: Computed based on figures from Office of the Textile Commissioner, in CITI, *Handbook of Statistics on Textile Industry* (2008) up to 2005–06; and www.txcindia.gov.in (last accessed on 15 February 2016) for recent years.

in production away from cotton towards non-cotton and blended fabrics in response to an increase in their demand.

The fact that spinning continued to remain dominated by cotton due to its inherent properties indicates growth in demand for cotton textiles. The major sources of increasing demand for cotton textiles since the 1990s were the richer sections at home and exports. The richer sections at home, who accounted for a major proportion of overall increase in the demand for textiles, continued to spend almost the same percentage of their total MPCP of textiles on cotton textiles.[8] The increasing demand for cotton textiles by the richer sections at home resulted in stabilisation of the long-term fall in the per capita demand for cotton textiles. In addition to this rising demand at home, the fast growth in the export of cotton yarn, cotton fabric, and cotton garments and made-ups during the period meant that there was an externally driven derived demand for cotton yarn,[9] which accompanied the growth in domestic demand.

---

[8] For details, see Chapter 1, 'Trends in Domestic Demand and their Implications'.

[9] For details, see Chapter 3, 'Exports: The New Driver of Growth?'.

However, in the more recent period, the ratio of spun yarn to filament yarn production has increased as production of cotton yarn has been increasing, while production of filament yarn has declined due to inter-fibre shifts in demand.

Inter-sectoral Changes

The textile industry also seems to have undergone important inter-sectoral changes during the period under consideration. The performance of the sectors has been analysed using data obtained from the Textile Commissioner's office. Although the problems associated with the conversion rates, as pointed out by several researchers, suggest that they may not provide accurate estimates of production, the broad trends that emerge from the data are indicative. The data point to a continuing fall in the share of the mill sector since 1980. As a result, almost the entire cloth is currently produced in the decentralised sector. Overall, the highlights of inter-sectoral changes during the period, as indicated by the data, are: continuing decline of mill sector; fast growth of hosiery sector; decline of handloom sector; rise of power loom sector; division of textile sector with spinning in organised and weaving in unorganised sectors; and continuing existence of few modern mills in fabric production.

Continuing Decline of Mill Sector

The share of the mill sector in fabric production has been declining roughly from the 1970s. Table 4.1 depicts the sector-wise performance of the textile industry since the 1980s. More than 30 per cent of the total fabric was produced in the mill sector during the early 1980s, which fell to about 11 per cent by the early 1990s (Table 4.2). The weaving capacity of the mills, which had been stagnant for a number of years, started declining after the middle of the 1980s. The number of installed looms, which varied between 200,000–210,000 till the mid-1980s, declined at the rate of -4.9 per cent per annum from 1985–86 to 2013–14.[10] The removal of restrictions on capacity

---

[10] Average annual compound rate of growth computed based on figures from CITI, *Handbook of Statistics on Textile Industry* (2008) and www.txcindia.gov.in (last accessed on 15 February 2016) for recent years.

expansion, flexibility of fibre use, and easy import of polyester fibre and capital equipment and technology during the course of rapid restructuring after the NTP (1985) could not reverse the declining scenario and the mill sector continued to experience a negative growth rate of –2.94 per cent per annum between 1990–91 and 2005–06 (Table 4.1). The production started improving thereafter with the revival of cotton after 2003–04,[11] but with the production in the other sectors expanding fast, the share of the mill sector in total fabric production remained low. The share of mill sector production came down from about 11 per cent in the early 1990s to around 3–4 per cent in recent years (Table 4.2). As a result, the mill sector currently produces only an insignificant proportion of the total fabric produced. This points to the declining competitiveness of composite mills in comparison to the power looms and the hosiery units in the decentralised sector, which is analysed later in this section.

Fast Growth of Hosiery Sector

The period since the 1990s was marked not only by a shift from cotton textiles towards synthetic and blended textiles, but also by a shift from woven towards knitted textiles within the cotton textiles. According to Market Research Wing, Textiles Committee, GoI (various years), the per capita purchase of hosiery cotton textiles at the all-India level increased from 0.69 m in 1983 to 1.32 m by 2000, which further increased to 2.87 m by 2012. As a percentage of overall per capita purchase of cotton textiles, this implied an increase from 6.8 per cent in 1983 to 18.57 per cent in 2000, and further to 26.35 per cent by 2012. In addition to this, there was a substantial growth in external demand for the products of hosiery sector after the mid-1980s. According to the DGCIS data, the export of knitted and crocheted garments grew at a rate of 17.36 per cent per annum during 1985 to 2013–14.[12] The export of knitted and

[11] For details, see Chapter 1, 'Trends in Domestic Demand and their Implications, and Chapter 2, 'Availability and Cost of Raw Materials'.

[12] For details see Figure 3.5 of Chapter 3, 'Exports: The New Driver of Growth?'.

Table 4.1   Sector-wise Production of Fabric (million sq. m), Revised Series

Year	Mill	Handloom	Power loom	Hosiery	Total
1980–81	4,533	3,109	4,802	–	12,444
1985–86	3,544	4,135	9,534	–	17,213
1990–91	2,589	4,295	13,348	2,696	22,928
1995–96	2,019	7,202	17,201	5,038	31,460
2000–01	1,670	7,506	23,803	6,696	39,675
2005–06	1,656	6,108	30,626	10,418	48,808
2010–11	2,205	6,907	38,015	14,634	61,761
2013–14	2,531	7,104	36,790	16,199	62,624

Sources: Office of the Textile Commissioner (1996) for 1980–81 and 1985–86; CITI (2008) for 1990–91, 1995–96, and 2000–01; Annual Reports, CITI, *Handbook of Statistics on Textile Industry* (2006) for 2005–06; and www.txcindia. gov.in (last accessed on 15 February 2016) for recent years.

Note: The cloth produced by the hosiery sector is included in the cloth produced by the power loom sector up to 1989–90. Figures are exclusive of khadi, silk, and wool fabric.

crocheted fabric grew fast from the late 1980s to roughly the middle of the 1990s, after which it registered a decline up to 2004–05.[13] It then increased fast at the rate of 18.73 per cent per annum. Casual wear, including men's T-shirts, fancy ladies T-shirts, night suits for ladies, sportswear, and jogging suits, dominated the textile demand structure in the post-reform period. Hosiery, which had a marginal existence in the 1980s, became an accepted form of wear. With the increase in jeans and denims, T-shirts or a knit garment were considered the perfect accompaniment. Clearly, it was another prominent sector catering to the needs of both domestic and export markets. The shift towards knitted textiles was mainly driven by the inherent qualities of the knitted textiles over the woven textiles, which include softness, coolness, easy maintenance, sweat absorbency, and durability.

Hosiery production rose sharply in the 1990s and after, as it started becoming increasingly popular among consumers. The data

[13] For details, see Chapter 3, 'Exports: The New Driver of Growth?'.

Table 4.2 Sectoral Share in Production of Fabric (%), Revised Series

	Sectoral shares in cotton fabric production				Sectoral shares in blended fabric production				Sectoral shares in 100 per cent non-cotton fabric production				Sectoral shares in total fabric production			
	M	PL	HL	H	M	PL	HL	H	M	PL	HL	H	M	PL	HL	H
1985–86	22	35	32	11	50	42	4	5	0	97	1	1	21	47	24	9
1990–91	12	45	28	16	29	66	1	5	1	95	2	2	11	58	19	12
1995–96	6	37	33	24	15	78	0	7	3	83	11	3	6	55	23	16
2000–01	6	33	33	28	5	80	2	13	2	89	6	3	4	60	19	17
2006–07	5	37	22	37	4	74	2	21	1	93	4	3	3	63	12	22
2010–11	5	38	19	39	6	71	2	21	0	93	4	3	4	62	11	24
2013–14	5	40	18	37	8	71	1	20	1	90	4	6	4	59	11	26

Source: Computed based on figures from the Office of the Textile Commissioner, in ICMF, *Handbook of Statistics on Cotton Textile Industry* (2001) for 1985–86; CITI, *Handbook of Statistics on Textile Industry* (2008) for 1990–91, 1995–96, 2000–01; CITI, *Annual Reports* (2007) for 2006–07; and www.txcindia.gov.in (last accessed on 15 February 2016) for 2010–11 and 2013–14.

Notes: 1. M: Mill sector; PL: Power loom sector; HL: Handloom sector; H: Hosiery.

2. All the figures in table are rounded of.

for the hosiery sector was, in fact, not available in official statistics till the 1980s, as it was shown as cloth produced by the power loom sector. The available data since the 1990s indicate that there was a continuous and sustained growth in this sector (at about 9 per cent per annum). As a result, the sector, which accounted for 11.8 per cent of fabric production by 1990–91, registered a rise in its share to 25.87 per cent of total fabric produced in 2013–14. In an overall scenario where demand was shifting away from cotton textiles towards synthetic and blended textiles, it was creditable for this sector to have more than doubled its share in cotton cloth production from 15.86 per cent in 1990–91 to 37.32 per cent by 2013–14 at the cost of the share of all the other sectors (Table 4.2). The sectoral share of hosiery in the blended cloth production also increased from 4.6 per cent in 1990–91 to 19.70 per cent by 2013–14. Locations like Tirupur, Bengaluru, Chennai, Delhi, and Ludhiana have become names synonymous with the knitwear industry.

Thus, the hosiery sector in India made considerable progress during the 1990s and its products seem to have good potential in the future also due to their inherent qualities. The transformation of Tirupur from a largely agrarian economy to the 'knitwear capital of India', within a very short span of three to four decades, is a perfect example depicting the process of growth of hosiery, while continuing its operations as a small-scale industry in the unregistered sector. The city contributes 51 per cent of the total knitwear export from India and provides employment to about 0.3 million people.[14] Two important factors explaining the fast growth of Tirupur are enterprise and technology. The people of Tirupur have developed their skills according to the changing business trends. First, they were cotton cultivators. From cotton cultivation, they went to ginning; from ginning to spinning; from spinning to weaving; and then, from weaving to knitting. The growth of spinning mills in nearby Coimbatore region also ensured the availability of specialised hosiery yarn (Shivakumar 2007). And this is how the entire area moved ahead.

Though the Tirupur entrepreneurs have started using modern machinery and upgraded technology with many of the units going in

[14] Source: http://www.fibre2fashion.com/industry-article/64/overview-of-tirupur-knitwear-industry (last accessed on 1 July 2016).

for computerisation and use of software technologies, they continue to be tiny and small-scale enterprises operating in the unregistered sector with very low capital base. For every single processing/manufacturing activity—knitting, bleaching, dyeing, printing, drying, embroidery—there are a number of independent operators. Being small-scale enterprises, they continue to be predominantly one-man shows (Sakthivel 2004). It is easy for the person concerned to control one manufacturing process, expand and modernise that, and become an expert in that activity. Thus, these tiny experts of Tirupur have been able to increase their exports, especially when the textile and garment manufacturing started shifting from the developed economies to the less developed and labour-abundant economies, including India.[15]

Decline of Handloom Sector

Regarding the trends in the handlooms, there are contradictory indications. The data from the Textile Commissioner's office indicate that the handloom sector performed well during the 1980s even when home demand for textiles was declining. According to the data, it continued to perform remarkably well from 1990–91 to 1997–98, recording 8.5 per cent annual growth rate. Its share in total fabric production is reported to have increased from about 18.73 per cent in 1990–91 to 22.89 per cent in 1995–96. The share declined in the following years, but it is reported that the production continued to remain high roughly up to 2000–01 (Table 4.1). The data indicate substantial reduction in production thereafter.

In contrast to this evidence, the data from the surveys on unorganised manufacturing and the employment and unemployment by NSSO indicate that the handloom production increased up to the late 1980s, but registered a fall thereafter. According to the NSSO surveys on unorganised manufacturing, the real Gross Value Added (GVA) in the weaving of cotton cloth in the handlooms at the all-India level was increasing during 1978–79 to 1989–90, but registered a decline thereafter. The real GVA in handlooms in the urban areas started falling during the 1980s, but it continued to increase in the rural areas. The real GVA declined substantially in the rural areas during 1989–90

[15] For details, see Chapter 3, 'Exports: The New Driver of Growth?'.

to 1994–95 (Table 4.3). Though there was some improvement in the real GVA generated in urban handlooms, the real GVA at the all-India level in 1994–95 was much lower than that in 1989–90.

According to the NSS data from employment–unemployment surveys,[16] the usual status employment (PS + SS) in handlooms at the all-India level increased from 1983 to 1987–88. The handlooms recorded a fall in employment thereafter. Clearly, there are contrary indications regarding the trends in the handlooms. While one source shows decline in the late 1980s, the other points to such a decline only since 2002–03, indicating that handloom sector was performing well during the 1990s.

The present study relies on the data from the surveys on unorganised manufacturing and employment and unemployment by NSSO for two reasons. First, there is absence of any evidence of increase in demand for the products of handloom sector during the 1990s. According to the data from the Textiles Committee, GoI, monthly per capita purchase of cotton textiles from the handloom sector at the all-India level declined from 1.68 m in 1993 to 1.06 m in 1998. The figures on the export of cotton fabric from handloom sector did not show any improvement during this period. The sector, which exported 85.66 million sq. m of cotton fabric in 1992–93, recorded a decline to 43.01 million sq. m in 1997–98, and further to 40.07 million sq. m by the end of the 1990s (ICMF, *Handbook of Statistics on Cotton Textile Industry* 2001). Further, data from the Apparel Export Promotion Council, published in the *Handbook of Export Statistics*, on the garment exports from the handloom sector indicate substantial reduction during the 1990s. The export of cotton garments declined from above 10 million pieces during the early 1980s to less than 5 million pieces towards the end of the 1990s. The analysis of the DGCIS data indicates that the value of exports of cotton made-ups of the handloom sector (with base year 1990–91) increased from Rs 1,191.51 million in 1990–91 to Rs 4,478.25 million in 1998–99 at a rate of about 18 per cent per annum.[17] But, overall, it does not

---

[16] For details, see Chapter 5, 'The Employment Fall Out'.

[17] Figures from code 63 are used for the exports of made-ups. The unit value index of export of cotton yarn, calculated from DGCIS data, is used as deflator.

Table 4.3   Real GVA with Base Year 1993–94 in Weaving of Cotton Cloth (Rs million)*

Year	Handlooms			Power Looms		
	Rural	Urban	All-India	Rural	Urban	All-India
1978–79	3,357.9	2,065.9	5,423.8	318.8	1,398.7	1,717.5
1989–90	5,915.0	1,638.8	7,553.8	1,187.8	3,233.8	4,421.6
1994–95	3,738.2	1,823.5	5,561.7	2,021.8	3,607.3	5,629.1
2005–06	2,035.0	2,074.9	4,100.9	1,888.3	2,642.8	4,531.1

Sources: Computed based on figures from NSSO (1987, 1995, 1998); CSO (1985, 1995); NSSO, unit-level data on unorganised manufacturing sector in India, 2005–06; and Office of Economic Advisor, GoI (for figures before 1993–94: *Index Numbers of Wholesale Prices in India*; for figures of 1993–94 onwards: http://www.eaindustry.nic.in/download_data_9394.asp [last accessed on 11 February 2016]).

Notes: 1. For 1978–79, following NIC-1970, codes (For details of NIC codes, refer Appendix C) 235 and 236 are used for handlooms and power looms respectively. For 1989–90 and 1994–95, following NIC-1987, codes 233 and 234 are used for handlooms and power looms respectively. For 2005–06, following NIC-2004, code 17133 is used for handlooms and code 17115 for weaving (excluding handloom and khadi) is used for power looms (as weaving in unorganised sector includes khadi, handlooms, and power looms).

2. The WPI of cotton textiles with base 1993–94 is used to deflate GVA in weaving of cotton textiles in handlooms as well as in power looms.

3. *Concordance tables between NIC-1970 and NIC-1987, NIC-1987 and NIC-1998, and NIC-1998 and NIC-2004 are used for computing the figures.

indicate growing demand for the products of the handloom sector in the light of decline in domestic demand as well as exports of cotton fabric and garments produced by handlooms. In the absence of an evidence of increase in demand for the products of the handloom sector, it seems that the handloom production started declining in the late 1980s.

Second, doubts have been raised regarding the reliability of sector-wise estimates obtained on the basis of data reported by the Textile Commissioner's office, particularly in identifying the relative contribution of power looms and handlooms to the growth in the decentralised sector. There are no separate reliable estimates for either handloom or power loom output. The data suffer from basic asymmetry in the method of estimation of cloth in the organised and the decentralised sectors (Bedi 2000; Misra 1993). Production figures for the mill sector are based on the returns filed by the industrial mills, but there are no firm statistics on the actual production of cloth in the decentralised sector. The production of cloth in the decentralised sector is calculated on the basis of delivery of various types of yarn to the decentralised sector and their conversion rates. Conversion rate of fabric from yarn is the number of square metres of cloth produced per kilogram of yarn. Therefore, the accuracy of production estimates based on yarn delivery statistics for the decentralised sector depends crucially on the accuracy of the conversion ratios. These conversion ratios are arbitrary and not scientifically derived. The values of these ratios remain fixed for a number of years and are not responsive to changes in the structure of the industry. No distinction is made in the application of these conversion rates between the power loom sector and the handloom sector despite significant dissimilarities in the yarn consumed as well as in the cloth woven in these two sectors (Table 4.4).

In addition to this, there is an inherent snag in the sector-wise estimates of production derived by the official agencies due to the diversion of hank yarn to the power looms, as suggested by several studies (Bedi 2000; Misra 1993). This results in large-scale overestimation of output in the handloom sector and corresponding underestimation of output in the power loom sector. In the light of all this discussion, it appears that the official figures that point to a creditable performance of the handlooms during the 1990s are not reliable. It seems that the trend of decline of handlooms started in the late 1980s. The increased disadvantages of handlooms in comparison to other sectors since the 1990s confirm this view.

Several studies have pointed to similar results. A comparison of a few indicators from the *Census of Handloom Weavers for 1987–88* (Development Commissioner for Handlooms 1990) and the *Joint Census of Handlooms and Powerlooms* for *1995–96* (NCAER 2004) confirms the view that handloom weaving was declining from 1987–88 to 1995–96. The number of units operating as handlooms as well as the number of looms fell during this period. The number of units operating as handlooms declined by 15.20 per cent. The number of looms fell by 7.73 per cent. The production of handloom[18] cloth also

---

[18] Excluding Meghalaya and Mizoram.

Table 4.4 Conversion Rate for Decentralised Sector

Type of Yarn	Old (m/kg)	Revised (m/kg)	Revised (sq. m/kg)
Cotton yarn	10	10.75	12.4
Blended yarn	8	11.1	12.9
100 per cent non-cotton yarn	9.06	11.1	12.9
Filament yarn	–	–	–
Cellulosic (viscose)	9.06	13	16
Synthetic	14	–	–
Nylon	–	25	31

Source: Office of the Textile Commissioner (1996: 44).

registered a fall of 12.76 per cent. The number of workers engaged in handlooms fell by 2.81 per cent over the period. The comparison also shows a decline in the productivity per loom and per worker. The production per day per worker declined from 1.48 m to 1.33 m and the production per day per loom declined from 2.63 m to 2.49 m during the period. This, together with the decline in the number of weavers and looms, resulted in an overall decline in the production of fabric in the handloom sector. A comparison of the figures from the *Census of Handlooms for 1995–96 and 2009–10* (NCAER 2010) points to a further decline of handloom weaving at the all-India level. The number of handloom weavers declined from 3.27 million to 2.91 million during the period. The number of looms declined to 2.38 million by 2010.

An analysis of unit-level data from the NSS 62nd round on unorganised manufacturing reveals similar findings. The comparable figures indicate a decline of –2.73 per cent per annum from 1994–95 to 2005–06 in the real GVA in handlooms engaged in weaving of cotton cloth at the all-India level (Table 4.3). The rate of decline was far higher from the late 1980s to the mid-1990s (–5.94 per cent per annum) when the overall demand for textiles was also falling.

Various attempts to explain the disadvantages of handlooms in comparison to other sectors since the 1970s highlight the low productivity of the sector. Several studies have established that while the handloom sector had lower wage rates, lower fixed capital cost, and lower overhead costs than the power looms, it was at a disadvantage in terms of productivity, which was one-third of that of power looms. Though the wages paid to handloom weavers per day were lower, wages paid per metre of cloth for weaving alone were higher in handlooms than those incurred for similar operations in power looms. As a result, handloom cloth was costlier than power loom cloth by 14 per cent (SITRA 1982). Studies have indicated that the productivity of handloom was low not only in weaving but also in the preparatory process. All power loom-processed cloth was cheaper than handloom-processed cloth.

However, the real GVA in the handlooms sector continued to increase till the late 1980s, even when overall demand for textile products was falling. After this, it declined substantially. By 1994–95, it was slightly lower than that in power looms (Table 4.3). Later, when the demand increased but there was a shift to synthetic textiles, the real GVA declined in the production of cotton cloth in both the sectors. By 2005–06, the real GVA in power looms was far higher than that in handlooms.

However, the problems faced by the handlooms have multiplied since the 1990s. There was a massive increase in consumer demand for synthetics and blended textiles, but they were almost entirely produced by the power looms. Though there was some shift towards synthetic and blended fabric production by the handlooms, no significant progress took place in this area (Table 4.2). In this scenario, the nature of competition that handlooms faced from the power looms requires a comparison of their real GVA in the weaving of cotton combined with synthetic cloth. The comparison points to a clear decline of handlooms, which continued to be dominated by the production of cotton cloth (Table 4.5). Power looms diversified significantly, responding to the shift in demand towards synthetic textiles. Only one-fifth of the total real GVA of power looms was generated in the production of cotton cloth during 2005–06.

Further, the period since the 1990s was characterised by changing consumer demand towards knitted and crocheted fabrics due to their comfort and inherent qualities. The handlooms produced mainly woven cloth of cotton. They faced tough competition from the hosiery sector, which grew fast during the period.

On the supply side, the lack of diversification of handlooms to MMFs meant that they continued to depend on spun yarn for their principal input. This dependency was debilitating because, besides being adversely affected by the shift away from cotton fabrics, handlooms had to bear the burden of an increase in the price of hank yarn as cotton became more expensive. The handlooms also faced problems of availability of yarn. A sharp increase was recorded in the export of cotton yarn due to the emphasis on exports after the announcement of the NTP (1985), when the ceiling on the exports of cotton yarn of counts 41s and above was removed and that for count group 1–40s was raised. The exports of cotton yarn increased from 125.54 million kg in 1992–93 to 442.94 million kg by 1996–97, leading to an increase in the share of exported yarn in total yarn produced from about 8 per cent to 20.62 per cent in the respective years. The share further increased to about 33.44 per cent in 2013–14 (computed based on DGCIS various years; TCO various years). Further, there was a substantial increase in the export of all kind of textile products,

Table 4.5   Real GVA with Base Year 1993–94 in Weaving of Cloth (Rs million), 2005–06

	Handlooms			Power looms		
	Rural	Urban	All-India	Rural	Urban	All-India
Cotton	2,035.0	2,074.9	4,109.9	1,888.3	2,642.8	4,531.1
Cotton and synthetic	2,264.6	2,167.7	4,432.3	2,266.2	14,224.2	16,490.4

Sources: Computed from unit-level data from NSS 62nd round on Unorganised Manufacturing Sector in India; and Office of Economic Advisor, GoI (for figures before 1993–94: *Index Numbers of Wholesale Prices in India*; for figures of 1993–94 onwards: http://www.eaindustry.nic.in/download_data_9394.asp [last accessed on 11 February 2016]).

Notes: 1. Following NIC-2004, codes (For details of NIC codes, refer Appendix C) 17133 and 17137 are used for weaving in handlooms using cotton and synthetic fibres respectively.

2. Codes 17115 and 17118 for weaving (excluding handloom and khadi) are used for weaving in power looms (as weaving in unorganised sector includes khadi, handlooms, and power looms) using cotton and synthetic fibres respectively.

3. The WPI of cotton textiles with base 1993–94 is used to deflate GVA in weaving of cotton textiles in handlooms and in power looms. The WPI of man-made textiles is used to deflate GVA in weaving of synthetic textiles in handlooms and in power looms.

including fabrics, garments, and made-ups, since the early 1990s. As the mills concentrated on supplying their production to more lucrative markets, this seems to have impacted the domestic availability of yarn, in an appropriate form (hanks), to the handloom weavers. Although the hank yarn obligation of the spinning mills was 50 per cent of the total yarn production until 2002,[19] the data from the Textile Commissioner's office indicate that the cotton hank yarn delivered since the 1990s did not exceed 30 per cent.[20]

Earlier, state intervention had been a major source of support to the sustenance of the handlooms. A number of items were reserved for production in the handloom sector. A development commissioner for handlooms coordinated the central government's initiatives in supporting and promoting this sector. A National Handloom Development Centre was also established. Some tax concessions were extended and several state governments gave active support to the formation of weavers' cooperative marketing support system. However, the state policy towards the handlooms changed since the 1990s. The state support was gradually reduced (National Commission for Enterprises in the Unorganised Sector [NCEUS] 2007). The number of items reserved for the sector was also curtailed and special scheme for the production and procurement of cheaper cloth under Janata Cloth Scheme was dissolved in 1996. The tax concessions enjoyed by Handlooms sector were also withdrawn. All this made the overall scenario more unfavourable for the handlooms and favourable for the power looms since the 1990s.

Continuing Rise of Power Loom Sector

From the given discussion, it is clear that the growth of the power loom sector was a major breakthrough in the development of the Indian textile industry. Power looms began when some prosperous handloom weavers set up looms discarded by mills in their workshops. The idea was to improve efficiency and productivity and reduce the strain of operation. Then, medium- and big-sized power loom units were set up in the 1930s and 1940s by a new class of entrepreneurs.

---

[19] Hank yarn obligation was slashed by 20 per cent from January 2003.

[20] Office of the Textile Commissioner, in CITI, *Handbook of Statistics on Textile Industry* (2008: 26).

Thus, the capacity in the power loom sector increased substantially every year since the 1950s. The conversion scheme (handlooms to power looms) introduced by the government did not succeed and instead, unauthorised growth occurred without any government protection and assistance (Uchikawa 1998). The fast growth of power looms affected not only the growth of handlooms but also led to the decline of the mill sector engaged in fabric production, which faced tough competition from the cloth produced by the power looms. As a result, the share of the mill sector in production of cloth started declining fast. The power loom sector continued to increase its production and share in total production even after the difference in excise duties levied on the mill and the power loom sectors was removed in 1985. Cloth production in the mill sector showed a steep fall from the early 1990s due to severe competition from the power loom sector. The power loom sector, that had already acquired a lion's share (58.2 per cent) of total fabric production by 1990–91, continued to grow throughout at an impressive rate of 4.66 per cent per annum till 2010–11. However, the production has declined in recent years after the demand for 100 per cent non-cotton textiles declined. Currently, it produces about 59 per cent of the total fabric production, and almost the entire output of non-cotton cloth is produced in the power looms sector (Table 4.2).

The growth of power looms and the consequent decline of mills over the last few decades seem to be the result of several cost advantages due to organisational differences between mills and power looms. They continue to operate in the unregistered sector either as own account enterprises (OAEs) or as non-directory or directory establishments. The power loom units consist of mainly two types: the owner proprietary type (weaver working on his own) and the master weaver type. In the first, the weaver purchases yarn, manufactures fabrics, and sells them. He owns less than 12 looms and undertakes weaving as a means of livelihood. In the master weaver type of activity, a weaver carries out the manufacturing task but receives only the conversion cost. The master weaver supplies the yarn to the weaver, gets it woven by him, and sells fabrics in the market. The master weaver owns about 12 or more looms and may not even manage the business himself. He may appoint an intermediary for this purpose. This relationship gives him the benefit of paying lower wages and obtaining yarn cheaply in bulk, adjusting the pattern of production, and better marketing (Nalavade et al. 1986). Therefore, an exclusive group of producers of MMFs has emerged that is linked with power looms through a management and production system (Patel 1990, cited in Uchikawa 1998: 104). The organisational differences between mills and power looms meant continuing cost advantages[21] to the power looms. The wage cost per metre was lower in power looms by about 50–70 per cent. The cost of fabric processing in power looms was 20 per cent lower in independent processing houses and 40 per cent lower in hand processing units than that in the organised process houses attached to the textile mills (ATIRA 1985).

Since the 1990s, the substantial growth in the demand for the products of textile and clothing—especially for synthetics, which are entirely produced by the power looms—has speeded up the growth of power looms. Increasing use of machinery in the power looms has resulted in technology improvement. The power loom units have established themselves in the international market as well. With a much higher growth rate (12 per cent per annum from 1993–94 to 1999–2000) of fabric exported than that of the mill sector (9.17 per cent per annum during the same period) (Office of Textile Commissioner 1999, 2000), power looms have become the leading suppliers of fabric in the world market. While reaping the full advantage of lower wage and other costs due to their unorganised structure of production, power looms have assimilated the latest designs and trends and have grown at the expense of mills and handlooms.

Organised in Spinning and Unorganised in Weaving

Overall, power looms have flourished in the unorganised sector over the years and have increased their share to about 59 per cent of the

---

[21] In 1985, as against Rs 50 per operative per shift in the mill sector, wage rates prevailing in the power loom sector varied between Rs 10 per operative per shift for workers in the preparatory process and Rs 25 per operative per shift for weavers. However, the wage cost per metre was lower in power looms by about 50 to 70 per cent as the gap in wage rates was offset by higher productivity of mills to some extent.

overall fabric produced currently. The hosiery sector, which was reserved under small-scale industries until 2005, continues to operate mainly in the unregistered sector and produces about 26 per cent of the overall fabric. Handlooms currently account for 11 per cent of the overall fabric produced (Table 4.2). Clearly, techno-economic factors seem to have been working over the last few decades towards ensuring a process of division of the textile sector, which is now near complete. Spinning is undertaken in the organised sector, while almost the entire weaving, either in power looms, or in hosiery, or in handlooms, is undertaken in the unorganised sector. Hand spinning by charkhas has disappeared over the years and the mill sector barely produces about 4 per cent of the overall cloth production. There is a boom in the textile industry, but the data from the Textile Commissioner's Office indicate a continuous fall in the number of installed looms from 177,800 in 1990–91 to 51,000 in 2013–14 in textile mills,[22] suggesting that almost the entire growth in demand for fabric is met by the unorganised sector. While power looms have specialised in the production of synthetic fabric, capturing almost the entire increase in demand for synthetic and blended fabric, the hosiery sector has increased its share in the production of cotton fabric. Handlooms have been losing their importance since the late 1980s.

The mills in the organised sector have continued to shrink. Many of the composite mills in the organised sector continued to make losses, and hence have closed down since the 1990s. The revival of demand for T&C from the early 1990s did not reverse the loss-making scenario in the mills. Many of these loss-making units closed down in Gujarat and Maharashtra. Maneklal Harilal, Navjyoti Investment, Maheshwari, Vishaldeep Spinning Mills Ltd, Standard Industries Ltd, Matulya, Arvind Polycot Ltd, and Svadeshi are examples of some of the mills that saw production of fabric declining after 1990.

Some of the composite mills which were closed down during the 1990s were the mills which had registered a decline in their production roughly since the middle of the 1980s or even earlier. Ahmedabad Manufacturing Calico Printing Co. Ltd, Maheshwari,

[22] Published in CITI, *Handbook of Statistics on Textile Industry* (2008: 2) and www.txcindia.gov.in (last accessed on 15 February 2016) for recent years.

Ahmedabad Kaiser-i-Hind Mills, Standard Industries Ltd, and Khatau are some examples of such mills. Some of the mills invested heavily in order to build capacity during the first half of the 1990s, for example, Arvind Polycot Ltd (during 1992), Maheshwari (during 1991), Svadeshi (during 1992), and Standard Industries Ltd (during 1994) (Bombay Stock Exchange Foundation various years). However, the cloth production continued to decline in spite of implementing modernisation-cum-expansion programmes in these mills. Clearly, competition from the power loom and hosiery units has been the main reason for the closure of the composite mills after 1990.

Modern Mills in Fabric Production

However, the discussion given here does not imply that the entire mill sector has performed poorly during the period. The number of shuttleless looms embodying more advanced technology, including Air Jet, Gripper, and Rapier installed in the mills, has grown from 3,860 in 1991 to 7,920 in 2004 (Textile Commissioner's Office, in CITI, *Handbook of Statistics on Textile Industry* 2008: 15). This points to the continuing existence of islands of excellence engaged in fabric production, which have expanded and modernised during the period. As in the 1970s and 1980s,[23] there continue to exist two different market segments: a high-volume, 'unbranded', cheap cloth market; and a higher-value, brand name market. However, contrary to the earlier period, the high-volume, unbranded, cheap cloth market catering to the bulk of the population is dominated by the synthetic textiles, while the higher-value, brand name market is almost wholly served by the cotton textiles. The mills that continue to do well cater to the high-value, brand name market segment and face no competition from the power looms. They include Arvind Mills, Raymond Ltd, Century Textiles, Morarjee Mills, GTN Textiles, Ginni Filaments, Birla Group, Banswara Syntex, S Kumar Synfab Ltd, Bombay Dyeing Ltd, KG Denim, LNJ Bhilwara Group, Mafatlal Textiles, etc. (US International Trade Commission 2001). These mills are making huge profits and have benefited from the growth of the industry during the period. These are the mills with both international and local brands

[23] Refer Goswami (1990) for this period.

and they are leading players in the domestic ready-made garment industry. They have the rights to market international brands such as Arrow, Lee, and Flying Machine in India. They have their own popular brands, such as Newport, Ruggers, Excalibur, and Ruf and Tuf.

The limited market had restricted modernisation in many of these mills during the 1970s and 1980s. But the spurt in external demand since the 1990s for cotton T&C seems to have led these mills to adopt a strategy that gives priority to exports. The growing demand for cotton textiles due to the rapid rise in incomes of the rich at home also provided incentive to expand. They have introduced a large number of shuttleless looms to avail economies of scale and compete with other exporting countries in the world market. These mills have diversified, and they have also entered into joint ventures with foreign firms based in the US, Switzerland, Germany, Italy, Australia, France, Scotland, and the UK. Their expansion and modernisation include expansion of existing capacity, opening new manufacturing units, modernising processing facilities, quality improvement, upgrading marketing and finishing, and downstream integration into processing, dyeing, finishing, and garment making. For example, Arvind Mills invested USD 270 million to increase denim capacity to 100 million m; USD 83 million in new capacity to produce cotton and blended shirt fabrics; USD 33 million to manufacture voiles; and USD 70 million on home furnishing. It also invested to increase production capacity to produce Lee jeans and Lee apparel, Arrow shirts, bed linen, and towels. For their modernisation and capacity building, these fast-modernising mills mostly rely on imported machinery. Some of these, like LNJ Bhilwara, Mafatlal Textiles, and Modern Group, have started 100 per cent Export Oriented Units (EOUs) during the period (US International Trade Commission 2001).

The remarkable increase in the average unit value realisation on exports of mill-made fabric since the 1990s has ensured the viability of investments in modernisation of the composite mills. Competition in such high-value, brand name markets is more in terms of quality, brand images, and fashion than in prices. These mills have been able to increase their exports and have successfully tapped the increasingly prosperous, fashion-conscious urban market and have earned large enough margins to recoup costs and reinvest in even better equipment. According to the data from the Cotton Textiles Export Promotion

Council,[24] the average unit value realised on the export of mill-made cotton cloth, which was about 58 per cent higher than the export of power loom cotton cloth in the early 1990s, grew much faster and was about 94–108 per cent higher in the late 1990s. Some of these mills also service part of the fast-growing demand for high-priced textile goods arising in the top 20 per cent of the population that accounts for about 40 per cent of the increase in overall demand for T&C since the early 1990s. The price of cloth sold by the mill sector has risen much faster than that sold by the other sectors. According to the data from the Textiles Committee published in Textile Commissioner's Office's Compendium of Textile Statistics 1999 and 2000, the retail price of mill-made cotton cloth was about two to four times, blended cloth was about two-and-a-half to six times, and synthetic cloth was about three-and-a-half to eight times more expensive in comparison to respective cloth produced in the power loom sector during 1992–93 to 1997–98. During this period, the prices of cloth sold by the mill sector rose much faster than those sold by the power loom sector. For example, the retail price of cotton cloth sold by the mill sector grew at a rate of 13 per cent per annum, while the price of that sold by the power looms grew at about 5 per cent per annum. The retail prices of blended cloth sold by the mill sector rose at a rate of about 7 per cent per annum, while that sold by the power looms grew at about 2 per cent per annum. The retail price of man-made cloth sold by the mill sector continued to rise at 6.25 per cent per annum, while it declined at a rate of –8.16 per cent per annum for the man-made cloth sold by the power looms.

Overall, though some of the composite mills continued to perform well, they are few in number. In the changing global scenario after the removal of MFA quota regime, these mills have been facing severe competition from low-cost international firms. Only those mills which are competitive in terms of price, cost, and quality, and enjoy economies of scale, have survived and the smaller and loss-making textile mills have been forced to exit the market. This has increased the concentration of the mills in the Indian textile industry. An analysis of the growth of exports as a percentage of total sales

[24] Published in ICMF, *Handbook of Statistics on Cotton Textile Industry* (2004: 105).

for multi-market textile and apparel manufacturing mills in India from 1991 to 2013 suggests that the concentration of mills, which was declining in the early 1990s and was almost stable during the transitory regime, increased during the post-MFA regime. Though it declined from 2007–08 to 2010–11, it experienced a fast growth thereafter, suggesting that the smaller mills are finding it difficult to coexist with the bigger ones after the withdrawal of quota regime. The mill-level concentration in the post-MFA regime was further reinforced by the regional concentration of activities in terms of number of textile mills and value of sales across the states, which enhanced regional inequalities in total labour income across the various states in India (Kar 2015).

Capacity Building and Modernisation in the Spinning Sector

The inducement to invest, which was lacking in the capital-intensive spinning sector since the mid-1960s, was provided by the increase in external demand after the mid-1980s. The changed scenario, when the ceiling on the exports of cotton yarn of counts 41s and above was removed and that for count group 1–40s was raised, led to a fast growth in the export of cotton yarn. The exports of cotton yarn, which declined during the first half of the 1980s, registered growth between 1985–86 and 1989–90.[25] The exports of cotton fabric, which fluctuated in the first half of the 1980s, also showed consistent improvement during this period. Though there was hardly any growth in the export of woven garments, the export of knitted and crocheted garments registered growth during this period. Clearly, with the home demand falling during the 1980s, investment in the spinning sector during the second half of the 1980s was driven by the external demand.

Huge investments were undertaken by the cotton mills in spinning after 1990 to meet the continuing growth of external demand, coupled with growth in home demand for textile products. According to the DGCIS data, the growth in the external demand for cotton T&C industry during this period was led by the export of ready-made garments and made-ups of cotton. The direct export of cotton yarn continued to grow after the 1980s. The increase in export of

[25] For details, see Chapter 3, 'Exports: The New Driver of Growth?'.

cotton fabric, which was followed by a decline after the mid-1990s, expanded fast in the recent years.[26]

Two important policy changes after the 1980s which affected capacity expansion in and modernisation of the spinning sector were: (i) delicensing in July 1991; and (ii) withdrawal of protection for the industry producing textile machinery by reducing customs duties on the import of machinery. The total customs duty on machinery for cotton and synthetic textiles (other than those imported under export obligation) was reduced from 90 per cent ad valorem in 1988–90 to 37.86 by 1997–98.[27] A natural response of the industry to these policy changes, in view of the increase in overall demand, was an investment boom in the mill sector, resulting in capacity creation and the associated economies of scale and increasing mechanisation. According to ASI data, real gross fixed investment in cotton mills at 1980–81 prices, which fluctuated between Rs 700–Rs 2,700 million during most of the 1980s, registered substantial growth after the middle of the 1980s and reached very high levels of Rs 5,700–Rs 12,900 million during 1992–93 to 1997–98 (Table 4.6).

Improved access to imported technology, spare parts, and textile machinery facilitated modernisation and technological upgradation in spinning during the period. Studies indicate that the increased investment since the 1990s led to improvement in productivity in the spinning sector. Bedi (2003) analysed the structural change in the spinning industry because of policy changes after the NTP, 1985. He worked out the age composition of the working or installed spindles and explained how installation of new and modern spindles changes the age composition of the working spindles and results in technological progress. The technological progress reduces the number of spindles required to produce the given volume and count composition of various types of spun yarns.

However, the fact that spinning involves the use of old as well as new and modern spindles reflects a lack of technological progress in spinning. As a result of this technological gap between the working

---

[26] For details, see Chapter 3, 'Exports: The New Driver of Growth?'.

[27] This was later increased to 53.82 per cent by 2000–01 (CITI, Annual Reports various years).

Table 4.6   Real Gross Fixed Investment in Cotton Mills with Base Year 1980–81 (Rs million)

Year	Gross investment in fixed capital in cotton mills at current prices (Rs million)	WPI for textile machinery for spinning and weaving	Real gross investment in fixed capital in cotton mills (Rs million)
1980–81	1,887	100.00	1,887.00
1982–83	3,337	125.02	2,669.17
1984–85	1,703	130.03	1,309.70
1986–87	1,063	141.87	749.28
1988–89	3,026	154.86	1,954.02
1990–91	5,807	184.23	3,152.04
1992–93	11,941	208.49	5,727.37
1994–95	24,730	247.21	10,003.64
1996–97	22,618	298.70	7,572.15
1997–98	40,186	312.14	12,874.33

Sources: CSO (various years) for gross investments; Office of Economic Advisor, GoI (for figures before 1993–94: *Index Numbers of Wholesale Prices in India* ; for figures of 1993–94 onwards: http://www.eaindustry.nic.in/download_data_9394.asp [last accessed on 11 February 2016]) for WPIs.

Note: Investments in tth year are calculated as difference in the stocks of gross fixed capital in tth year and t^{-1}th year.

spindles and spindles of latest technology, excess spindles (compared to the minimum required at the latest available technology) are used to produce the given count composition. However, this excess use of heterogeneous quality of spindles could be due to low utilisation of working spindles as well. In order to estimate the excess spindles used due to technological differences alone, Bedi made suitable adjustments for underutilisation of the working spindles by estimating the number of working spindles assuming 100 per cent utilisation of all spindles.[28]

[28] However, the 'normal' level of utilisation of equipment in industry is never 100 per cent, in order to accommodate for demand fluctuations across season and time.

The implications of the technological gap between the working spindles and best-practice spindles for productivity were studied by comparing the ratio of production to number of working spindles at 100 per cent utilisation with ratio of production to minimum number of spindles required of latest available technology of 1996. This indicated the difference in productivity of the installed spindles when they are fully utilised and the productivity of modern spindles of latest technology due to the technological gap between the working spindles and modern spindles. The change in relative productivity, thus estimated, pointed to the growth in productivity of installed spindles over time due to reduction in technological gap between the working spindles and modern spindles.

According to Bedi (2003), the increase in external demand for yarn due to the opening up of yarn export during the first phase of economic reforms, after NTP (1985), was largely met by better utilisation of existing spindles, as the investment in new and modern spindles was not sufficient to support the rise in demand. For example, the active spindles increased by 4.35 million during 1983–88, while the new spindles installed were only 2.18 million. Thus, the greater reliance on the old spindles widened the technological gap between working spindles and the spindles of modern technology during this period. As a result, the excess spindles used as a per cent of installed spindles due to technological gap increased from 14.72 per cent in 1983 to 18.01 per cent in 1990.

However, the continuing growth of external demand, coupled with a rise in domestic demand, due to the cuts in excise and customs duties on textile products during the second phase of economic reforms led to a huge investment in new and modern spindles after 1990. This modernisation process reduced the technological gap. The excess spindles used due to technological gap over the minimum required at latest available technology of 1996 as percentage of installed spindles declined from 18.01 per cent in 1990 to 8.06 per cent in 1996. The productivity of spindles, which increased at a low rate of 0.09 per cent per annum from 1983 to 1990, improved at an annual rate of 2.85 per cent between 1990 and 1996.

Similarly, results of a year-wise comparison of major spinning productivity parameters over the 1990s, carried out by SITRA (Rajamanickam et al. 2003), also highlight significant growth in productivity in the spinning sector. A comparison of the average hours of workers required to produce 100 kg of yarn (HOKs) in spinning, in different years, is presented in Table 4.7. The averages are based on all the mills[29] that participated in each of the surveys. The study indicates that between 1990 and 2000, the labour productivity in spinning showed an impressive increase of about 42 per cent. The average HOK fell from 37.7 in 1990 to 26.5 in 2000. Approximately half of this improvement was attributable to the participation of new mills with high levels of labour productivity as well as to the closure of old mills with very low levels of productivity. And the remaining half of this increase was ascribed to the improvement registered in labour productivity in the same mills from year to year. The productivity per spindle in the year 2000 was higher by about 9 per cent relative to 1990, the increase being particularly steep since 1994. The spindle utilisation had also increased by about 6 per cent points, reaching as high as 94 per cent in 2000.

Since the 1990s, spinning mills such as Century Textiles, Morarjee Mills, Indo Rama, Vardhman Group, GTN Textiles, Ginni Filaments Ltd, Modern Group, Banswara Syntex, Birla Group, and Hanil Era Textiles Ltd diversified, expanded, and modernised their spinning capacity (US International Trade Commission 2001). These mills mainly relied on imported machinery, and entered into joint ventures with foreign firms based in South Korea, Japan, Italy, etc. Several mills, like Vardhman Group, GTN Textiles, Modern Group, and Hanil Era Textiles Ltd, started 100 per cent EOUs. In addition to this, there were some new mills which set up additional spindleage. These included Royal Classic Mills, Santosh Mills, Ranger Mills, Kiwi Kotspin, Raji Mills, Bhuwaneshwari Card Spinning, Best Cotton Mills, Balu Spinning, SKT Textiles, Arvind Sivakumaran, Jayavishnu Mills, and Kuruji Textiles. As a result, there was a substantial increase in the number of spindles installed, which increased from 21.23 million in 1980–81 to 26.25 million in 1987–88, and crossed 49.46 million by 2013–14.[30]

---

[29] On an average, about 250 mills participated each year.

[30] Provisional estimates, available at www.txcindia.gov.in (last accessed on 15 February 2016).

Table 4.7   Average HOKs, Average Production Per Spindle, and Spindle
Utilisation, 1990–2000

Year	Average HOK	Production per spindle–8 hours (40s count) (g)	Spindle utilisation (%)
1990	37.7	78	87.5
1992	36.5	76.5	87.7
1994	33.3	77.5	91.7
1996	31.9	79.5	90.8
1998	29.2	83.4	91.2
2000	26.5	84.9	93.7
Productivity increase in 2000 over 1990	42%	8.80%	7.10%

Source: Rajamanickam et al. (2003: 5–7).

More recently, the industry has been relying on Technology Upgradation Fund Scheme (TUFS), introduced in April 1999, for their investment plan in view of 5 per cent compensation available under the scheme. Figures on segment-wise progress under TUFS indicate that out of Rs 188,084.1 million loan amount sanctioned from 1999 to 2006 against Rs 425,828.5 million project cost, about Rs 63,384.8 million (about 34 per cent) was sanctioned to spinning against project cost of Rs 125,800 million. Segment-wise progress under Restructured Technology Upgradation Fund Scheme, for the period from 28 April 2011 to 31 March 2014, indicates that out of Rs 219,611.9 million loan amount sanctioned against Rs 376,246.2 million project cost, about Rs 59,650.9 million (27.16 per cent) was sanctioned to spinning against project cost of Rs 96,427.8 million.[31] The mills that had created spinning capacity using TUFS assistance include Ambica Cotton Mills Ltd, Bannari Amman Spinning Mills, Suryajyoti Spinning Mills, Mahavir Spinning Mills, Suryalakshmi Cotton Mills Ltd, and Super Spinning Mills. The lowering of the minimum economic size for spinning mills eligible for TUFS assistance from 25,000 to 12,000 spindles in case of new investment and

---

[31]   Available at www.txcindia.gov.in (last accessed on 15 February 2016).

from 12,000 to 8,000 spindles in case of existing ones, allowing the import of second-hand machinery, and doing away with the stipulation that the stand-alone spinning units seeking TUFS assistance should also invest on downstream value addition are some of the steps which seem to have improved the investment sentiment of the stand-alone small-scale spinning enterprises.

Overall, the spinning sector was doing well. The increase in demand led to substantial capacity expansion and modernisation in spinning. New units were set up at an unprecedented pace.[32] The number of spinning mills increased from 777 in 1990–91 to 1,564 in 1997–98, and further to 1,771 by 2012–13. The existing mills were also expanding rapidly. As a result, despite the expansion in demand, the industry was characterised by excess capacity because of 'overexpansion'. This seems to have affected the inducement to invest and modernise some of the mills in the industry. Thus, while the productivity of the spinning sector as a whole increased substantially, there was variation in the level of modernisation and technological competence within the mill sector, which widened during the period of high investments. Based on information from the 120 spinning mills for the period April–June 2007, Shanmuganandam and Sreenivasan (2008) constructed an overall modernisation index (OMI) for each mill. The OMI is a single measure of overall modernisation of machines working in various departments of the mills and is used to compare the level of modernisation of different mills. Based on the type of machines working in all the mills, a suitable level of modernisation was fixed for the standard mill.[33] The OMI was estimated for each of the 120 mills and compared with that of the standard mill. The results of the study indicated a large variation in the level of modernisation of the mills (Table 4.8). The best mill's OMI (107) was four times higher than the last mill's OMI (26). The level of modernisation in one-fourth of the mills was less than 50 (or

[32] www.txcindia.gov.in (last accessed on 15 February 2016).

[33] Standard mill is a hypothetical mill producing a certain number of counts of yarn with a given complement of machinery, which is operated with the best organisation and maximum efficiency attainable without affecting the quality of the product.

Table 4.8   OMI of the Mills

OMI group	OMI average	Mills (%)
Up to 40	33	14
41–50	46	11
51–60	56	8
61–70	67	6
71–80	75	9
81–90	85	19
Above 90	97	33
Overall average	74	100

Source: Shanmuganandam and Sreenivasan (2008).

half of the standard mill). The overall modernisation of the mills was only 74 (or less than three-fourth of the standard mill). In one-third of the mills, the OMI was almost close to the standard mill. The average OMI of these mills was high at 97.

The level of modernisation affects the productivity of workers. The differences in the level of technology and automation in spinning have resulted in differences in the level of labour productivity. The 30th productivity survey in spinning conducted by SITRA for September 2004, covering 180 mills, showed that labour productivity (HOK) up to spinning varied very widely (over 500 per cent) among the mills. The total HOK or the average hours of workers required to produce 100 kg of yarn was 7.5 for the most productive mill, while it was 51.5 for the least productive mill. The average HOK for the top 20 per cent of the mills (productivity wise) was 11.5, while the average based on all the mills was 21.7. Similarly, the labour productivity index varied between 200 and 29. The machine productivity index, which is a combined measure of production per spindle and spindle utilisation, also varied from 49 to 118, and the average for all the mills was 84 (Shanmuganandam and Mariappan 2007).

Under these circumstances, the mills which chose not to modernise (or invest less in modernisation) could not compete with the stronger and fast-expanding mills that had modernised and enjoyed economies of scale. For example, few mills like Bombay Rayon Fashions Ltd, Vardhman Textiles Ltd, S. Kumars Nationwide Ltd, Alok Industries Ltd, and Loyal Textiles Mills Ltd, with large-scale capacity and a sound capital base, continued to do well and earn good profits, while others like JJ Exports, Adinath Textiles Ltd, Raymond Ltd, Hanil Era Textiles Ltd, and Supertex Industries Ltd, with medium or small capital base, suffered losses. The firms with large-scale capacity and a sound capital base were more responsive and adaptive to the required changes and could perform well when competition increased in the post-MFA regime. On the other hand, the firms with medium or small capital base faced either capital or technology constraints and remained economically weak (Chaudhary 2011). Similarly, several spinning mills operating under cooperative sector, like Akot Taluka Sahakari Soot Girni Ltd and Jawahar Shetkari Sahakari Roto Soot Girni Ltd, which did not allocate funds for modernisation of plant and machinery and technological upgradation, could not face increased competition. Many of these units had started accumulating losses because of recession in demand during the 1970s and 1980s, which increased substantially during the 1990s, and ultimately led to the closure of the units after the administration could not pay the electricity bills and salary to the employees.

Thus, the revival of demand for textiles led to an investment boom in the mill sector since the 1990s, resulting in capacity creation and the associated economies of scale and increasing mechanisation. Delicensing in July 1991 and improved access to imported technology, spare parts, and textile machinery facilitated modernisation and technological upgradation in spinning, which led to growth of productivity. Overall, the spinning sector performed well. But, there were differences with respect to the level of modernisation within the mills, which had implications for the level of productivity of these mills. Mills which did not allocate adequate funds for modernisation remained technologically incompetent and qualitatively poor. They could not compete with the modern fast-expanding mills, and were forced to close down.

Growth of Ready-made Garments Production

Another important structural change that took place in the textile industry since the middle of the 1990s was the substantial growth of the ready-made garment sector. Since the garment industry in India was reserved for the small-scale sector (until 2005–06), almost the entire garment sector continued to exist in the unregistered sector.

Table 4.9   Real GVA in the Unorganised Garment Sector with Base Year 1993–94 (Rs million)

Year	Rural	Urban	All-India
1989–90	675.9	4,596.0	5,271.9
1994–95	742.0	5,902.6	6,644.6
2000–01	1,844.5	12,858.4	14,702.9
2005–06	2,061.8	11,993.7	14,055.5
2010–11	1,813.0	18,893.2	20,706.1

Sources: Computed based on figures from NSSO (1995, 1998), CSO (1995); unit-level data from NSS 56th and 62nd rounds on Unorganised Manufacturing Sector in India, unit level data from NSS 67th round on Unincorporated Nonagricultural Enterprises (Excluding Construction) in India; and Office of Economic Advisor, GoI (for figures before 1993–94: *Index Numbers of Wholesale Prices in India* ; for figures of 1993–94 onwards: http://www.eaindustry.nic.in/download_data_9394. asp [last accessed on 11 February 2016]).

Notes: 1. Since most of the garment production continues to exist in the unorganised sector, the real GVA in the garment sector is based on the data from the surveys on unorganised manufacturing. The GVA is obtained as GVA per enterprise multiplied by the number of enterprises.

2. For the years 1989–90 and 1994–95, code 265 in the NIC-1987 provides data on garment sector.

3. For the year 2000–01, following NIC-1998, 5-digit code 18101 is considered. For the year 2005–06, code 18101 is used following NIC-2004. For the year 2010–11, following NIC-2008, code 14101 is used.

4. The WPI of textiles is used as deflator.

5. Concordance tables between NIC-1987 and NIC-1998, NIC-1998 and NIC-2004, NIC-2004, and NIC-2008 are used for computing the figures.

According to the NSSO surveys on unorganised manufacturing, the garment sector generated real GVA (with 1993–94 as base) of about Rs 5,270 million in the year 1989–90, which then increased at the rate of 4.74 per cent per annum during 1989–90 to 1994–95 (Table 4.9).

The sector saw spectacular growth with real GVA growing at a high rate of about 14 per cent per annum thereafter, from 1994–95 to 2000–01. Much of the increase (about 86 per cent) in real GVA was in the urban areas with better infrastructure in the form of banking, electricity, transportation, communication, and so on. Finally, an analysis of the comparable figures from the 62nd round of NSS suggests that real GVA of Rs 14,055.5 million was generated in the garment sector in 2005–06, which was slightly lower than the value for the year 2000–01 (Table 4.9). However, the real value increased to Rs 20,706.1 million in 2010–11.

The poor performance of the garment sector before the mid-1990s is explained by a fall in home demand coupled with low exports. The NSS data indicate a fall in the demand for T&C in all sections of the population from 1983 to 1993–94. The export of garments remained low during the most of the 1980s and picked up only afterwards. The growth in the export of garments from the late 1980s to the first half of the 1990s seems to have led to some improvement in the real GVA in the garment sector.

The high growth of the garment sector since the middle of the 1990s is explained by an increase in home demand as well as in the external demand for garments. According to the Textiles Committee's Market Research Wing, the aggregate household consumption of ready-made garment in quantity terms increased at a high rate of 6.34 per cent per annum from 1993 to 2006 (Textiles Committee various years).[34] Increasing incomes, increasing fashion orientation, and fast-changing lifestyle seem to have led to a shift from tailor-made goods to ready-made garments. The period after 1990–91 is marked by a substantial increase in the export of ready-made garments. The data indicate massive increase in the numbers of all types and varieties of garments[35] exported during the period. They include overcoats, jackets, trousers, suits, skirts, shirts, nightshirts and pyjamas, T-shirts, tracksuits, dresses, undergarments, shawls, and scarves. Overall, the period since the 1990s was marked by a spectacular growth of the ready-made garment sector.

* * *

Thus, based on the overall analysis of the structural changes in the Indian textile industry, it can be concluded that the period since the 1990s was marked by important inter-fibre and inter-sectoral

---

[34] *National Household Surveys* published by Textiles Committee were previously called *Consumer Purchase of Textiles*.

[35] For details, see Chapter 3, 'Exports: The New Driver of Growth?'

changes. The decline in the relative price of synthetic fabric led to a shift in demand from cotton fabric to blended and synthetic fabric. However, the spinning sector continued to depend heavily on cotton. The shift away from cotton in weaving was made possible by the increased dependence of weaving on the rapidly growing synthetic fibre and filament yarn industry.

Also, several factors worked over the last few decades to ensure a process of division of the textile sector into spinning and weaving, where spinning is undertaken in the organised sector and almost the entire weaving forms part of the unorganised sector. The share of the mill sector in fabric production continued to decline during the period since the 1990s. This was mainly due to declining competitiveness of composite mills in comparison to the power looms and the hosiery units in the decentralised sector. However, a few modern mills engaged in fabric production have continued to do well as they produce branded fabric and cater to the export market and increasingly prosperous domestic urban market.

The growth of the power loom sector was a major breakthrough in the development of the Indian textile industry. The growth of power looms and the consequent decline of mills over the last few decades was the result of several cost advantages due to organisational differences between mills and power looms. The hosiery sector grew fast as its products became popular among consumers due to their inherent qualities. The handlooms suffered a setback after the 1980s. The problems faced by the handlooms multiplied since the 1990s. The handlooms faced tough competition from the power looms and hosiery sector as there was a massive increase in consumer demand for the products of these sectors. On the supply side, handlooms faced problems of availability of yarn due to a sharp increase in the export of cotton yarn after 1985.

The growth in home demand and exports led to an investment boom in the mill sector from the 1990s. The boom was facilitated by delicensing in July 1991 and improved access to imported technology, spare parts, and textile machinery, which resulted in modernisation and technological upgradation in spinning and led to growth of productivity. However, the spinning mills differed with respect to their degree of modernisation and productivity. Further, the mills which did not modernise and expand capacities could not compete with the modern fast-expanding mills, and were forced to close down.

There was a spectacular growth of the ready-made garment sector during the period since the 1990s. The growth in the sector was the result of an increase in home demand and in the export of ready-made garments. Ready-made garment have substituted for tailor-made goods, reflecting fast growth of incomes and increasing fashion orientation and fast-changing lifestyle.

5

The Employment Fall Out

This chapter discusses the changes in the extent and pattern of employment in the Indian textile industry since 1980s. As the textile industry is considered to be labour intensive and is a major source of manufacturing employment, it is expected that any growth of textile production would be accompanied by growth of employment. A boom in textiles is thus expected to create jobs for the poor. Hence, for many economists, the textile industry in India typifies the low-end, labour-intensive manufacturing sector, the growth of which would improve the lives of low-skilled, impoverished citizens, who have been largely bypassed by India's high-end growth, by creating more jobs and better working conditions.

In the overall context of a falling employment intensity of production in an otherwise fast-growing economy since the early 1990s, the focus of this chapter is to examine whether employment in the industry is growing at a rate warranted by the growth rate of output. Changes in the structure of employment in the textile industry are also analysed. The major sources of data are the NSSO surveys on employment and unemployment[1] for the years 1983, 1987–88,

---

[1] As they provide employment estimates at the all-India level (organised as well as unorganised sectors).

1993–94, 1999–2000, 2004–05, and 2009–10. Since the National Industrial Classification-1970 (NIC-1970) was used for the 38th and 43rd rounds of NSS (1983 and 1987–88 respectively), NIC-1987 was used for 50th round of NSS (1993–94), NIC-1998 was used for the 55th and 61st rounds of NSS (1999–2000 and 2004–05 respectively), and NIC-2004 was used for the 66th round of NSS (2009–10), the concordance from 3-digit levels of NIC-1987 to NIC-1970, from 4-digit level of NIC-1998 to 3-digit level of NIC-1987, and from 4-digit level of NIC-2004 to 4 digit level of NIC-1998 was used for ensuring comparability of employment data over time. Further, since the focus, here, is to compare employment figures in textiles according to the use of fibre (cotton and/or synthetic) or according to process of manufacturing (spinning, weaving, or garment manufacturing), disaggregation of NIC-1998 at 5-digit level was also necessary.

Two different estimates of employment in the textile industry are generated. These estimates are based on the usual status approach used in classification of the activity status of the persons employed. The employment estimates provide:

1. The number of persons employed in the industry according to their usual status (PS), that is, by considering usual principal activity or those who work in the textile industry for a relatively longer part of the 365 days preceding the date of survey.
2. The number of persons employed in the industry according to the usual status (PS + SS), that is, by considering usual principal and subsidiary activity together. This estimate of employment includes the persons who: (i) worked in the textile industry for a relatively longer part of the 365 days preceding the date of survey; and (ii) also those persons from among the remaining population who had worked in this industry for at least 30 days during the reference period of 365 days preceding the date of survey.

Trends in Employment

The textile industry was under the grip of stagnation roughly since the mid-1960s. The revival of the industry in terms of demand, production, and exports from the early 1990s was expected to lead to growth in employment, but the NSS data indicate that employment has continued to decline. The revival of the industry has failed to reverse the continuing fall in usual status employment in the textile industry.[2] According to the data, the number of usual status employees engaged in the production of cotton and man-made (including blended) textiles at the all-India level fell continuously from the early 1980s from about 4.16 million in 1983 to 3.13 million by 1999–2000 (Table 5.1). It more or less stagnated from 1999–2000 to 2004–05, but declined thereafter to 2.86 million by 2009–10. The rural sector, however, registered an increase from 1983 to 1987–88, but such employment showed a decline thereafter. The urban sector employment fluctuated during the 1980s and the 1990s. Though it increased after the 1990s, it remained far below the levels attained in the 1980s and the early 1990s.

The period since the early 1990s saw remarkable growth in the ready-made garment industry. The bulk of the garment sector continued to exist in the unregistered sector as the entire garment industry was reserved under the small-scale sector until 2005–06. The sector saw spectacular growth with real gross value added (GVA)[3] growing at a high rate of about 16 per cent per annum from 1994–95 to 2000–01. Despite the fast growth of the garment sector during the 1990s and after, the employment in the garment sector in the 1990s was much lower when compared to the 1980s. The situation improved in 2004–05 in both the rural and the urban areas (Table 5.2). Employment in the urban areas in 2004–05 was higher than what it was during the 1980s, but it continued to be below the 1980s level in the rural areas. The sudden decline, beginning in the late 1980s, occurred in both the rural and the urban areas. It got reversed after 1993–94 when usual status employment grew in the garment sector. However, about 60 per cent of the increase in employment occurred in the urban areas as much of the increase (about 87 per cent) in real GVA during the period occurred

---

[2] The discussion in the chapter is based on usual status employment (PS + SS) unless mentioned otherwise.

[3] For details, see Chapter 4, 'Structural Changes in the Indian Textile Industry'.

Table 5.1 Usual Status Employment in Production of Textiles (lakhs)

Year	Urban			Rural			All-India		
	PS	SS	PS + SS	PS	SS	PS + SS	PS	SS	PS + SS
1983	20.24	1.81	22.05	16.33	3.17	19.50	36.5-8	4.97	41.55
1987–88	17.35	1.14	18.49	20.04	2.46	22.50	37.39	3.60	40.99
1993–94	19.18	1.64	20.82	16.30	2.95	19.25	35.49	4.59	40.08
1999–2000	13.76	0.46	14.22	15.49	1.55	17.04	29.25	2.01	31.26
2004–05	15.83	0.91	16.74	13.71	1.72	15.43	29.54	2.63	32.17
2009–10	16.34	0.80	17.14	10.24	1.15	11.39	26.58	1.95	28.55

Source: Computed from unit-level data from the NSS 38th, 43rd, 50th, 55th, 61st, and 66th rounds on employment–unemployment for the years 1983, 1987–88, 1993–94, 1999–2000, 2004–05, 2009–10 respectively.

Notes: 1. One lakh is equal to a hundred thousand.

2. For calculating employment in the textile sector for 1983 and 1987–88, following NIC-1970, codes 231, 233, 234, 235, 236, 247, and 260 are used (details of NIC codes are given in Appendix C).

3. For 1993–94, following NIC-1987, codes 231, 232, 233, 234, 235, 247, and 260 are considered.

4. For 1999–2000 and 2004–05, following NIC-1998, digit codes 17111, 17114, 17115, and 17118, and 1730 are used.

5. For 2009–10, following NIC-2004, codes 17111, 17114, 17115, 17118, 17131, 17132, 17133, 17137, and 1730 are used for calculating employment in the textile sector.

6. The figures in the Table include workers engaged in preparation and spinning of cotton and MMFs (including blended), weaving of cotton and man-made textiles (including blended), and manufacture of knitted and crocheted fabrics and articles. Employment in the manufacture of knitted and crocheted textile products of other fibers (mainly woolen) is included for all the years as, given the NIC, fibre-wise estimates cannot be obtained for the period prior to 1999–2000.

Table 5.2 Usual Status Employment in Garment Sector (lakhs)

Year	Urban			Rural			All-India		
	PS	SS	PS + SS	PS	SS	PS + SS	PS	SS	PS + SS
1983	13.01	2.64	15.65	12.65	3.72	16.36	25.66	6.36	32.01
1987–88	13.54	2.87	16.41	14.99	3.30	18.29	28.53	6.17	34.70
1993–94	5.84	0.59	6.44	2.50	0.71	3.21	8.34	1.30	9.64
1999–2000	10.28	0.67	10.93	8.30	0.68	8.98	18.58	1.35	19.91
2004–05	17.19	0.96	18.15	8.60	2.14	10.24	25.79	3.10	28.39
2009–10	9.48	0.46	9.94	3.06	0.42	3.48	12.54	0.88	13.42

Source: Computed from unit-level data from NSS 38th, 43rd, 50th, 55th, 61st, and 66th rounds on employment–unemployment for 1983, 1987–88, 1993–94, 1999–2000, 2004–05 and 2009–10 respectively.

Notes: 1. One lakh is equal to a hundred thousand.

2. For the 38th and 43rd rounds of NSS for 1983 and 1987–88, following NIC-1970, code 264 is used for calculating employment in the garment sector.

3. For the 50th round (1993–94), using NIC-1987, code 265 is used.

4. For the 55th and 61st rounds for 1999–2000 and 2004–05, following NIC-1998, code 18101 is used.

5. For the 66th round of NSS for 2009–10, following NIC-2004, code 18101 is used.

6. The figures in the Table include workers engaged in manufacture of textile garments and clothing accessories only.

in these areas.[4] The employment declined considerably in 2009–10 in both the rural and the urban areas. Overall, it grew slowly during the period 1993–94 to 2009–10 at 2.09 per cent per annum.

Overall, the increase in production in the textile and garment industry led to a slight improvement in the usual status employment during the 1990s at the all-India level (Table 5.3). The employment grew at a rate of 3.4 per cent per annum from 1999–2000 to 2004–05, but the results do not appear to be satisfactory as it continued to fall short of the levels attained in the 1980s. Though the employment in the urban areas in the textile and garment sector in 2004–05 was comparable to that attained in the 1980s, the employment in the rural areas was much below the 1980s levels. However, the employment declined considerably in 2009–10 in both the rural and the urban areas and was at its lowest level since the 1980s. Thus, though the industry grew remarkably well from the early 1990s with spun yarn, fabric, and garment production growing at about 4 per cent, 4.5 per cent, and 7.36 per cent per annum respectively, the performance of the industry on the employment front was far from satisfactory.

Analysis of Fall in Employment in Textile Industry

Fall in Employment in Mill Sector

One of the reasons for the dissatisfactory performance of the textile industry on the employment front is the continuous decline in employment in the mill sector. Although the mills (spinning as well as composite) form part of the organised (or the formal) sector, they employ formal (organised) as well as informal (unorganised) workers. These informal workers are the unprotected wage workers without any job or social security. They consist of substitute (*badli*) workers[5] and casual or contract workers who are completely flexible. The regular workers without the social security benefits also form part of the informal workers.

[4] For details, see Chapter 4, 'Structural Changes in the Indian Textile Industry'.

[5] After the 1982 textile strike in Bombay, permanent labourers were replaced by casual labourers.

Table 5.3 Usual Status Employment in Textile (cotton and man-made) and Garment Sector Combined (lakhs)

Year	Urban			Rural			All-India		
	PS	SS	PS + SS	PS	SS	PS + SS	PS	SS	PS + SS
1983	33.25	4.45	37.70	28.98	6.89	35.86	62.24	11.33	73.56
1987–88	30.89	4.01	34.90	35.03	5.76	40.79	65.92	9.77	75.69
1993–94	25.02	2.23	27.26	18.80	3.66	22.46	43.83	5.89	49.72
1999–2000	24.04	1.13	25.15	23.79	2.23	26.02	47.83	3.36	51.17
2004–05	33.02	1.87	34.89	22.31	3.86	25.67	55.33	5.73	60.56
2009–10	25.82	1.26	27.08	13.3	1.57	14.87	39.12	2.83	41.95

Source: Computed from Tables 5.1 and 5.2.

Note: One lakh is equal to a hundred thousand.

Although home demand for textiles increased after the early 1990s, much of this increase was for synthetic and blended textiles. The shift in demand towards non-cotton and blended textiles was reflected in terms of a fall in the share of cotton yarn and cotton cloth produced in the mill sector. However, the mills continued to be largely dominated by cotton as a fibre and were bypassed by the significant growth in demand, which occurred for the synthetic and blended textiles. The production of a proportion of the total yarn consumed in weaving started shifting from the spinning sector to the sector producing filament yarn, which formed part of the chemical industry.[6] Further, the mills could not compete with the cloth produced in the power looms and the hosiery units in the unregistered sector and consequently, the production of cloth continued to shift away from the mill sector.

The boom in demand for the T&C industry since the early 1990s was expected to lead to a tremendous increase in the production of spun yarn and to create additional jobs in the spinning sector. The production of spun yarn increased in response to the increase in external and domestic demand, but it could not reverse the fall in employment in spinning. There were several reasons that resulted in a continuation of the fall in employment in the spinning sector.

Though much of the increase in demand occurred for the synthetic and blended textiles, the rich at home or abroad continued to prefer cotton over non-cotton and blended textiles due to its inherent properties.[7] The rich (or the top 20 per cent of the population) at home accounted for about 40 per cent of the increase in demand from 1993–94 to 2004–05. Since they continued to spend almost the same proportion of their textile expenditure on cotton textiles and clothing (T&C) and since the export of cotton yarn (either direct or indirect in the form of cloth, garments, and made-ups) also

[6] For details, see Chapter 4, 'Structural Changes in the Indian Textile Industry'.

[7] For details, see Chapter 1, 'Trends in Domestic Demand and their Implications'.

grew fast,[8] the demand for cotton T&C continued to grow during the period. Collectively, these trends resulted in an increase in demand for cotton yarn, which led to higher investments in the spinning sector.[9]

The increase in investment was accompanied by substantial modernisation and a consequent improvement in productivity in the spinning sector during the 1990s. Bedi (2003) concluded that there was huge investment in modern spindles after 1990, which reduced the technological gap and resulted in substantial increase in productivity of spindles.[10] A study by SITRA (Rajamanickam et al. 2003) also highlighted a significant growth in productivity in the spinning sector. The study suggested that both the labour and capital productivity in spinning increased between 1990 and 2000.[11]

The increase in productivity of workers in spinning due to a rapid expansion in capacity using techniques of more recent dates and due to modernisation was reflected in an increase in the real GVA per worker. The ASI data for the mills engaged in manufacture of cotton textiles show an increasing trend in the real GVA per worker (with base 1993–94) since the mid-1980s. According to the data, the real GVA per worker, that varied in the range of Rs 38,000–46,000 in the first half of the 1980s, increased considerably to around Rs 80,000–86,000 after the mid-1990s (Table 5.4).[12] Further, the ASI data for the entire factory sector, engaged in the manufacturing of all types of textiles (using all types of fibres), indicate an increase in the real GVA per worker from Rs 0.11 million in 1998–99 to more than about 0.3 million by 2012–13 (Table 5.5). The increase in the real GVA per worker in modernised mills reflected the lower requirement of workers for performing the same tasks in the mills as all

---

[8] For details, see Chapter 1, 'Trends in Domestic Demand and their Implications' and Chapter 3, 'Exports: The New Driver of Growth?'.

[9] For details, see Chapter 4, 'Structural Changes in the Indian Textile Industry'.

[10] For details, see Chapter 4, 'Structural Changes in the Indian Textile Industry'.

[11] For details, see Chapter 4, 'Structural Changes in the Indian Textile Industry'.

[12] Due to change of NIC, figures in Table 5.4 are not comparable with those in Table 5.5.

Table 5.4 Employment, Real GVA, and real GVA per Worker in the Mills Engaged in Manufacture of Cotton Textiles (with base year 1993–94)

Year	Number of workers	Number of man-days–workers (thousands)	GVA at current prices (Rs billion)	GVA per worker at current prices (Rs thousand)	Real GVA (Rs billion)	Real GVA per worker (Rs thousand)
1980–81	732,846	234,929	13.4	18.32	33.7	46.04
1982–83	706,592	226,473	11.8	16.71	26.8	38.00
1984–85	670,828	225,798	14.2	21.11	29.3	43.71
1986–87	601,869	206,732	17.1	28.46	34.8	57.77
1988–89	508,909	172,137	17.7	34.80	20.4	40.13
1990–91	545,802	190,130	30.9	56.55	41.9	76.77
1992–93	509,199	172,505	30.7	60.26	33.4	65.63
1994–95	496,435	171,154	48.7	98.01	36.7	73.98
1996–97	507,197	176,074	60.3	118.91	43.5	85.82
1997–98	495,750	NA	56.4	113.70	39.6	79.88

Sources: Computed based on figures from Economic and Political Weekly Research Foundation (2002) and Office of Economic Advisor, GoI (for figures before 1993–94: *Index Numbers of Wholesale Prices in India*; for figures of 1993–94 onwards: http://www.eaindustry.nic.in/download_data_9394.asp [last accessed on 11 February 2016]) for WPI.

Notes: 1. The 3-digit code 235 based on NIC-1987 is considered.
2. The WPI of cotton textiles with base 1993–94 is used as deflator.

purely manual work became redundant (Chakravarty 2002). Several case studies suggest that there was a significant fall in the need for the usual skills required for handling usual operations, which were routine, repetitive, and monotonous. Technological modernisation led to a significant amount of retrenchment of workers in the organised mills (Choudhary 1996; Dutta 1996). Even formal employment was affected as a number of vacancies created after the retirement of the workers were not filled during the first phase of technological modernisation around the mid-1980s. Later, a voluntary retirement scheme was offered to the workers who became redundant in the course of computerisation and automation. This resulted in a substantial fall in employment in the mills.

Table 5.5 Employment, Real GVA, and Real GVA per Worker in the Factory Sector Engaged in Manufacturing of Textiles (with base year 1993–94)

Year	Number of workers	Number of man-days–workers (thousands)	GVA at current prices (Rs billion)	GVA per worker at current prices (Rs thousand)	Real GVA (Rs billion)	Real GVA per worker (Rs thousand)
1998–99	893,634	291,674	117.1	131.06	102.4	114.56
2000–01	810,290	269,876	125.6	155.03	104.8	129.34
2002–03	732,712	245,428	124.5	169.86	101.8	138.95
2003–04	696,353	231,349	121.1	173.93	92.0	132.14
2004–05	696,556	267,901	129.8	186.38	95.6	137.30
2006–07	766,677	288,906	187.7	244.79	137.2	178.89
2008–09	726,632	282,244	172.2	236.99	122.9	169.18
2010–11	811,212	312,248	342.9	422.73	211.2	260.33
2012–13	792,170	301,844	418.3	528.04	234.7	296.32

Sources: Computed based on figures from CSO, *Annual Survey of Industries* (various years); Office of Economic Advisor, GoI (for figures before 1993–94: *Index Numbers of Wholesale Prices in India*; for figures of 1993–94 onwards: http://www.eaindustry.nic.in/download_data_9394.asp [last accessed on 11 February 2016]) for WPI.

Notes: 1. The 4-digit code 1711, based on NIC-1998, is considered for 1998–99, 2000–01, and 2002–03; 4-digit codes 1711 and 1713, based on NIC-2004, are considered for 2004–05 and 2006–07; and 4-digit codes 1311 and 1312, based on NIC–2008, are considered for 2008–09, 2010–11, and 2012–13.

2. The WPI of textiles with base 1993–94 is used for deflating GVA.

According to ASI data, the number of workers employed in the mills engaged in the manufacture of cotton textiles declined from above 0.7 million in the early 1980s to about 0.5 million after the mid-1990s (Table 5.4). The total number of man-days employed annually declined from about 226 million in the year 1984–85 to less than 180 million after 1990–91. Further, the data available indicate that the number of workers employed in the manufacture of all kinds of textile in the factory sector declined from 0.89 million in 1998–99 to about 0.70 million by 2003–04. The number of man-days (workers) employed declined from about 292 million in 1998–99 to 231 million by 2003–04 (Table 5.5). The employment improved somewhat during the period of high growth after 2003–04 when the production of cotton textiles increased fast in response to increase in its demand,[13] but the number of workers employed remained lower than what they were during the late 1990s.

The wage per worker (and the wage per man-day) in monetary terms increased during this period (Tables 5.6 and 5.7). But the real wage rate,[14] which increased in the late 1980s, did not show any further increase in the mills engaged in the manufacture of cotton textiles. It remained almost the same in the first half of the 1990s and declined later in 1996–97 and 1997–98. A similar tendency was observed from 1998–99 to 2009–10 in the factory sector engaged in the manufacture of all kinds of textiles. There was some increase after 2009–10, but the real wages remained far below than what they were during the period from 1998–99 to 2004–05.

Apart from remaining almost stable, the real wages lagged far behind labour productivity, which increased fast due to substantial modernisation in the sector. As a result, the share of wages in the GVA (at current prices),[15] which was high in the 1980s (between 0.47 and 0.59), declined after the late 1980s (between 0.32 and 0.47) in the mills engaged in the manufacture of cotton textiles (Table 5.6). Similarly, the share of wages in GVA at current prices declined in the factory sector engaged in manufacture of all kinds of textiles from 0.29 in 1998–99 to 0.17 in the recent years (Table 5.7). In real terms, the fall was from 0.59 in the year 1980–81 to 0.40 in the 1990–91, and further to only 0.35 in 1997–98, in the mills engaged in the manufacture of cotton textiles (Table 5.6). In the manufacture of all

[13] For details, see Chapter 4, 'Structural Changes in the Indian Textile Industry'.

[14] The Consumer Price Index Number for Industrial Workers (CPIN-IW) with base 1993–94 is used as deflators.

[15] Kar (2015), while relating trade and labour market outcomes based on firm-level empirical analysis during 1998–2012, also suggests that increase in capital stock, that leads to increase in exports, lowers the employment, the wage bills, and total labour costs for all firms taken together.

Table 5.6 Real Wage Rate and the Share of Wages in GVA in the Mills Engaged in Manufacture of Cotton Textiles (with base year 1993–94)

Year	Number of workers	Total wages to workers (Rs billion)	Wages per worker (Rs thousands)	Wages per man-day (Rs)	Real wages per man-day at 1993–94 prices (Rs)	Real wages per worker (Rs thousand)	Total real wages (Rs billion)	Wages/ GVA at current prices	Real wages/ real GVA
1980–81	732,846	6.29	8.58	26.75	84.87	27.20	19.94	0.47	0.59
1982–83	706,592	6.90	9.77	30.48	79.77	25.57	18.07	0.58	0.67
1984–85	670,828	8.41	12.54	37.26	81.44	27.41	18.39	0.59	0.63
1986–87	601,869	9.27	15.39	44.81	84.55	29.04	17.48	0.54	0.50
1988–89	508,909	9.32	18.31	54.13	85.85	29.04	14.78	0.53	0.72
1990–91	545,802	12.40	22.71	65.20	87.19	30.37	16.58	0.40	0.40
1992–93	509,199	14.43	28.34	83.65	89.95	30.47	15.52	0.47	0.46
1994–95	496,435	16.10	32.44	94.08	85.45	29.46	14.63	0.33	0.40
1996–97	507,197	19.13	37.72	108.70	81.95	28.45	14.43	0.32	0.33
1997–98	495,750	19.80	39.93	—	—	28.18	13.97	0.35	0.35

Sources: Computed based on figures from Economic and Political Weekly Research Foundation (2002); Ministry of Labour and Employment, GoI (various years) for CPIN; and Office of Economic Advisor, GoI (for figures before 1993–94: *Index Numbers of Wholesale Prices in India*; for figures of 1993–94 onwards: http://www.eaindustry.nic.in/download_data_9394.asp [last accessed on 11 February 2016]) for WPI.

Notes: 1. The 3-digit code 235, based on NIC-1987, is considered.

2. The CPIN-IW with base 1993–94 is used for deflating wages. The WPI of cotton textile with base 1993–94 is used for deflating GVA.

Table 5.7 Real Wage Rate and the Share of Wages in GVA in the Factory Sector Engaged in Manufacturing of Textiles (with base year 1993–94)

Year	No. of workers	No. of man-days–workers (thousand)	Wages per worker (Rs)	Wages per man-day (Rs)	Real wages per man-day at 1993–94 prices (Rs)	Real wages per worker (Rs thousand)	Total real wages (Rs billion)	Wages/GVA at current prices	Real wages/real GVA
1998–99	893,634	291,674	37,691.3	115.47	72.04	23.51	21.01	0.29	0.21
2000–01	810,290	269,876	43,851.2	131.66	76.51	25.48	20.65	0.28	0.20
2002–03	732,712	245,428	46,411.1	138.56	74.17	24.84	18.20	0.27	0.18
2004–05	696,556	267,901	47,392	123.22	61.14	23.51	16.37	0.25	0.17
2006–07	766,677	288,906	47,589	126.29	56.89	21.44	16.43	0.19	0.12
2008–09	726,632	282,244	54,722	140.38	54.71	21.25	15.44	0.23	0.13
2010–11	811,212	312,248	72,299	187.83	58.84	22.65	18.37	0.17	0.09
2012–13	792,170	301,844	90,321.1	237.04	61.44	23.41	18.54	0.17	0.08

Sources: Computed based on figures from GoI, *Annual Survey of Industries* (various years); Ministry of Labour and Employment, GoI (various years) for CPIN; and Office of Economic Advisor, GoI (for figures before 1993–94: *Index Numbers of Wholesale Prices in India*; for figures of 1993–94 onwards: http://www.eaindustry.nic.in/download_data_9394.asp [last accessed on 11 February 2016]) for WPI.

Notes: 1. The 4-digit code 1711, based on NIC-1998. is considered for 1998–99, 2000–01, and 2002–03; 4-digit codes 1711 and 1713, based on NIC-2004, are considered for 2004–05 and 2006–07; 4-digit codes 1311 and 1312, based on NIC-2008, are considered for 2008–09, 2010–11, and 2012–13.

2. The CPIN-IW with base 1993–94 is used for deflating wages. The WPI of textile with base 1993–94 is used for deflating GVA.

kinds of textiles, the share of real wages in real GVA declined from 0.21 in 1998–99 to 0.08 by 2012–13 (Table 5.7). Though there was some increase in the real wages in the recent period, the real wages continued to lag behind labour productivity. Thus, the changes in the structure of the industry and technology use had serious implications for the level of employment and the share of wages in the mill sector.

Thus, the technological modernisation of the spinning process in most of these mills led to a fall in employment. The fall in the number of persons employed reduced the wage cost of the mills. The salary and wage cost varied from a low of 1.5 per cent to a high of over 20 per cent of sales turnover depending on differences in labour productivity, wage rate, and sales turnover (Shanmugnanandam and Mariappan 2007).

The 30th productivity survey conducted by SITRA examined the implications of the increase in productivity in 187 spinning mills for their salary and wage costs during the period September 2004. The study indicated that if the labour productivity was maintained at a high level, even at a higher wage rate (of Rs 250 per day), a salary and wage cost of 5–6 per cent of sales turnover was possible to achieve. The mills operating with lower wage levels (of below Rs 150 per day) could maintain the salary and wage cost at no more than 2–3 per cent of sales by achieving high labour productivity (Shanmugnanandam and Mariappan 2007).

An analysis of the salary and wage cost of 183 spinning mills which participated in a study conducted by SITRA for the period of October–December 2005 pointed to the low ratio of salary and wage cost to sales turnover. The salary and wage cost averaged 8.1 per cent of sales turnover. In about 80 per cent of the spinning mills, the wage costs were less than 11 per cent of sales. In about 30 per cent of the mills, it was at a level of below 5 per cent. It was found to be low at below 3 per cent of sales turnover in EOUs and high-tech mills, which constituted about 5 per cent of the mills (Shanmugnanandam and Mariappan 2007).

While substantial modernisation in most of the mills led to a fall in employment due to significant automation, the absence or lack of modernisation adversely affected several other spinning mills as they chose not to expand and modernise due to overexpansion in spinning.[16] As a result, these mills could not exploit the advantages

[16] For details, see Chapter 4, 'Structural Changes in the Indian Textile Industry'.

that accrue to the mill due to modernisation. Higher level of modernisation increases not only the level of labour and machine productivity, it also affects sales turnover and profits. Based on their study of 120 spinning mills, Shanmuganandam and Sreenivasan (2008) suggested that sales turnover registers an increasing trend with increase in the level of modernisation. The net profits relative to sale turnover also show a fairly steep (from 7 per cent to 25 per cent) increase for mills with an up to 70 overall modernisation index (OMI). Above 70 OMI, the net profits remain almost constant at about 25 per cent the sales turnover. The production per spindle also shows a fairly close association ($r = 0.64$) with the level of modernisation. The HOK (that is, the average hours of workers to produce 100 kilograms of yarn) registers a declining trend with increase in the level of modernisation. The study showed that in one-fourth of the mills, in which the level of modernisation was less than one-half of the standard mill, the HOK was almost 50 per cent more than the all mills' average at 32. Thus, the level of modernisation of machines largely influences the profit margins as well as labour and machine productivity in the spinning mills. As a result, the mills which do not modernise or the mills with low levels of modernisation find it difficult to compete with the highly modernised spinning mills. As mentioned earlier, Akot Taluka Sahakari Soot Girni Ltd and Jawahar Shetkari Sahakari Roto Soot Girni Ltd are examples of some mills which did not allocate funds for modernisation of plant and machinery and technological upgradation. They found it difficult to sustain the pressure and compete with the modern mills and were ultimately forced to close down. According to figures from the Textile Commissioner's office, the number of closed spinning mills increased from 46 in December 1984 to 77 in December 1994, but it then increased to 378 by May 2004, and further to 457 by April 2014.[17] The closure of the mills led to a further decline in the number of workers in spinning.

The fall in employment in spinning was also reflected in the employment data collected by the NSS through its employment–unemployment surveys (Table 5.8). The data indicate that the usual

[17] ICMF, *Handbook of Statistics on Cotton Textile Industry* (2001: 91–8) up to May 2004; and www.txcindia.gov.in (last accessed on 15 February 2016) for recent years.

Table 5.8   Usual Status Employment in Spinning of Yarn (lakhs)

All-India	1993–94		1999–2000		2004–05		2009–10	
	PS	PS+SS	PS	PS+SS	PS	PS+SS	PS	PS+SS
Total yarn	7.49	8.86	7.23	7.57	5.36	6.53	5.47	5.74
Cotton yarn	5.62	6.97	5.88	6.18	4.72	5.36	5.00	5.66
Man-made yarn	1.87	1.89	1.35	1.4	0.64	1.17	0.07	0.08
Rural	PS	PS+SS	PS	PS+SS	PS	PS+SS	PS	PS+SS
Total yarn	2.47	3.33	3.38	3.63	2.85	3.44	2.07	2.39
Cotton yarn	1.9	2.75	3.05	3.28	2.7	3.18	2.04	2.35
Man-made yarn	0.57	0.58	0.33	0.36	0.15	0.26	0.03	0.04
Urban	PS	PS+SS	PS	PS+SS	PS	PS+SS	PS	PS+SS
Total yarn	5.02	5.53	3.85	3.94	2.51	3.09	3.00	3.35
Cotton yarn	3.72	4.22	2.83	2.9	2.02	2.18	2.96	3.31
Man-made yarn	1.3	1.31	1.02	1.04	0.49	0.91	0.04	0.04

Source: Computed from unit-level data from NSS 50th, 55th, 61st, and 66th rounds on employment–unemployment.

Notes: 1. One lakh is equal to a hundred thousand.

2. The figures in the table include persons engaged in spinning of cotton and man-made yarn.

3. The employment estimates in cotton spinning for 1993–94 are based on NIC codes 231 and 235 (based on NIC-1987). Skill codes are observed for the persons employed in code 235 during 1993–94. Total employment minus the weavers (skill code 05) in cotton mills are considered to be engaged in cotton spinning.

4. Similarly, estimates are generated for employment in the spinning of man-made yarn for the year 1993–94 using NIC code 247.

5. For 1999–2000 and 2004–05, following NIC-1998, 5-digit codes 17111 and 17114 are used for spinning of cotton yarn and man-made yarn respectively.

6. For 2009–10, following NIC-2004, 5-digit codes 17111 and 17131 are used for spinning of cotton yarn. Code 17114 is used for spinning of man-made yarn.

status employment in the spinning of yarn (cotton and synthetic) declined after 1993–94 at the all-India level. The decline in employment during 2009–10 was also partly a result of the September 2008 crisis—which started in the US and soon spread to the other developed economies—that affected India's exports adversely.

In the rural areas, it fluctuated at around 0.35 million up to 2004–05, but declined to 0.24 million in 2009–10. The urban areas recorded a substantial fall in employment from 0.55 million in 1993–94 to 0.31 million in 2004–05, which later increased to 0.34 million in 2009–10. The data also point to a continuing dominance of cotton in spinning in spite of a substantial increase in the demand for synthetic and blended textiles since the 1990s. About 80 per cent of the persons continued to remain engaged in the spinning of cotton yarn.

Clearly, although the period after 1993–94 was marked by a revival of the home demand for textile and clothing in all the three sections (bottom 40 per cent, middle 40 per cent, and top 20 per cent) of the population, as well as by a substantial growth in the exports of textile and clothing leading to growth in the production of spun yarn,[18] employment fell in the spinning sector.

In addition to this, the closure of composite mills during this period had an adverse impact on employment. The number of closed composite mills, which stood at 59 in March 1993, increased to 106 by March 1999, rising further to 134 by March 2003.[19] About 110 of these were closed for a period of more than 5 years.[20] This was mainly because of their declining competitiveness in comparison to the power looms and hosiery units in the decentralised sector. The power looms, which continued to operate in the unregistered sector either as own account enterprises or as non-directory or directory establishments, had several cost advantages due to organisational differences between mills and power looms. The weaving capacity of the mills, which had been stagnant for a number of years, started

---

[18] For details, see Chapter 1, 'Trends in Domestic Demand and their Implications'; Chapter 3, 'Exports: The New Driver of Growth?'; and Chapter 4, 'Structural Changes in the Indian Textile Industry'.

[19] The number has been falling thereafter, and about 81 composite mills were closed at the end of 2013–14, www.txcindia.gov.in (last accessed on 15 February 2016).

[20] For details, see Chapter 4, 'Structural Changes in the Indian Textile Industry'.

declining after the middle of the 1980s. The number of installed looms, which was almost stagnant till the mid-1980s, declined thereafter. Rapid restructuring of the industry after NTP (1985), involving removal of restrictions on capacity expansion, flexibility of fibre use, and easy import of polyester fibre and modern technology, could not counter the declining scenario. The fabric produced in the mill sector continued to experience negative growth since the early 1990s. The share of the mill sector declined further from about 11 per cent of the total fabric in early 1990s to about 3.5 per cent by 2004–05 and fluctuated around this level. Though few composite mills, like Arvind Mills, Raymond Ltd, Century Textiles, Morarjee Mills, GTN Textiles, and Ginni Filaments, continued to do well and cater to the high-value, brand name market segment, a majority of them failed to compete with the cloth produced in the unorganised sector.[21] Some of the mills experienced a decline in production of fabric during the 1990s. But there were others like Ahmedabad Manufacturing Calico Printing Co. Ltd, Maheshwari, Ahmedabad Kaiser-i-Hind Mills, and Khatau which experienced a decline in their production since the 1980s, which could not be recouped during the period of revival. The increasing number of closures of the composite mills since the 1990s affected employment adversely.

Decline of Handlooms

Another explanation for the decline in employment in the Indian textile industry during the period of its revival was the decline of handlooms. The rapid growth of the power loom sector posed a serious threat not only to the composite mills but also to handlooms as there was hardly any demand for the handloom workers, with traditional skills, in the power loom sector. The power looms started with the setting up of looms discarded by mills by some prosperous handloom weavers in their workshops. Though production in the power loom sector increased substantially every year since the 1950s, the real GVA in cotton weaving in the handlooms remained more than three times that in the power looms till the late 1970s. The real

[21] For details, see Chapter 4, 'Structural Changes in the Indian Textile Industry'.

GVA in the handlooms in the urban areas declined during the 1980s, but overall, there was an increase in real GVA at the all-India level up to the 1980s.[22] However, when the handlooms in the rural areas suffered a serious setback after the late 1980s, the real GVA declined in the handloom sector at the all-India level. The real GVA in the weaving of cotton cloth in the power loom sector was higher than that in the handloom sector at the all-India level by the mid-1990s.

The analysis of data from the NSS rounds on employment–unemployment indicates changes in the employment scenario in the power loom, handloom, and cotton mill sectors from the early 1980s to the early 1990s (Table 5.9). This data, combined with the results from the NSS surveys on unorganised manufacturing, indicates that the employment trends in the handloom sector mirror those in the real GVA generated in the sector. Though handlooms remained the major source of employment, the employment in urban handlooms started falling after the early 1980s. It continued to increase in rural handlooms. At the all-India level, the employment declined in handlooms after 1987–88 when the real GVA in rural handlooms recorded a downward trend.

Though the inter-sectoral analysis of the employment scenario is not permitted after 1993–94 due to change in NIC, with focus shifting from sector to process of manufacturing, the decline of handlooms, which started in the late 1980s, seems to have continued throughout the 1990s. While the official data indicate remarkable increase in the output of handloom cloth during 1990–91 to 1997–98, they suffer from various lacunae. There is an inherent problem in the sector-wise estimates of production derived by the official agency due to the diversion of hank yarn to the power looms. There is hardly any evidence of increase in internal or external demand for the products of the handloom sector.[23] The data from the Textiles Committee, GoI, point to the decline of the monthly per capita purchase of cotton textiles from the handloom sector at the all-India level from 1993 to 1998. The data recorded by the DGCIS and the Apparel

[22] For details, see Chapter 4, 'Structural Changes in the India Textile Industry'.

[23] For details, see Chapter 4, 'Structural Changes in the Indian Textile Industry'.

Table 5.9 Usual Status Employment in Cotton Mills, Handlooms, and Power Looms (lakhs)

	1983			1987–88			1993–94		
All-India	PS	SS	PS+SS	PS	SS	PS+SS	PS	SS	PS+SS
Cotton mills	11.87	0.92	12.79	9.36	0.65	10.01	5.26	0.22	5.48
Handlooms	15.44	2.1	17.54	16.48	2.66	19.14	13.57	2.87	16.44
Power looms	3.95	0.14	4.08	5.99	0.16	6.14	7.08	0.32	7.4
Urban	PS	SS	PS+SS	PS	SS	PS+SS	PS	SS	PS+SS
Cotton mills	8.41	0.31	8.72	5.64	0.08	5.71	3.36	0.08	3.45
Handlooms	6.44	0.59	7.03	5.72	0.6	6.31	5.49	0.73	6.22
Power looms	2.75	0.08	2.83	2.7	0.1	2.8	4.57	0.13	4.69
Rural	PS	SS	PS+SS	PS	SS	PS+SS	PS	SS	PS+SS
Cotton mills	3.46	0.61	4.07	3.73	0.58	4.3	1.89	0.14	2.03
Handlooms	9	1.51	10.51	10.77	2.06	12.83	8.07	2.15	10.22
Power looms	1.2	0.06	1.25	3.29	0.06	3.34	2.51	0.2	2.71

Source: Computed from unit-level data from NSS 38th, 43rd, and 50th rounds on employment–unemployment.

Notes: 1. One lakh is equal to a hundred thousand.

2. For the 38th and the 43rd rounds conducted in 1983 and 1987–88, following NIC-1970, codes 231, 235, and 236 are used for calculating employment estimates in the cotton mills, handlooms, and power looms respectively.

3. For the 50th round conducted in 1993–94, following NIC-1987, codes 233, 234, and 235 are used for calculating employment estimates in the handlooms, power looms, and cotton mills.

Export Promotion Council indicate substantial reduction in exports of handloom fabric and garments during the 1990s. Although the value of export of cotton made-ups from the handloom sector, calculated at 1990–91 prices, increased from 1990–91 to 1995–96, the overall demand for the products of the handloom sector seems to have declined.

Similar results are reported by a comparison of the censuses of handlooms conducted in 1987–88 and 1995–96. Handloom weaving declined between 1987–88 and 1995–96. A comparison of the results from the *Census of Handlooms*, 1995–96 and *Census of Handlooms*, 2009–10 indicates a further decline of handloom weaving at the all-India level. Further, an analysis of the unit-level data from the NSS 62nd round on unorganised manufacturing sector (2005–06) suggests that the fall of handlooms continued after the mid-1990s as well.[24]

Handlooms were always at a disadvantage because of lower productivity in comparison with power looms and mills that use similar techniques of production. However, in spite of this disadvantage, they continued to remain a large employer from the 1960s to the late 1980s. Besides producing the coarse and medium category of cotton cloth, the sector specialised in the production of some exquisite cloth showing excellent craftsmanship. While the former were demanded by the relatively poor in local markets, the latter had national and international markets. However, after the NTP (1985), both types of products seem to have suffered a setback, which further exacerbated the problem of lower productivity. A massive shift in consumer demand towards synthetics and blended textiles in the domestic economy and a substantial increase in the export of cotton yarn and other cotton products since the 1990s aggravated the problem of low productivity faced by handlooms.[25] The state support to the sector was also gradually reduced.

In addition to this, handlooms, engaged mainly in weaving of cotton cloth, suffered because of changing consumer demand

[24] For details, see Chapter 4, 'Structural Changes in the Indian Textile Industry'.

[25] For details, see Chapter 4, 'Structural Changes in the Indian Textile Industry'.

towards knitted textiles due to their comfort and inherent qualities. There was a continuous increase in production in the hosiery sector since the 1990s.[26] The share of the hosiery sector increased in cotton as well as blended cloth production. This led to increase in employment in the hosiery sector. According to the NSS data, the usual status employment in the hosiery sector at the all-India level increased after the late 1980s. It declined somewhat in 1999–2000, but grew substantially by 2004–05. However, the employment declined sharply in the year 2009–10 (Table 5.10). The decline in 2009–10 can be attributed to fall in exports of knitted and

Table 5.10   Usual Status Employment in Hosiery Sector (lakhs)

Year	Urban		Rural		All-India	
	PS	PS+SS	PS	PS+SS	PS	PS+SS
1983	0.46	1.00	0.27	0.37	0.73	1.37
1987–88	1.13	1.24	0.06	0.12	1.19	1.36
1993–94	2.18	2.39	0.50	0.59	2.68	2.98
1999–2000	1.28	1.31	0.56	0.60	1.84	1.91
2004–05	3.32	3.36	0.71	0.81	4.03	4.17
2009–10	1.98	2.18	0.47	0.52	2.45	2.70

Source: Computed from unit-level data from NSS 38th, 43rd, 50th, 55th, 61st, and 66th rounds on employment–unemployment.

Notes: 1. One lakh is equal to a hundred thousand.

2. For the 38th and 43rd rounds of NSS, conducted in 1983 and 1987–88, following NIC-1970, code 260 is used to calculate the employment estimates in the hosiery sector.

3. For the 50th round of NSS, conducted in 1993–94, following NIC-1987, code 260 is used.

4. For the 55th and 61st rounds of NSS for 1999–2000 and 2004–05 respectively, following NIC-1998, 4-digit code 1730 is used for calculating employment in the hosiery sector.

5. For the 66th round of NSS for 2009–10, following NIC-2004, 4-digit code 1730 is used for calculating employment in the hosiery sector.

[26] For details, see Chapter 4, 'Structural Changes in the Indian Textile Industry'.

crocheted garments to the developed economies as these economies were hit by the financial crisis in September 2008. Figures from the DGCIS indicate that the value of India's exports of knitted and crocheted garments of cotton with base year 1990–91, which increased from Rs 8,738.87 million in 1990–91 to Rs 89,205.10 million by 2008–09, declined thereafter to Rs 58,738.79 million by 2010–11.[27] The employment in the hosiery sector continued to be much higher in the urban sector compared to the rural sector during this period. Increase in demand for knitted products affected the handloom sector adversely.

An analysis of the unit-level data from the NSS employment–unemployment surveys shows that the overall scenario which emerged since 1993–94 was one in which there was a substantial fall in the number of persons engaged in weaving. Table 5.11 shows the employment scenario in weaving from 1993–94 to 2009–10. About 2.90 million persons were employed in woven cloth production in the usual status at the all-India level in 1993–94. The numbers fell after 1993–94. Clearly, the fall in the number of persons engaged in weaving in the composite mills and the handlooms since the 1990s was much greater than the increase in employment in the power loom sector. Similar trends were observed in the rural and urban areas during the 1990s. Subsidiary employment continued to fall since 1993–94. The urban areas recorded some improvement after the 1990s, though the rural areas continued to experience a decline.

Clearly, modernisation of the spinning sector and the decline of composite mills and handlooms led to a fall in the number of persons employed in the textile industry. Though employment increased in the hosiery sector, the fall in employment in the weaving sector was much sharper. Overall, there was a decline in the number of employees in the textile sector. The industry performed well in terms of growth of output, but the structural changes in the spinning as well as the weaving sectors constrained the accompanying growth in employment.

---

[27] For details, see Figure 3.5 in Chapter 3, 'Exports: The New Driver of Growth?'.

Table 5.11 Usual Status Employment in Weaving of Cloth (lakhs)

All-India	1993–94		1999–2000		2004–05		2009–10	
	PS	PS+SS	PS	PS+SS	PS	PS+SS	PS	PS+SS
Total cloth	25.3	28.95	20.2	21.75	20.1	21.45	18.33	19.38
Cotton cloth	22.6	26.2	18.9	20.32	17.6	18.76	14.19	15.14
Man-made cloth	2.69	2.75	1.25	1.45	2.58	2.68	4.5	4.61
Rural	PS	PS+SS	PS	PS+SS	PS	PS+SS	PS	PS+SS
Total cloth	13.3	16.06	11.5	12.8	10.1	11.16	7.01	7.79
Cotton cloth	11.9	14.53	11	12.15	9.71	10.68	6.9	7.58
Man-made cloth	1.47	1.53	0.51	0.67	0.41	0.47	0.46	0.57
Urban	PS	PS+SS	PS	PS+SS	PS	PS+SS	PS	PS+SS
Total cloth	12	12.89	8.62	8.95	10	10.29	11.32	11.59
Cotton cloth	10.8	11.67	7.88	8.17	7.84	8.08	7.29	7.56
Man-made cloth	1.22	1.22	0.74	0.78	2.17	2.22	4.04	4.04

Source: Computed from unit-level data from NSS 50th, 55th, 61st, and 66th rounds on employment–unemployment.

Notes: 1. One lakh is equal to a hundred thousand.

2. The employment estimates in cotton cloth production are obtained for the 50th round of NSS conducted in 1993–94 using codes 232, 233, 234, 235, and 247, following NIC-1987. Skill codes are observed for the employed persons in code 235 in 1993–94. The weavers (skill code 05) in cotton mills are considered to be engaged in cotton cloth production.

3. Similarly, estimates are generated for employment in the production of man-made cloth in 1993–94 using NIC code 247.

4. For the 55th and 61st rounds of NSS conducted in 1999–2000 and 2004–05 respectively, the estimates are based on NIC-1998. The 5-digit code 17115 is used for cotton cloth and 5-digit code 17118 is considered for man-made cloth.

5. For the 66th round of NSS conducted in 2009–10, the estimates are based on codes 17115 and 17133 for cotton cloth. Codes 17118 and 17137 are used for man-made cloth.

6. Usual status employment in weaving of cotton as well as man-made cloth is considered in this table.

Changing Structure of Employment

In addition to the fall in employment in the textile industry since the 1980s, there were other changes in the structure of employment, which were of equal concern. One such change was a fall in the number of regular employees and an increase in the number of casual employees. Such changes point to a deterioration in the quality of employment since the 1990s.

Informalisation of the Formal Spinning Sector

An analysis of the NSS data on composition of employment in spinning since 1993–94 suggests that the mills not only reduced employment, they were able to adjust the composition of employment and reduce the share of the regularly employed, who were costlier. The data indicate that the regular employment, which accounted for 55 per cent of total employment in spinning in 1993–94 at the all-India level, declined to 50 per cent in 1999–2000, and further to 46 per cent in 2004–05. The decline was sharper in the urban areas from 69 per cent in 1993–94 to 51 per cent in 1999–2000, and further to 38 per cent in 2004–05. The number of casual workers also declined in the urban areas, but the fall was of a much lower extent. The overall impact of this was a rise in the share of casual employees, which grew from 16 per cent to 19 per cent, and further to 26 per cent, in the respective years in the urban areas. These changes point to the increase in the informalisation of the spinning sector, as a result of a reduction in the number of regular workers, who continued to be unprotected with no job or social security and formed part of informal employment. After 2004–05, the number of regular workers continued to decline further, but there was an increase in the number of casual workers at the all-India level (Table 5.12). As a result, the share of casual employees increased from 19 per cent in 2004–05 to 22 per cent in 2009–10.

The increase in casualisation of employment in the spinning sector seems to be the result of increase in privatisation and the drive to maximise profits. The data from the Textile Commissioner's office indicate that while the production of spun yarn in the private sector

Table 5.12   Usual Status Employment in Spinning of Cotton and Man-made
Yarn according to Category of Employment (lakhs)

All-India	1993–94		1999–2000		2004–05		2009–10	
	PS	PS+SS	PS	PS+SS	PS	PS+SS	PS	PS+SS
Self	1.09	1.99	1.84	2.15	1.62	2.28	0.99	1.54
Regular	4.8	4.83	3.83	3.83	2.87	3.01	2.85	2.93
Casual	1.6	2.04	1.57	1.6	0.89	1.26	1.21	1.28
Total	7.49	8.86	7.24	7.58	5.37	6.53	5.05	5.75
Rural	PS	PS+SS	PS	PS+SS	PS	PS+SS	PS	PS+SS
Self	0.56	1.15	0.75	1	0.83	1.13	0.23	0.51
Regular	1.01	1.02	1.8	1.8	1.71	1.84	1.01	1.03
Casual	0.9	1.16	0.83	0.83	0.32	0.46	0.84	0.87
Total	2.46	3.33	3.38	3.63	2.87	3.44	2.08	2.40
Urban	PS	PS+SS	PS	PS+SS	PS	PS+SS	PS	PS+SS
Self	0.53	0.84	1.09	1.15	0.77	1.12	0.79	1.04
Regular	3.79	3.81	2.03	2.03	1.16	1.17	1.85	1.91
Casual	0.7	0.88	0.73	0.77	0.57	0.8	0.36	0.41
Total	5.02	5.53	3.85	3.95	2.5	3.09	3.01	3.35

Source: Computed from unit-level data from NSS 50th, 55th, 61st, and 66th
rounds on employment–unemployment.
Notes: 1. One lakh is equal to a hundred thousand.
2. Self: Self-employed; Regular: Regularly employed; Casual: Casual workers.
3. Status codes 11, 12, and 21 are used for calculating the number of self-
employed. Code 31 is used for calculating regularly employed. Codes 41 and 51
provide the number of casual workers.
4. Industry codes: For the year 1993–94, the employment estimates in cotton
spinning are based on NIC codes 231 and 235 (based on NIC-1987). Skill
codes are observed for the persons employed in code 235 during 1993–94. Total
employment minus the weavers (skill code 05) in cotton mills are considered to
be engaged in cotton spinning. Similarly, estimates are generated for employment
in the spinning of man-made yarn for the year 1993–94 using NIC code 247.
For 1999–2000 and 2004–05, following NIC-1998, 5-digit codes 17111 and
17114 are used for spinning of cotton yarn and man-made yarn respectively.
For 2009–10, following NIC-2004, 5-digit codes 17111 and 17131 are used for
spinning of cotton yarn. Code 17114 is used for spinning of man-made yarn.

increased[28] at a high rate of growth of 6.23 per cent per annum during 1990–91 to 2013–14, the production declined in the public sector[29] at a rate of –7.75 per cent per annum during the same period.[30] Clearly, the increase in privatisation and the drive to maximise profits of the textile mills since the 1990s resulted in increase in casualisation of the spinning sector.

Shift from Self-employment to Wage Employment in Weaving

Another important change in the structure of employment, which is revealed by the data and which later resulted in increased casualisation of the textile industry, is the shift from self-employment to wage employment in weaving, where employment fell substantially since the 1990s. A majority (about 60 per cent) of the workers were self-employed in the early 1990s (Table 5.13) at the all-India level. The number of self-employed declined substantially during the 1990s in the rural and the urban areas. In terms of share, there was a continuous fall in the percentage of the self-employed from 59 per cent in 1993–94 to 47 per cent in 2004–05, and further to 43 per cent in 2009–10, at the all-India level. The share of casual employees declined substantially during the 1990s but increased thereafter.

The substantial shift in weaving away from self-employment is reflected in the decline of OAEs. An analysis of the NSS rounds on unorganised manufacturing sector[31] shows that the real GVA (with base year 1993–94) in the OAEs engaged in weaving at the all-India level declined from 1989–90 to 1994–95 (Table 5.14). Though it increased later from 1994–95 to 2000–01, it declined substantially

---

[28] From 1,269.35 million kg in 1990–91 to 5,099.98 million kg in 2013–14, see www.txcindia.gov.in (last accessed on 15 February 2016).

[29] From 327.25 million kg in 1990–91 to 51.16 million kg in 2013–14, see www.txcindia.gov.in (last accessed on 15 February 2016).

[30] CITI, *Handbook of Statistics on Textile Industry* (2008) and www.txcindia.gov.in (last accessed on 15 February 2016) for recent years.

[31] The NSSO surveys on unorganised manufacturing provide data on OAEs, NDEs, and DMEs in the unorganised manufacturing sector of the economy, and about 95 per cent of the woven cloth production takes place in the unorganised sector.

Table 5.13   Usual Status Employment in Weaving of Cloth according to Category of Employment (lakhs)

All-India	1993–94		1999–2000		2004–05		2009–10	
	PS	PS+SS	PS	PS+SS	PS	PS+SS	PS	PS+SS
Self	13.96	17.13	10.4	11.83	9.14	10.11	7.93	8.57
Regular	6.12	6.17	7	7.02	7.41	7.49	7.45	7.56
Casual	5.24	5.79	2.75	2.93	3.6	3.87	3.67	3.75
Total	25.32	29.09	20.2	21.78	20.2	21.46	19.04	19.88
Rural	PS	PS+SS	PS	PS+SS	PS	PS+SS	PS	PS+SS
Self	9.32	11.63	7.17	8.27	6.21	7.03	4.81	5.20
Regular	1.68	1.73	2.59	2.59	1.45	1.45	1.48	1.59
Casual	2.34	2.88	1.78	1.95	2.48	2.68	1.39	1.46
Total	13.34	16.24	11.5	12.82	10.1	11.17	7.68	8.25
Urban	PS	PS+SS	PS	PS+SS	PS	PS+SS	PS	PS+SS
Self	4.64	5.5	3.25	3.56	2.93	3.07	3.12	3.37
Regular	4.43	4.43	4.41	4.43	5.95	6.03	5.97	5.97
Casual	2.9	2.91	0.97	0.97	1.12	1.19	2.28	2.29
Total	11.98	12.86	8.63	8.96	10	10.29	11.36	11.63

Source: Computed from unit-level data from NSS 50th, 55th, 61st, and 66 rounds on employment–unemployment.

Notes: 1. One lakh is equal to a hundred thousand.

2. The figures in the table include persons engaged in weaving of cotton and man-made cloth. However, the figures include employment in the weaving of knitted and crocheted textile products of other fibres (mainly woollen) as well for all the years as, given the NIC, fibre-wise estimates cannot be obtained for the period prior to 1999–2000.

3. Self: Self-employed; Regular: Regularly employed; Casual: Casual workers.

4. Status codes 11, 12, and 21 are used for calculating the number of self-employed. Code 31 is used for calculating regularly employed. Codes 41 and 51 provide the number of casual workers.

5. Industry codes: For the 50th round of NSS conducted in 1993–94, the employment estimates in cotton cloth production are obtained following NIC-1987, using codes 232, 233, 234, 235, and 247. Skill codes are observed for the persons employed in code 235 during 1993–94. The weavers (skill code 05) in cotton mills are considered to be engaged in cotton cloth production. Similarly, estimates are generated for employment in the production of man-made cloth in 1993–94 using NIC code 247. For the 55th and 61st rounds of NSS conducted in 1999–2000 and 2004–05, the estimates are based on NIC-1998. The 5-digit code 17115 is used for cotton cloth and 5-digit code 17118 is considered for man-made cloth. For the 66th round of NSS for 2009–10, the estimates are based on NIC-2004, using codes 17115, 17132, and 17133 for cotton textiles. Codes 17118 and 17137 are used for man-made cloth.

Table 5.14 Real GVA (with base year 1993–94) according to Type of Enterprise in Weaving of Cotton and Man-made Cloth (Rs billion)

	1978–79			1989–90			1994–95			2000–01			2005–06			2010–11		
	R	U	AI	R	U	AI	R	U	AI	R	U	AI	R	U	AI	R	U	AI
OAE	NA	NA	NA	4.96	1.90	6.87	3.48	1.32	4.80	4.95	2.35	7.30	3.03	1.57	4.60	6.56	2.64	9.20
NDE	NA	NA	NA	1.06	6.35	7.42	0.96	2.46	3.42	0.90	4.88	5.79	0.52	3.39	3.91			
DME	1.31	2.78	4.10	1.82	4.48	6.30	2.59	5.92	8.51	2.36	10.51	12.86	1.01	11.44	12.46	5.39*	31.14*	36.53*
Overall	4.23	4.33	8.56	7.85	12.74	20.58	7.04	9.70	16.74	8.21	17.74	25.95	4.56	16.41	20.96	11.95	33.78	45.73

Sources: Computed based on figures from NSSO (1987, 1995, 1998) and CSO (1985, 1995); unit-level data from NSSO 56th and 62nd rounds on Unorganised Manufacturing Sector in India for 2000–01 and 2005–06; unit-level data from NSSO 67th round on Unincorporated Non-agricultural Enterprises (Excluding Construction) in India for 2010–11; and Office of Economic Advisor, GoI (for figures before 1993–94: *Index Numbers of Wholesale Prices in India*; for figures of 1993–94 onwards: http://www.eaindustry.nic.in/download_data_9394.asp [last accessed on 11 February 2016]).

Notes: 1. R: Rural; U: Urban; AI: All-India.

2. *(NDE + DME). In the *Survey on Unincorporated Non-agricultural Enterprises (Excluding Construction) in India* for 2010–11, the enterprises are divided in two categories: OAE and Establishments.

3. Industry codes: For 1978–79, 3-digit codes 231, 234, 235, and 236 are used for the production of cotton cloth, using NIC-1970. Code 231 is considered as it includes mainly weaving in the unorganised sector. Code 247 is considered for synthetic cloth as it mainly includes weaving in the unorganised sector. For 1989–90 and 1994–95, 3-digit codes 232, 233, 234, and 235 are used for the production of cotton cloth, using NIC-1987. Code 247 is considered for synthetic cloth as it mainly includes weaving in the unorganised sector. For the year 2000–01, 5-digit code 17115, based on NIC-1998, is used for cotton cloth. The 5-digit code 17118 is considered for synthetic cloth. For 2005–06, following NIC-2004, codes 17133 and 17137 are used for handlooms for cotton and man-made cloth respectively. Codes 17115 and 17118 for weaving (excluding handloom and khadi) are used for power looms for cotton and man-made cloth respectively (as weaving in unorganised sector includes khadi, handlooms, and power looms). Code 17132 is used for cotton khadi. For 2010–11, following NIC-2008, codes 13121 and 13124 are used for weaving of cotton and man-made cloth respectively.

(*Contd*)

Table 5.14 (*Cont'd*)

4. Enterprise codes: OAE-1, NDE-2, and DME-3.

5. The WPIs (with base 1993–94) for cotton textiles and man-made textiles are used as deflators for the cotton cloth and synthetic cloth respectively.

6. Concordance tables between NIC-1970 and NIC-1987, NIC-1987 and NIC-1998, NIC-1998 and NIC- 2004, and NIC-2004 and NIC-2008 are used for computing the figures.

thereafter from 2000–01 to 2005–06. As a result, real GVA in 2005–06 in OAEs was lower than that in 1994–95. But, the real GVA in the DMEs, which hire workers, grew consistently since 1978–79. By 2000–01, it was almost double of that in 1989–90. Though the real GVA declined in the DMEs in 2005–06, the decline was only marginal. The revival of cotton which started after 2003–04, and picked up fast after 2009–10, led to increase in real GVA in OAEs in 2010–11, but their share in real GVA in weaving of cloth has continued to decline.

The shift from self-employment to wage employment, which is reflected in the decline of OAEs, was the result of the decline of handlooms and expansion of power looms and hosiery units. Handlooms operated mainly as OAEs. According to an analysis of the unit-level data from the 62nd round of the NSS on unorganised manufacturing sector for 2005–06, OAEs accounted for about 67 per cent of the real GVA (with base year 1993–94) in the handloom sector at the all-India level. The share of NDEs and DMEs was 12 per cent and 21 per cent respectively. Production grew fast in the power looms, which worked mainly as DMEs that hire workers. The DMEs accounted for about 70 per cent of the real GVA (with base year 1993–94) in the power loom sector in 2005–06. The share of NDEs was about 20 per cent and OAEs accounted for less than 10 per cent.

Increasing Casualisation of Employment in the Textile Industry

Although the employment was declining in the period from 1983 to 1987–88 in the overall cotton and synthetic textile industry, it was characterised by increasing regularisation (Table 5.15) as the number of regularly employed increased, and casually employed declined, at the all-India level. Rural areas showed similar trends. The urban areas also experienced a substantial fall in casual employment. However, the period from the late 1980s to the early 1990s saw a reversal of this trend when casual employment increased and regular employment declined in percentage terms.

Later, the period from 1993–94 to 1999–2000 was characterised by a substantial fall in employment of almost all types of workers in the textile industry. But the largest fall occurred in the case of the casual employees (Table 5.16). As a result, there was an increase

Table 5.15 Usual Status Employment in Production of Textiles according to Category of Employment (lakhs) (from the early 1980s to the early 1990s)

	1983		1987–88		1993–94	
All-India	PS	PS+SS	PS	PS+SS	PS	PS+SS
Self	16.08	19.51	16.7	19.58	15.92	19.68
Regular	12.15	12.26	13.77	14.04	12.25	12.29
Casual	8.35	9.78	6.92	7.38	7.32	8.1
Total	36.58	41.55	37.39	40.99	35.49	40.08
Rural	PS	PS+SS	PS	PS+SS	PS	PS+SS
Self	11.39	14.11	11.72	13.87	10.17	12.53
Regular	1.86	1.91	4.41	4.54	2.79	2.81
Casual	3.08	3.48	3.92	4.1	3.35	3.92
Total	16.33	19.5	20.05	22.5	16.31	19.25
Urban	PS	PS+SS	PS	PS+SS	PS	PS+SS
Self	4.69	5.39	4.98	5.71	5.75	7.16
Regular	10.28	10.35	9.37	9.51	9.45	9.48
Casual	5.27	6.3	3	3.28	3.97	4.18
Total	20.24	22.05	17.35	18.49	19.18	20.82

Source: Computed from unit-level data from NSS 38th, 43rd, and 50th rounds on employment–unemployment.

Notes: 1. One lakh is equal to a hundred thousand.

2. Self: Self-employed: Regular: Regularly employed; Casual: Casual workers.

3. Status codes 11, 12, and 21 are used for calculating the number of self-employed. Code 31 is used for calculating regularly employed. Codes 41 and 51 provide the number of casual workers.

4. Industry codes: For 38th and 43rd rounds of NSS for 1983 and 1987–88, following NIC-1970, codes 231, 233, 234, 235, 236, 247, and 260 are used for calculating employment in the textile sector. For the 50th round of NSS for 1993–94, following NIC-1987, codes 231, 232, 233, 234, 235, 247, and 260 are considered (Details of the status codes and industry codes are given in Appendix C).

5. The figures in this table include usual status employment in the production of cotton and man-made textiles. However, the figures include employment in the manufacture of knitted and crocheted textile products of other fibers (mainly woolen) as well for all the years as, given the NIC, fiber-wise estimates cannot be obtained for the period prior to 1999–2000.

in the percentage of regularly employed, combined with a fall in the percentage of casually employed, both in rural and urban areas. However, the trend seems to have been reversed after the 1990s. While overall employment in the textile industry at the all-India level almost stagnated from 1999–2000 to 2004–05 and declined thereafter from 2004–05 to 2009–10, there was increasing casualisation of employment in the textile industry. The share of casual employment at the all-India level increased from 16.53 per cent in 1999–2000 to 18.34 per cent in 2004–05, and further to 19.7 per cent by 2009–10. Both the rural and the urban areas showed similar trends.

The increase in casualisation of employment in the textile industry is, in part, an outcome of an increase in privatisation of the industry. The data from the Textile Commissioner's office indicate increasing privatisation of the spinning as well as weaving sector. While the quantity of cloth produced in the private sector mills remained almost unchanged, the cloth produced in the mills under the public sector declined from 1,003 million sq. m in 1990–91 to 517.3 million sq. m in 1994–95, and further to a mere 26.82 million sq. m by 2005–06.[32] However, the share of the mill sector in total cloth production declined rapidly during the period. About 96 per cent of the cloth output is currently produced in the power loom, hosiery, and handloom units, which form part of the unregistered sector. While the number of handlooms, which generate self-employment, declined, the power looms and the hosiery units, which hire workers, flourished during the period, leading to increasing casualisation. Overall, there were several forces working simultaneously towards changing the structure of India's textile industry roughly since the 1990s, which resulted in increase in casualisation of the industry. These included: the decline of the mill sector vis-à-vis the unorganised sector in cloth production; increasing infomalisation of employment within the mill sector; and increasing wage employment in the unorganised weaving sector. Clearly, the period which was characterised by growth of demand, production, and exports of the industry not only led to a fall in employment in the textile industry but also to a deterioration in the quality of employment. Casual employment, which is characterised by lack of job security, frequent changes in

---

[32] Office of the Textile Commissioner, in CITI, *Handbook of Statistics on Textile Industry* (2008: 27).

Table 5.16   Usual Status Employment in Textile Production according to
Category of Employment (lakhs) (since the early 1990s)

All-India	1993–94		1999–2000		2004–05		2009–10	
	PS	PS+SS	PS	PS+SS	PS	PS+SS	PS	PS+SS
Self	15.92	19.68	12.6	14.34	11.4	13.15	8.95	10.09
Regular	12.25	12.29	11.7	11.75	12.9	13.12	10.31	10.49
Casual	7.32	8.10	4.97	5.18	5.2	5.9	4.87	5.03
Total	35.49	40.08	29.3	31.27	29.5	32.17	24.13	25.51
Rural	PS	PS+SS	PS	PS+SS	PS	PS+SS	PS	PS+SS
Self	10.17	12.53	8.06	9.43	7.18	8.36	5.04	5.69
Regular	2.79	2.81	4.71	4.71	3.52	3.65	2.49	2.61
Casual	3.35	3.92	2.73	2.9	3.02	3.42	2.23	2.33
Total	16.31	19.25	15.5	17.05	13.7	15.43	9.76	10.63
Urban	PS	PS+SS	PS	PS+SS	PS	PS+SS	PS	PS+SS
Self	5.75	7.16	4.51	4.91	4.27	4.79	3.91	4.40
Regular	9.45	9.48	7.01	7.04	9.38	9.47	7.82	7.88
Casual	3.97	4.18	2.23	2.27	2.18	2.48	2.64	2.70
Total	19.18	20.82	13.8	14.22	15.8	16.74	14.37	14.88

Source: Computed from unit-level data from NSS 50th, 55th, 61st, and 66th
rounds on employment–unemployment.
Notes: 1. One lakh is equal to a hundred thousand.
2. Self: Self-employed; Regular: Regularly employed; Casual: Casual workers.
3. Status codes 11, 12, and 21 are used for calculating the number of
self-employed. Code 31 is used for calculating regularly employed. Codes 41
and 51 provide the number of casual workers.
4. Industry codes: For the 50th round of NSS for 1993–94, following NIC-1987,
codes 231, 232, 233, 234, 235, 247, and 260 are considered for calculating
employment in the textile industry.
For the 55th and 61st rounds of NSS for the years 1999–2000 and 2004–05,
following NIC-1998, codes 17111, 17114, 17115, 17118, and 1730 are used. For
the 66th round of NSS for the year 2009–10, following NIC-2004, 17111, 17131,
17114, 17115, 17132, 17133, 17118, 17137, and 1730 are used for calculating
employment in the textile industry.
5. The figures in the table include employment in the production of cotton and
man-made textiles. However, they include employment in the production of knitted
and crocheted textile products of other fibers (mainly woollen) as well for all the
years as, given the NIC, fiber-wise estimates cannot be obtained for the period prior
to 1999–2000.

work place, increasing exposure to exploitative informal contrac-
tual arrangements, intermittent nature of work, and a high level of
income instability, grew during the period.

Thus, the rapid growth of the textile industry since the 1990s did
not result in the expected growth of employment. It led to changes
in the structure of employment, which included increase in the informalisation of the spinning sector, a shift from self-employment to
wage employment in the weaving sector, and increase in casualisation
of employment in the overall textile sector.

Continuing Dominance of Self-employment and Signs of Increasing Regular Employment in the Garment Sector

There was increasing casualisation of employment in the textile sector. However, the growth pattern of the garment sector was quite
different (Table 5.17). The remarkable growth in the garment sector
created more jobs, especially in the urban areas. The workforce in the
garment sector continued to be dominated by self-employed workers
up to 2004–05. Though the sector observed growth in employment
of all types of workers, it was self-employment which grew at the
highest rate from 1993–94 to 2004–05 in the rural areas. The number of regular employees increased at a high rate, closely followed by
that of casual workers, in the urban areas during this period. At the
all-India level, the share of regular employment increased and that of
self-employment and casual employment declined after the 1990s.

The employment declined substantially in garment production in
2009–10 when the garment exports to the developed economies suffered after the financial crisis.[33] The rate of decline was highest in the
self-employed in both the rural and the urban areas. As a result, the
percentage of self-employed declined and that of regular employees
increased in 2009–10. Thus, garment production in 2009–10 was
dominated by the regular employees at the all-India level. The urban
areas followed a similar trend, but production in the rural areas
continued to be dominated by self-employed. The percentage of self-
employed in the rural areas declined, however, from 82 per cent in
2004–05 to 50 per cent in 2009–10.

---

[33] For details, see Chapter 2, 'Exports: The New Driver of Growth?'.

Table 5.17   Usual Status Employment in Garment Production according to Category of Employment (lakhs)

	1993–94		1999–2000		2004–05		2009–10	
All-India	PS	PS+SS	PS	PS+SS	PS	PS+SS	PS	PS+SS
Self	5.12	6.21	11.23	12.52	12.76	15.34	4.12	4.92
Regular	2.47	2.53	5.05	5.06	10.87	11.16	7.39	7.41
Casual	0.75	0.91	2.31	2.33	2.17	2.38	1.03	1.09
Total	8.34	9.64	18.58	19.91	25.80	28.88	12.54	13.42
Rural	PS	PS+SS	PS	PS+SS	PS	PS+SS	PS	PS+SS
Self	1.74	2.33	6.39	7.05	7.05	8.88	1.53	1.88
Regular	0.39	0.39	1.05	1.05	1.01	1.01	1.32	1.34
Casual	0.37	0.49	0.87	0.88	0.54	0.75	0.21	0.26
Total	2.50	3.21	8.30	8.98	8.60	10.64	3.06	3.48
Urban	PS	PS+SS	PS	PS+SS	PS	PS+SS	PS	PS+SS
Self	3.38	3.87	4.84	5.47	5.71	6.46	2.58	3.04
Regular	2.08	2.14	4.00	4.01	9.86	10.15	6.07	6.07
Casual	0.38	0.42	1.44	1.45	1.63	1.63	0.83	0.83
Total	5.84	6.44	10.28	10.93	17.20	18.24	9.48	9.94

Source: Computed based on unit-level data from NSS 50th, 55th, 61st, and 66th rounds on employment–unemployment.

Notes: 1. One lakh is equal to a hundred thousand.

2. Self: Self-employed; Regular: Regularly employed; Casual: Casual workers.

3. Status codes 11, 12, and 21 are used for calculating the number of self-employed. Code 31 is used for calculating regularly employed. Codes 41 and 51 provide the number of casual workers.

4. Industry Codes: For the 50th round (1993–94), using NIC-1987, code 265 is used. For 1999–2000 and 2004–05, following NIC-1998, code 18101 is used. For 2009–10, following NIC-2004, code 18101 is used.

5. The figures in the table include workers engaged in manufacture of textile garments and clothing accessories only.

* * *

Thus, the analysis of trends in employment of the Indian textile industry suggests that a boom in the ostensibly labour-intensive textile industry in terms of demand, production, investment, and exports since the early 1990s did not lead to the expected growth of employment. Instead employment declined in both the spinning and the weaving sectors. Technological progress and modernisation in the spinning sector led to an increase in productivity, which adversely affected employment. The decline of handlooms, which used to account for a significant share of employment in textile industry, led to the fall in employment in the weaving sector. The decline of the composite mills also reduced employment in the weaving sector. The quality of employment in the textile industry also deteriorated. There was increasing informalisation of the formal spinning sector. Weaving sector was characterised by a shift from self-employment to wage employment as handlooms declined and power looms and hosiery units flourished during this period. The key outcomes of these changes were a decline in the share of regular employment and an increase in the casualisation of employment in the textile industry. This, in turn, led to job insecurity and high level of income instability. Although overall employment increased in the textile and garment industry from the early 1990s to 2004–05, it remained below the levels attained in the 1980s. The employment declined substantially in the year 2009–10. Overall, the performance of the industry on the employment front remained unsatisfactory both in terms of numbers and quality.

6

Concluding Observations

Despite the industry-specific nature of many of the tendencies discussed in the book, they reflect more general trends that have been operative at an economy level. The book attempts to present the results of an analysis of the growth of the textile industry in the context of the character and pace of growth of the Indian economy as a whole, and the Indian industrial sector in particular. After a period of deceleration since the mid-1960s, Indian industry entered a period of growth roughly since the mid-1980s. While the GDP at factor cost (with base year 2004–05) in the industrial sector grew at a rate of 4.66 per cent per annum between 1965–66 and 1985–86, growth during the period 1985–86 to 2013–14 amounted to 6.39 per cent per annum.[1] An increase in domestic demand and exports provided the stimulus for industrial growth. Changes in industrial policy also facilitated that growth.

The increase in domestic demand reflected an increase in income at a higher rate. Since the increase in income was largely experienced

---

[1] The rates are the average annual compound growth rates calculated using data from RBI (2014) by applying the formula r = power $(X_t/X_0, 1/n)$-1 using excel, where X_t is the value of X variable in the tth year and X_0 is the value of the X variable in the initial year 0 and n is the number of years between years 0 and t.

by workers in the service and manufacturing sectors, the benefits of growth remained limited to a small section of the population mainly in the urban areas. The agricultural sector, accounting for about 60 per cent of the workforce, lagged behind, widening the inequalities in the distribution of income. Overall, the increase in domestic demand came mainly from the upper income groups of the population, who were the beneficiaries of growth. However, given the size of the population, it meant a huge increase in the overall demand.

This increase in home demand coupled with growing exports provided the inducement to invest in the industrial sector. The dismantling of government controls on capacity creation, production, and pricing practices of even large firms and groups; improved access to imported capital equipment, raw materials, and intermediates; easier possibilities of technical and financial collaboration with foreign entrepreneurs; and disinvestments of public equity to private players had facilitated private investment since the 1990s.

The increase in output was expected to lead to an increase in employment. Scholars suggest that export pessimism and an inward-looking import substitution policy up to the mid-1980s had discouraged employment-intensive export production and led to high-cost, capital-intensive production, which had low linkages with the rest of the economy. Opening up the economy to more liberal external trade and foreign investment was expected to restructure production towards areas of international comparative advantage and lead to restructuring of production towards more labour-intensive avenues. This was not only expected to lead to a higher rate of growth of output but also to generate substantial increase in employment (Chandrasekhar and Ghosh 2000).

However, substantial capacity expansion and modernisation of the industrial sector, which was facilitated by the reductions in the customs duties on the import of technology, machinery, and other inputs, led to capital using technical change, which resulted in a significant growth of productivity in the Indian manufacturing industries after 1990–91. These include machine tools and instruments industries, pharmaceuticals, automobiles, synthetic fibres, and soap and detergents industries (Pattanayak and Thangavelu 2003). As a result, the average labour productivity in manufacturing grew so fast that the effects of the higher rate of increase in output on employment growth were more than neutralised. According to estimates quoted in the Planning Commission's Eleventh Plan Document, GDP per worker in manufacturing, which grew at 2.29 per cent per annum during 1983 to 1993–94, accelerated to 3.31 per cent between 1993–94 and 2004–05 (Planning Commission 2008, cited in Chandrasekhar and Ghosh 2008). The average labour productivity was much higher for the organised manufacturing sector, which grew at a higher rate of 6.72 per cent per annum from 1992–93 to 2004–05. This rate of growth was 5.78 per cent per annum during 1983–84 to 1991–92. Though employment increased in one set of organised industries that experienced employment-creating growth, the other set experienced employment-displacing growth. The job-creating industries, which experienced positive employment elasticities,[2] included leather tanning and dressing, paper and paper products, wearing apparel, dressing and dyeing of fur, rubber and plastic products, fabricated metal products, and furniture manufacturing, while the job-displacing industries, which experienced negative employment elasticities, included wood and wood products, textiles, publishing, printing, and other transport equipment. The overall picture that emerged in the organised manufacturing was one of 'jobless growth' due to the combined effects of these two trends that had countered each other (Kannan and Raveendran 2009).

Overall, the increased use of capital-intensive techniques of production implied that the acceleration in the growth of output was not accompanied by the acceleration in the growth of employment in the industrial sector. The growth rate of usual status employment at the all-India level in the secondary sector declined from 3 per cent per annum during 1983 to 1993–94 to 2.37 per cent per annum during 1993–94 to 1999–2000 (Bhattacharya and Sakthivel 2004). A similar scenario was observed in the other sectors as well. The declining trend is more striking in the primary sector, where the growth of usual status employment declined from 1.61 per cent per annum between 1983 and 1993–94 to 0.04 per cent per annum from 1993–94 to 1999–2000, implying a virtually stagnant agricultural workforce during the reform period. Also, the growth

[2] Measured as the ratio of percentage growth in employment to percentage growth in GVA.

of the service sector, being knowledge intensive, could not provide an outlet for the surplus labour in the agricultural sector. The usual status employment growth in the tertiary sector at the all-India level declined sharply from 3.94 per cent per annum during 1983 to 1993–94 to 2.8 per cent per annum during 1993–94 to 1999–2000. Overall, the 1990s was referred to as a decade of jobless growth. The aggregate usual status employment growth at all-India level declined sharply from 2.26 per cent during 1983 to 1993–94 to 1.01 per cent during 1993–94 to 1999–2000. Though the employment scenario improved from 1999–2000 to 2004–05, this was mainly in the form of self-employment and reflected inability to find adequately gainful paid employment (Chandrasekhar and Ghosh 2007). In addition to this, the period was characterised by increasing informalisation of the formal sector as the increase in employment in the organised sector was informal in nature, that is, without any job or social security (Mehrotra et al. 2012; NCEUS 2007). Later, the growth of the economy was affected by September 2008 crisis as exports and domestic demand declined in the following years. The employment scenario deteriorated again from 2004–05 to 2009–10 and was characterised by increase in casual employment. Overall, it implied a scenario in which the economy was booming in terms of demand, production, and exports, but the growth was not inclusive. Unemployment was increasing as the growth of output was not accompanied by the expected growth of employment. The quality of employment was also deteriorating. These, in brief, are the main features and implications of the process of growth of the Indian economy since the 1990s.

Similar tendencies operated in the textile industry as well. The industry was delicensed in 1991. The growth of incomes at a much higher rate led to an increase in the home demand for textile products after the early 1990s. The exports of all kinds of textile products also grew fast. Imports of capital goods, intermediates, and raw materials required by the industry were substantially liberalised during the first half of the 1990s by placing them under the Open General License (OGL) category. The industry benefited from the tariff reductions on a wide range of commodities, which resulted in a decline in protection given to the domestic synthetic fibre and filament yarn industry. The duty cuts on the imports of synthetic fibres and filament yarns during liberalisation increased the competition and reduced their prices in the domestic market. This ultimately resulted in reduced prices of synthetic textiles, which led to an increase in their demand. This further led to a substantial increase in the demand for synthetic fibres and filament yarns, thereby encouraging growth in their domestic capacity and domestic production, and made them widely available domestically at lower prices. This affected the prices of synthetic textiles, and further increased the demand for synthetic textiles. Thus, as a result of revival of demand, the textile industry—which was stagnating since the mid-1960s—experienced substantial growth roughly since the 1990s. Total cloth output, which was growing at the rate of 2.71 per cent per annum during 1975 to 1989, registered a much higher rate of growth of 4.46 per cent per annum during the period 1990–91 to 2013–14.

The growth of the textile industry, being a labour-intensive industry, was expected to lead to substantial increase in employment. However, as the growth of output in the industrial sector as a whole was not accompanied by the expected growth of employment, a similar tendency was reflected in the case of textile industry. The revival of growth in the textile industry could not reverse the fall in employment in the industry. According to the NSS data from the employment–unemployment surveys, the usual status employment in the textile industry (cotton and synthetic) at the all-India level fell continuously from about 4.16 million in 1983 to 3.13 million by 1999–2000. It almost stagnated during 1999–2000 to 2004–05 but declined thereafter, from 2004–05 to 2009–10. The rural sector, which employed about 48 per cent of the usual status employees, however, registered an increase from 1983 to 1987–88, but such employment showed a decline thereafter. Though urban sector employment, which was fluctuating during the 1980s and the 1990s, increased after the 1990s, it remained far below the levels attained in the 1980s and the early 1990s.

Further, the period since the early 1990s saw remarkable growth in the ready-made garment industry with real Gross Value Added (GVA) growing at a high rate of about 7.36 per cent per annum from 1994–95 to 2010–11.[3] Though output and employment in the

---

[3] For details, see Chapter 4, 'Structural Changes in the Indian Textile Industry'.

garment sector grew during the 1990s and after, the employment in the garment sector in the 1990s was much lower when compared to the 1980s. The employment situation seems to have improved during 1999–2000 to 2004–05 in both rural and urban areas. Employment in the urban areas in 2004–05 was higher than what it was during the 1980s; but it continued to be below the 1980s level in the rural areas. The employment declined considerably in 2009–10 in both the rural and the urban areas. Overall, it grew slowly during the period 1993–94 to 2009–10 at the all-India level.

Overall, as a result of a substantial increase in the production of India's textiles and clothing (T&C) industry since the early 1990s, employment grew slowly at 0.5 per cent per annum during the 1990s and then at a faster pace (3.4 per cent per annum) from 1999–2000 to 2004–05 at the all-India level, but the results were far from satisfactory as the rates continued to fall short of the levels attained in the 1980s. While the employment in the urban areas in 2004–05 was comparable to that obtained in the 1980s, the employment scenario in the rural areas deteriorated in comparison to the one in the 1980s. Further, this period of growth of employment after the 1990s did not last long as the economy was affected by the crisis in the developed economies and the employment in 2009–10 was reduced to its lowest levels since the 1980s.

Thus, despite substantial growth in various sectors of India's T&C industry since the early 1990s the performance of the industry on the employment front continued to remain unsatisfactory. There were changes in the underlying structure of the textile industry due to which the growth of output did not lead to growth of employment. These structural changes included the decline of the handlooms and the composite mills; shift from cotton to the synthetic textiles; and the consolidation and modernisation of the spinning sector with expansion of capacities.

The decline of handlooms after the mid-1980s resulted in a fall in employment in the weaving sector. A massive shift in consumer demand towards synthetics and blended textiles aggravated the problem of low productivity faced by handlooms as they specialised in the weaving of cotton cloth. A shift in preferences towards synthetic fabrics had been observed since the 1970s, but it remained limited due to the high prices as a result of very high import duties imposed on what were considered as items of luxury. The period since the 1990s saw a significant increase in demand for synthetic textiles, which had become cheaper due to the growth of the domestic synthetic fibre and filament yarn industry. However, the revival of cotton after 2003–04 proved favourable for the hand-looms and the handloom production is reported to have improved in the recent years.[4]

Further, the increasing popularity of hosiery products due to their inherent properties, both in the domestic economy and in the international market, affected the demand for the handloom products. There was a continuous and sustained growth in the hosiery sector (at about 8.1 per cent per annum) since 1990–91. As a result, the sector, which accounted for 11.8 per cent of fabric production by 1990–91, registered a rise in its share to 25.9 per cent of total fabric production in 2013–14. The share of this sector in cotton cloth production became more than double from 15.86 per cent in 1990–91 to 34.3 per cent by 2002–03, and increased further to about 37 per cent in the recent years. The sectoral share of hosiery in blended cloth production also increased from 4.6 per cent in 1990–91 to 16.6 per cent by 2003–04, and further to about 20 per cent by 2013–14. Since the handlooms specialised in the production of woven cloth, the increasing popularity of knitted and crocheted textiles adversely affected the demand for handloom products both in the domestic and the international markets.

In addition to these demand-side problems, handlooms faced supply-side problems related to availability of yarn. A sharp increase in the export of cotton yarn due to increase in emphasis on exports after the NTP (1985) affected the domestic availability of cotton yarn required by the handloom weavers. The share of exported yarn in total yarn produced which stood at about 8 per cent in 1992–93 increased to 20.5 per cent in the year 1996–97 and further to about 33.44 per cent per annum in 2013–14.[5] The increased exports by the mills to more lucrative international markets seem to have affected the domestic availability of yarn to the handloom weavers.

[4] Available at www.txcindia.gov.in (last accessed on 15 February 2016).
[5] Derived using figures from Chapter 3, 'Exports: The New Driver of Growth?' and Chapter 4, 'Structural Changes in the Indian Textile Industry'.

The handlooms always faced tough competition from the power looms due to their low productivity, but their products had unique characteristics and experienced sustained demand. However, the shifts in demand affected the growth of handlooms adversely. But these shifts were in favour of the growth of power looms, which produced almost the entire output of synthetic cloth. Since the power looms generate less employment for a given increase in output and since they are controlled not by independent weavers but by well-endowed entrepreneurs, overall the rise of power looms and the fall of handlooms resulted in a decline in employment. The decline of handlooms and expansion of power looms resulted in a shift from self-employment to wage employment in weaving as handlooms mainly operate as Own Account Enterprises (OAEs) and power looms as Directory Manufacturing Establishments (DMEs). This resulted in increased casualisation of the weaving sector.

Another reason for the unsatisfactory performance of the textile industry on the employment front was the continuous decline in employment in the mill sector. The production of spun yarn increased in response to the increase in external and domestic demand, but it could not reverse the fall in employment in spinning. There were several reasons responsible for this outcome.

There was a substantial increase in home demand for textiles after the early 1990s. However, much of the increase was for synthetic and blended textiles. This shift in demand resulted in a fall in the share of cotton yarn in the total yarn produced in the mill sector. But, the mills continued to remain dominated by cotton as a fibre due to which they were bypassed by the significant growth in home demand for the synthetic and blended textiles.

The textile industry was delicensed in July 1991. Protection to the industry producing textile-machinery was withdrawn during the 1990s via reductions in customs duties on the import of machinery. These changes were expected to affect capacity expansion and lead to increase in employment in the spinning sector. In view of the increase in overall demand, these policy changes led to an investment boom in the mill sector. Fixed investment in the sector registered substantial growth during the 1990s and reached very high levels. However, the rising investments in the sector involved modernisation and greater use of capital-intensive technologies, which led to an increase in labour productivity and affected the employment level adversely as fewer workers were required to accomplish the same task.

Further, several spinning mills entered the market during the period of expansion, modernisation, and growth of the spinning sector. This increased competition among the growing number of spinning mills, which differed with respect to their level of modernisation, and resulted in surplus production. As a result, the mills which chose not to modernise and expand capacities and the mills with low levels of modernisation could not compete with the stronger, fast-expanding mills, which had modernised, built-up capacities, and enjoyed economies of scale. Several spinning mills operating under the cooperative sector, such as Akot Taluka Sahakari Soot Girni Ltd and Jawahar Shetkari Sahakari Roto Soot Girni Ltd, are examples of such mills which were forced to close down. The closure of these mills affected employment adversely. In addition to this, the period since the 1990s was also characterised by increase in the informalisation of the spinning sector as a result of a decline in the share of the regularly employed and increase in the share of casually employed. The trend of increase in privatisation and the associated drive to maximise profits of the textile mills resulted in increase in casualisation of the spinning sector.

Further, the composite mills could not compete with the cloth produced in the power looms in the unregistered sector. The growth of power looms, and the consequent decline of mills over the last few decades, seem to be the result of several cost advantages due to organisational differences between mills and power looms. Power looms continue to operate in the unregistered sector either as OAEs or as non-directory or directory establishments. As a result of these organisational differences between mills and power looms, the wage cost per metre was lower in power looms by about 50 to 70 per cent. The cost of fabric processing was also lower in power looms by about 20 to 40 per cent than that in the organised process houses attached to the textile mills.

The substantial growth in the demand for synthetic T&C, almost entirely produced by the power looms, speeded up the growth of power looms since the 1990s. Increasing use of machinery in the power looms resulted in technology improvement. The power looms established themselves in the international market as well.

With a much higher growth rate (12 per cent per annum from 1993–94 to 1999–2000) of fabric exported than that of the mill sector (9.17 per cent per annum during the same period), the power looms have become the leading suppliers of fabric in the world market.[6] Clearly, the fast growth of the power looms has meant tough competition to the fabric produced in the composite mills both in the domestic and in the international market. The number of closed composite mills which were forced to close down increased fast during the period, rising from 59 in March 1993 to 106 by March 1999 and further to 134 by March 2003. About 110 of these were closed for a period of more than 5 years (ICMF, *Handbook of Statistics on Cotton Textile Industry* 2004). Though the revival of cotton after 2003–04 did prove favourable for the mill sector and the employment improved somewhat during the period of high growth, it continued to be lower than what it was during the late 1990s.

Thus, just as the capacity expansion and modernisation of the organised manufacturing sector as a whole led to capital-using technical change and restricted the growth of employment due to significant growth of labour productivity after 1990, it also resulted in similar tendencies in this specific case of the textile industry. The capacity expansion involving modernisation led to capital-using technical change in spinning, which resulted in a significant growth of labour productivity and restricted the growth of employment. The inability of the weaving sector to generate additional employment mainly due to the decline of handlooms was the result of several demand-side and supply-side changes. While the demand-side changes shifted the demand in favour of synthetic textiles and knitted products, the supply-side changes increased problems relating to cost and availability of the cotton yarn required by the handlooms, reflecting the increasing emphasis on exports and the neglect of agriculture.

---

[6] For details see Chapter 4, 'Structural Changes in the Indian Textile Industry'.

Appendices

Appendix A

Table A.1 Rural–Expenditure Group-wise Average Real MPCE on Clothing with Base Year 1983 Using CPI-AL for Clothing, Bedding, and Footwear as Deflator (Rs)

Year	1983	1993–94	2004–05
Bottom 40 per cent	1.95	1.05	1.54
Middle 40 per cent	6.22	4.03	4.59
Top 20 per cent	31.96	20.13	16.19
All classes	9.66	6.05	5.68

Source: Computed based on figures from NSSO (1986, 1996, and 2006) and Labour Bureau, GoI (2008) for CPI-AL for Clothing, Bedding, and Footwear.

Table A.2 Urban–Expenditure Group-wise Average Real MPCE on Clothing (with base year 1983) Using CPI-IW for Clothing, Bedding, and Footwear as Deflator (Rs)

Year	1983	1993–94	2004–05
Bottom 40 per cent	2.06	1.85	3.53
Middle 40 per cent	8.62	8.49	11.01
Top 20 per cent	41.23	37.22	36.82
All classes	12.52	11.5	13.14

Source: Computed based on figures from NSSO (1986, 1996, and 2006) and Labour Bureau, GoI (2001, 2004, and 2011) for CPI-IW for Clothing, Bedding, and Footwear.

Table A.3 Urban–Expenditure Group-wise Average Real MPCE on Clothing (with base year 1993–94) Using CPI-UNME for Clothing, Bedding, and Footwear as Deflator (Rs)

Year	1983	1993–94	2004–05
Bottom 40 per cent	NA	3.45	6.33
Middle 40 per cent	NA	15.8	19.75
Top 20 per cent	NA	69.25	66.06
All classes	NA	21.4	23.58

Source: Computed based on figures from RBI, *Handbook of Monetary Statistics of India*, available at https://rbi.org.in/scripts/PublicationsView.aspx?id=8250 (last accessed on 25 October 2015) for CPIN for UNMEs for Clothing, Bedding, and Footwear.

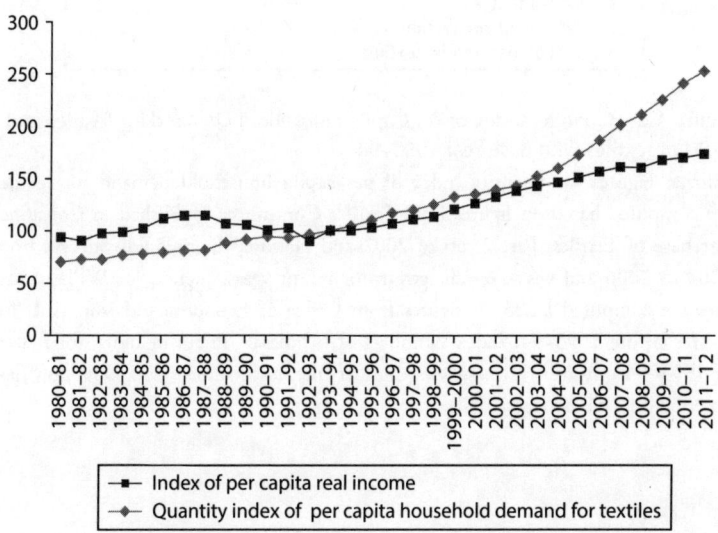

- ■ Index of per capita real income
- ◆ Quantity index of per capita household demand for textiles

Figure A.1 Indices of Per Capita Household Demand for Textiles and Real Per Capita Income with Base Year 1993–94

Sources: Figures for quantity index of per capita household demand for textiles are computed based on figures from Textiles Committee, published in *Consumer Purchase of Textiles*, Part 2, up to 2002 and National Households Surveys from 2003 to 2006 and www.txcindia.gov.in for recent years. Figures for Index for per capita real income are computed based on figures from GoI, National Accounts Statistics (2014).

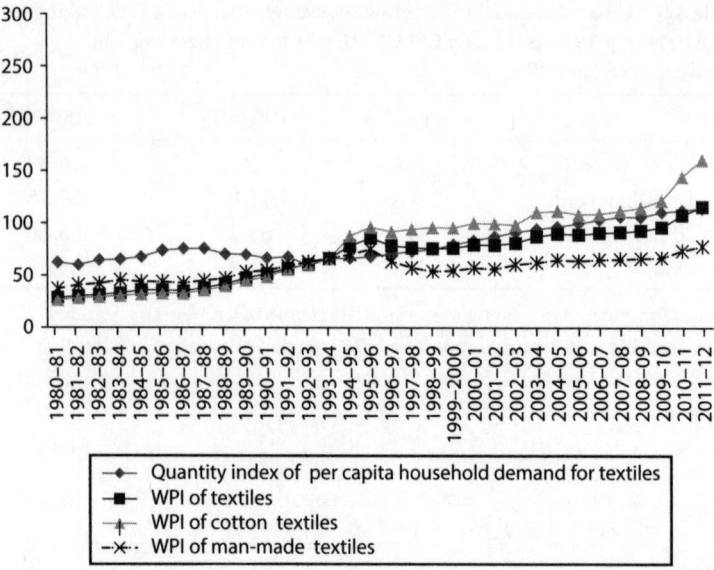

Legend:
- ◆ Quantity index of per capita household demand for textiles
- ■ WPI of textiles
- ▲ WPI of cotton textiles
- ✕ WPI of man-made textiles

Figure A.2 Quantity Index of Per Capita Household Demand for Textiles and WPIs of Textiles with Base Year 1993–94

Sources: Figures for quantity index of per capita household demand for textiles are computed based on figures from Textiles Committee, published in Consumer Purchase of Textiles, Part 2, up to 2002 and National Households Surveys from 2003 to 2006 and www.txcindia.gov.in for recent years. Figures for WPIs of textiles are computed based on figures from Office of Economic Advisor, GoI (for figures before 1993–94: Index Numbers of Wholesale Prices in India; for figures of 1993–94 onwards: http://www.eaindustry.nic.in/download_data_9394.asp [last accessed on 11 February 2016]).

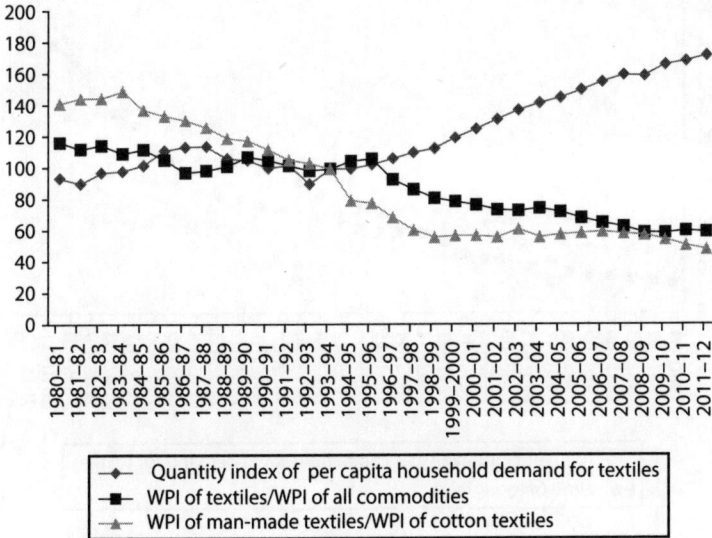

Figure A.3   Quantity Index of Per Capita Household Demand for Textiles, Ratio of WPI of Textiles to WPI of All Commodities, and Ratio of WPI of Man-made Textiles to WPI of Cotton Textiles (with base year 1993–94)

Sources: Figures for quantity index of per capita household demand for textiles are computed based on figures from Textiles Committee, published in Consumer Purchase of Textiles, Part 2, up to 2002 and National Households Surveys from 2003 to 2006 and www.txcindia.gov.in for recent years. Figures for ratios of WPIs are computed based on figures from Office of Economic Advisor, GoI.

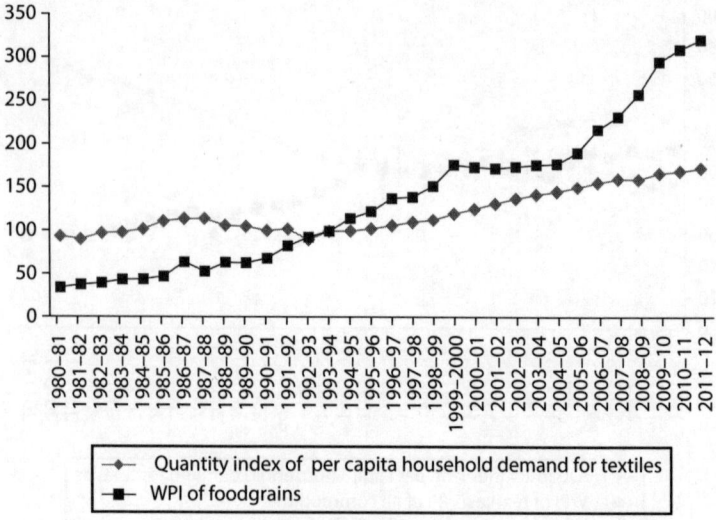

Figure A.4   Quantity Index of Per Capita Household Demand for Textiles and WPI of Foodgrains with Base Year 1993–94

Sources: Figures for quantity index of per capita household demand for textiles are computed based on figures from Textiles Committee, published in Consumer Purchase of Textiles, Part 2, up to 2002 and National Households Surveys from 2003 to 2006 and www.txcindia.gov.in for recent years. Figures for WPI of foodgrains are computed based on figures from Office of Economic Advisor, GoI.

Appendix B

Table B.1 Production (metric tons), Installed Capacity (metric tons), and Capacity Utilisation (%) of Other Staple Fibres

Year	Cellulosic Staple Fibres (Viscose/Modified Viscose/Polynosic/ Acetate/Other Rayons)			Acrylic Staple Fibre			Polypropylene Staple Fibre		
	Production	Installed Capacity	Capacity Utilisation	Production	Installed Capacity	Capacity Utilisation	Production	Installed Capacity	Capacity Utilisation
1980–81	82.7	97.4	85	10.1	16.0	63	0	0	0
1981–82	84.2	97.7	86	13.6	16.0	85	0	0	0
1982–83	49.3	97.7	50	16.2	16.0	101	0	0	0
1983–84	82.8	97.7	85	16.6	16.0	104	0	0	0
1984–85	102.018	107.7	95	20.9	20.0	104	0	0	0
1985–86	90.0	107.7	84	21.8	22.5	97	0	0	0
1986–87	96.3	112.7	85	23.1	22.5	102	0	0	0
1987–88	119.451	112.7	106	22.1	22.5	98	0	0	0
1988–89	125.702	116.7	108	26.3	36.0	73	0	0	0
1989–90	147.646	157.9	94	30.5	48.0	64	0	0	0
1990–91	160.173	176.1	91	42.5	63.0	67	1.0	4.3	23
1991–92	158.075	186.6	85	47.0	63.0	75	1.1	4.3	24
1992–93	162.453	186.6	87	55.0	87.0	63	1.1	5.3	20

(*Contd*)

Table B.1 (Cont'd)

Year	Cellulosic Staple Fibres (Viscose/Modified Viscose/Polynosic/Acetate/Other Rayons)			Acrylic Staple Fibre			Polypropylene Staple Fibre		
	Production	Installed Capacity	Capacity Utilisation	Production	Installed Capacity	Capacity Utilisation	Production	Installed Capacity	Capacity Utilisation
1993–94	183.335	223.0	82	68.4	87.0	79	1.1	5.8	27
1994–95	173.113	206.0	84	82.7	98.0	84	1.6	5.8	29
1995–96	194.340	220.7	88	74.1	98.0	76	1.7	5.8	32
1996–97	178.783	220.7	81	82.8	98.0	85	1.9	5.8	33
1997–98	188.399	288.0	65	79.4	98.0	81	2.0	7.8	25
1998–99	178.180	306.5	58	79.0	118.5	67	1.9	7.3	26
1999–2000	202.037	305.5	66	79.3	121.0	66	2.1	7.8	27
2000–01	236.170	305.5	77	99.4	137.5	72	2.3	7.8	29
2001–02	185.279	305.5	61	99.9	137.5	73	2.4	7.8	32
2002–03	224.610	305.5	74	105.010	137.5	77	2.5	7.8	34
2003–04	221.010	305.5	72	117.000	137.5	85	2.7	8.0	34
2004–05	247.950	336.6	74	127.610	145.0	88	2.9	8.0	36
2005–06	228.980	338.4	68	107.810	145.0	74	3.1	8.0	39
2006–07	246.833	345.7	71	97.1	151.5	64	3.5	8.7	40
2007–08	279.9	354.8	79	81.2	153	53	3.4	8.7	39

2008–09	232.8	418.7	56	79.5	153	52	3.4	8.7	39
2009–10	302.1	418.7	72	90.5	153	59	3.4	8.7	39
2010–11	305.1	418.7	73	79.5	155	51	3.7	8.7	43
2011–12	322.6	418.7	77	77.7	155	50	4.1	9.6	43
2012–13	337.5	418.7	81	73.6	167	44	4.3	13.2	33
2013–14	361.0	418.7	86	96.1	167	58	3.7	13.2	28

Source: CITI, *Handbook of Statistics on Textile Industry* (2008: 53) up to 2005–06 and www.txcindia.gov.in for recent years.

Table B.2 Production (million kg), Installed Capacity (million kg), and Capacity Utilisation (%) of Man-made Filament Yarn

Year	Cellulosic Filament Yarns (Viscose/Acetate/Cuprammonium/ Other Rayons)			Nylon Filament Yarn			Polypropylene Filament Yarn		
	Production	Installed Capacity	Capacity Utilisation	Production	Installed Capacity	Capacity Utilisation	Production	Installed Capacity	Capacity Utilisation
1980–81	41.4	41.8	99	20.7	21.7	95	0	0	0
1981–82	41.1	43.4	95	23.1	25.3	91	0	0	0
1982–83	33.2	43.4	76	25.5	30.0	85	0	0	0
1983–84	35.4	43.4	82	30.6	30.6	100	0	0	0
1984–85	32.9	43.4	76	34.5	34.0	102	0	0	0
1985–86	42.0	44.3	95	39.4	41.9	94	0	0	0
1986–87	44.6	45.2	99	36.7	43.5	84	0	0	0
1987–88	45.9	55.0	84	34.3	47.5	72	0	0	0
1988–89	44.4	55.0	81	35.8	68.2	52	0	0	0
1989–90	49.2	53.2	93	38.7	94.0	41	0.0	92.5	0
1990–91	50.9	60.4	84	39.8	97.6	41	24.1	92.5	26
1991–92	52.7	68.9	77	30.9	22.5	29	40.3	11.4	36
1992–93	48.0	66.5	72	32.5	22.5	30	68.7	39.3	17
1993–94	53.0	68.0	78	37.3	22.5	32	83.0	39.3	21
1994–95	58.6	69.9	84	39.4	22.5	34	11.9	41.6	29

Year									
1995–96	60.7	71.9	84	41.6	22.5	35	14.6	44.8	33
1996–97	57.3	71.9	80	38.0	22.5	32	13.0	44.8	29
1997–98	57.0	72.9	78	29.8	24.0	133	13.8	20.7	67
1998–99	60.9	75.2	81	28.6	24.0	119	15.4	16.3	95
1999–2000	49.5	75.2	66	26.1	24.0	108	17.2	16.5	104
2000–01	55.3	75.2	73	26.3	24.0	109	18.5	19.2	96
2001–02	48.3	75.2	64	27.8	24.0	116	19.8	17.4	114
2002–03	50.8	75.2	68	29.7	24.0	124	24.4	17.4	140
2003–04	53.2	75.2	71	31.0	24.0	129	20.8	17.4	120
2004–05	53.6	78.1	69	35.4	24.0	148	16.3	17.4	94
2005–06	53.1	79.7	67	36.8	24.0	154	13.6	17.4	78
2006–07	54.0	79.7	68	32.3	32.0	101	13.4	17.6	76
2007–08	51.1	79.7	64	27.6	32.0	86	10.5	17.6	60
2008–09	42.4	80.1	53	28.1	32.0	88	15.1	17.6	86
2009–10	42.7	80.1	53	30.4	32.0	95	14.8	17.6	84
2010–11	40.9	73.7	56	33.5	32.0	105	13.1	17.6	75
2011–12	42.4	76.2	56	28.0	32.0	87	13.2	17.6	75
2012–13	42.6	76.2	56	22.9	32.0	72	17.2	17.6	97
2013–14	44.0	79.5	55	24.1	32.0	75	12.9	17.6	73

Source: CITI, *Handbook of Statistics on Textile Industry* (2008: 54) up to 2005–06 and www.txcindia.gov.in for recent years.

Table B.3 Production of Raw Materials Required in the Production of PSF
(metric tons)

Year	DMT	MEG	PTA
1979–80		11,782	
1980–81	23,136	11,989	–
1981–82	27,317	15,491	–
1982–83	22,835	17,361	–
1983–84	25,063	18,018	–
1984–85	27,299	23,101	–
1985–86	53,496	20,840	–
1986–87	96,920	20,754	–
1987–88	114,982	18,158	–
1988–89	124,505	17,782	118,730
1989–90	123,392	24,854	125,009
1990–91	128,416	31,178	151,453
1991–92	128,457	52,539	162,679
1992–93	124,911	132,515	232,435
1993–94	113,734	164,574	255,505
1994–95	183,666	175,522	257,090
1995–96	207,203	197,926	248,518
1996–97	206,005	187,916	235,362
1997–98	190,611	363,638	659,341
1998–99	214,206	446,120	988,338
1999–2000	179,705	457,365	1,151,789
2000–01	190,522	556,298	1,488,218
2001–02	180,914	575,407	1,303,596
2002–03	199,077	611,233	1,704,682
2003–04	216,770	651,918	1,675,717
2004–05	238,635	713,434	1,737,927
2005–06	197,413	881,366	1,734,237
2006–07	27,532	872,473	2,379,197
2007–08	3,563	1,078,072	2,059,182
2008–09	–	783,203	2,154,021
2009–10	–	738,292	2,985,327
2010–11	–	746,322	3,190,593
2011–12	–	764,637	3,307,806
2012–13	–	1,054,000	3,390,000

Source: ASFI (various years).

Appendix C

Table C.1 Details of NIC Codes Used

NIC	Code	Details of NIC Codes Used
NIC-1970	231	Cotton spinning, weaving, shrinking, sanforising, mercerizing, and finishing of cotton textiles in mills.
	233	Cotton spinning other than in mills (charkha).
	234	Weaving and finishing of cotton khadi.
	235	Weaving and finishing of cotton textiles on handlooms.
	236	Weaving and finishing of cotton textiles on power looms.
	247	Spinning, weaving, and finishing of other textiles– synthetic fibres, rayons, nylons, etc.
	260	Manufacture of knitted and crocheted textile products.
	264	Manufacture of all types of textiles garments including wearing apparel.
NIC-1987	231	Cotton spinning other than in mills (charkha).
	232	Weaving and finishing of cotton khadi.
	233	Weaving and finishing of cotton textiles on handlooms.
	234	Weaving and finishing of cotton textiles on power looms.
	235	Spinning, weaving, and processing in mills.
	247	Spinning, weaving, and processing of man-made textile fibres.
	260	Manufacture of knitted and crocheted textile products.
	265	Manufacture of all types of textiles garments and clothing accessories n.e.c. (except by purely tailoring establishments) from not self-produced material (Note: in principle, the raw material is cut and sewn together in the establishments covered in this group).
NIC-1998	1711	Preparation and spinning of textile fibre including weaving of textiles
	17111	Preparation and spinning of cotton fibre including blended cotton.
	17114	Preparation and spinning of man-made fibre including blended fibre.

(Cont'd)

Table C.1   *(Cont'd)*

NIC	Code	Details of NIC Codes Used
	17115	Weaving and manufacture of cotton and cotton mixture fabric.
	17118	Weaving and manufacture of man-made fibre and man-made mixture fabric.
	1730	Manufacture of knitted and crocheted fabrics and articles.
	18101	Manufacture of all types of textile garments and clothing accessories.
NIC-2004	171	Spinning, weaving, and finishing of textiles.
	1711	Preparation and spinning of textile fibre including weaving of textiles (excluding khadi/handlooms).
	17111	Preparation and spinning of cotton fibre including blended cotton (excluding khadi/handloom).
	17112	Preparation and spinning of silk fiber including blended* silk.
	17113	Preparation and spinning of wool, including other animal hair and blended* wool, including other animal hair.
	17114	Preparation and spinning of man-made fibre including blended fibre (excluding khadi/handloom).
	17115	Weaving, manufacture of cotton and cotton mixture fabrics (excluding khadi/handloom).
	17116	Weaving, manufacture of silk and silk mixture fabrics.
	17117	Weaving, manufacture of wool and wool mixture fabrics.
	17118	Weaving, manufacture of man-made fibre and man-made mixture fabric (excluding khadi/handloom).
	17119	Preparation, spinning and weaving of jute, mesta, and other natural fibers including blended natural fibers n.e.c.
	1712	Finishing of textile excluding khadi/handloom (this class includes finishing of textiles of Class 1711 by operations such as bleaching, dyeing, calendering, napping, shrinking, or printing. No distinction is to be made between these activities carried out on a fee or contract basis or by purchasing the material and selling the finished products).

Table C.1   *(Cont'd)*

NIC	Code	Details of NIC Codes Used
	17121	Finishing of cotton and blended cotton textiles.
	17122	Finishing of silk and blended silk textiles.
	17123	Finishing of wool and blended wool textiles.
	17124	Finishing of man-made and blended man-made textiles.
	17125	Finishing of jute, mesta, and other vegetable textiles fabrics.
	17126	Activity related to screen printing.
	17129	Other activities relating to finishing of textile n.e.c.
	1713	Preparation and spinning of textile fiber including weaving of textiles (khadi/handloom).
	17131	Cotton spinning through charkha.
	17132	Weaving of cotton khadi.
	17133	Weaving of cotton textiles on handlooms.
	17134	Spinning of wool and silk through charkha.
	17135	Weaving of woollen and silk khadi.
	17136	Weaving of wool and silk on handlooms.
	17137	Weaving of artificial/synthetic textile fabrics on handlooms.
	17139	Preparation and spinning of textile fibre including weaving of textiles (khadi/handloom), n.e.c.
	1714	Finishing of textiles (khadi/handloom).
	17141	Bleaching, dyeing, and finishing of cotton cloth and yarn by hand.
	17142	Printing of cloth by hand.
	17143	Bleaching, dyeing, and finishing of woollen textiles by hand.
	17144	Bleaching, dyeing, printing, and finishing of silk textiles by hand.
	17145	Bleaching, dyeing, printing, and finishing of artificial/synthetic textile fabrics by hand.
	17149	Finishing of textiles (khadi/handloom), n.e.c.
	172	Manufacture of other textiles.
	1721	Manufacture of made-up textile articles, except apparel.
	17211	Manufacture of curtains, bedcovers, and furnishings.
	17212	Manufacture of crocheted made-up textile goods, except apparel.

(Cont'd)

Table C.1 (*Cont'd*)

NIC	Code	Details of NIC Codes Used
	17213	Manufacture of mosquito nets.
	17214	Manufacture of bedding, quilts, pillows, cushions, and sleeping bags (manufacture of coir foam mattresses and pillows is classified in class 3610).
	17215	Manufacture of tarpaulin.
	17219	Manufacture of other made-up textile goods except apparel n.e.c.
	1722	Manufacture of carpet and rugs other than by hand (manufacture of linoleum and other hard surface floor coverings is classified in Class 3699).
	17221	Manufacture of blankets, shawls.
	17222	Manufacture of cotton carpets.
	17223	Manufacture of woollen carpets.
	17224	Manufacture of silk carpets.
	17225	Manufacture of durries, druggets, and rugs.
	17226	Manufacture of carpets, rugs, and other covering of jute, mesta, and coir.
	17229	Manufacture of other floor coverings (including felt) of textile, sannhemp, and other kindred fibres, n.e.c.
	1723	Manufacture of cordage, rope, twine, and netting.
	17231	Manufacture of thread, including thread ball making.
	17232	Manufacture of jute/hemp rope and cordage.
	17233	Manufacture of coir rope and cordage.
	17234	Manufacture of other rope and cordage other of jute/mesta and coir.
	17235	Manufacture of nets (except mosquito net).
	17236	Manufacture of tapes, *newar*, and wicks.
	17239	Manufacture of other cordage, rope, nets, etc., n.e.c.
	1724	Embroidery work, zari work, and making of ornamental trimmings by hand.
	17241	Embroidery work by hand.
	17242	Zari work by hand.
	17243	Making of laces and fringes by hand.
	17249	Making of other ornamental trimmings by hand, n.e.c.
	1725	Manufacture of blankets, shawls, carpets, rugs, and other similar textile products by hand.

Table C.1 *(Cont'd)*

NIC	Code	Details of NIC Codes Used
	17251	Manufacture of blankets and shawls by hand.
	17252	Manufacture of cotton carpets by hand.
	17253	Manufacture of woollen carpets by hand.
	17254	Manufacture of silk carpets by hand.
	17255	Manufacture of durries, druggets, and rugs by hand.
	17259	Manufacture of blankets, shawls, carpets, rugs, and other similar textile products by hand, n.e.c.
	1729	Manufacture of other textiles n.e.c.
	17291	Embroidery work and making of laces and fringes other than by hand.
	17292	Zari work and making of other ornamental trimmings other than by hand.
	17293	Manufacture of linoleum and similar products.
	17294	Manufacture of gas mantles.
	17295	Manufacture of made-up canvas goods such as tents and sails, etc.
	17296	Manufacture of wadding of textile materials and articles of wadding such as sanitary towels and tampons.
	17297	Manufacture of metallised yarn or gimped yarn; rubber thread or cord covered with textile material; textile yarn or strip, impregnated, covered, or sheathed with rubber or plastics.
	17298	Manufacture of waterproof textile excluding tarpaulin.
	17299	Manufacture of other textiles/textile products n.e.c.
	173	Manufacture of knitted and crocheted fabrics and articles.
	17301	Manufacture of knitted and crocheted cotton textile products.
	17302	Manufacture of knitted and crocheted woollen textile products.
	17303	Manufacture of knitted and crocheted synthetic textile products.
	17309	Manufacture of knitted and crocheted textile products n.e.c.

(Cont'd)

Table C.1 (*Cont'd*)

NIC	Code	Details of NIC Codes Used
	181	Manufacture of wearing apparel, except fur apparel (this class includes manufacture of wearing apparel made of material not made in the same unit. Both regular and contract activities are included)).
	18101	Manufacture of all types of textile garments and clothing accessories.
	18102	Manufacture of rain coats of waterproof textile fabrics or plastic sheetings.
	18103	Manufacture of hats and caps from waterproof.
	18104	Manufacture of wearing apparel of leather and substitutes of leather.
	18105	Custom tailoring.
	18109	Manufacture of wearing apparel, n.e.c.
	182	Dressing and dyeing of fur; manufacture of articles of fur.
	18201	Scraping, curying, tanning, bleaching, and dyeing of fur and other pelts for the trade.
	18202	Manufacture of wearing apparel of fur and pelts.
	18203	Manufacture of fur and skin rugs and other similar articles.
	18204	Embroidering and embossing of leather articles.
	18205	Stuffing of animals' and birds' hides.
	18209	Manufacture of other leather and fur products, n.e.c.
NIC-2008	1311	Preparation and spinning of textile fibres.
	1312	Weaving of textiles.
	13121	Weaving, manufacture of cotton and cotton mixture fabrics.
	13124	Weaving, manufacturing of man-made fiber and man-made mixture fabrics.
	14101	Manufacture of all types of textile garments and clothing accessories

Source: Ministry of Statistics and Program Implementation, available at http://mospi.nic.in/Mospi_New/site/inner.aspx?status=2&menu_id=129 (last accessed on 25 January 2016).

Notes: 1. Blended yarn/fabrics means yarn/fabrics containing more than 50% of one fibre.

2. n.e.c. – Not elsewhere considered.

Bibliography

'Alvin L. Breen and Herbert G. Lauterbach, Appellants, v. Alfred Richmond, Robert Albert King and Alexander Henderson Gentle, Appellees, 366 F.2d 482 (C.C.P.A. 1966)', 6 October 1966, available at http://law.justia.com/cases/federal/appellate-courts/F2/366/482/160728/ (last accessed on 21 July 2016).

Apparel Export Promotion Council. various years. *Handbook of Export Statistics*. New Delhi: Apparel Export Promotion Council.

Association of Synthetic Fibre Industry (ASFI). various years. *Handbook of Statistics on Manmade/Synthetic Fibre/Yarn Industry, Part One*. Mumbai: ASFI.

Basu, Arindam and D. Shanmugasundaram. 2002. 'WTO and its Impact on the Indian Textile and Clothing Industry', SITRA research report, 47(1), Coimbatore.

Bedi, J.S. 2000. 'Economic Liberalisation and Changes in the Structure of the Indian Textile Industry', PhD thesis, Jawaharlal Nehru University, New Delhi.

———. 2003. 'Production, Productivity and Technological Changes in Indian Spinning Sector', *Indian Economic Review*, XXXVIII(2): 205–33.

Bhattacharya, B.B. and S. Sakthivel. 2004. 'Economic Reforms and Jobless Growth in India in the 1990s', available at http://www.iegindia.org/upload/publication/Workpap/wp245.pdf (last accessed on 10 May 2009).

Breen, Alvin L. 1957. 'Bulky Continous Filament Yarn, U.S. Patent No. 2783609A', Grant Report, available at https://www.google.com/patents/US2783609 (last accessed on 21 July 2016).

Bureau of Industrial Costs and Prices (BICP). 1994. *Report on Paraxylene, DMT and PTA*. New Delhi: Government of India.

Bureau of Industrial Costs and Prices (BICP). 1997. *Report on PSF*. New Delhi: Government of India.

Central Statistical Organisation (CSO). 1985. *DME Report for Enterprise Survey: Summary Results for Central Sample for 1978–79*. New Delhi: Ministry of Statistics and Programme Implementation, Government of India.

———. 1989. *Directory Manufacturing Establishment Survey: Detailed Results for 1984–85*. New Delhi: Government of India.

———. 1995. *Report on Unorganised Manufacture: Directory Establishments, Directory Manufacturing Establishments Survey for 1989–90*. New Delhi: Government of India.

———. 2007. *National Accounts Statistics: Back Series 1950–51 to 1999–00*. New Delhi: Government of India.

———. 2014. *National Accounts Statistics*. New Delhi: Government of India.

———. various years. *Annual Survey of Industries*, vol. 1, Industrial Statistics Wing. Kolkata: Ministry of Statistics and Programme Implementation, Government of India.

Chakravarty, D. 2002. 'Work Organisation and Employment Contracts: Technological Modernisation in Textile Firms', *Economic and Political Weekly*, XXXVII(8): 743–9.

Chandra, N.K. 2008. 'Is Inclusive Growth Feasible in Neoliberal India? Some Preliminary Notes on Fiscal and Credit Policy', available at http://www.networkideas.org/ideasact/sep08/Nirmal_Kumar_Chandra.pdf (last accessed on 15 January 2009).

Chandrasekhar, C.P. 1981. 'Growth and Technical Change in Indian Cotton Mill Industry: 1947–77', PhD thesis, Jawaharlal Nehru University, New Delhi.

———. 1984. 'Growth and Technical Change in Indian Cotton-Mill Industry', *Economic and Political Weekly* (Review of Political Economy), 19(4): PE-22–PE-39.

———. 2004. 'Behind the Agrarian Crisis of the 1990s', *People's Democracy*, 28(1), available at http://pd.cpim.org/2004/0104/01042004_eco.htm (last accessed on 12 February 2008).

Chandrasekhar, C.P. and J. Ghosh. 2000. *The Market that Failed: A Decade of Neoliberal Reforms in India*. New Delhi: Leftword Books.

———. 2007. 'Recent Employment Trends in India and China: An Unfortunate Convergence?', Paper presented at ICSSR–IHD–CASS Seminar on Labour Markets in India and China: Experiences and Emerging Perspectives, New Delhi, 28–30 March, available at http://www.macroscan.com/anl/apr07/pdf/India_China.pdf (last accessed on 10 May 2009).

Chandrasekhar, C.P. and J. Ghosh. 2008. 'Employment and the Pattern of Growth', *Macroscan*, October, available at http://www.macroscan.com/the/employment/oct08/emp08102008Employment.htm (last accessed on 10 May 2009).

Chaudhary, A. 2011. 'Changing Structure of Indian Textiles Industry after MFA (Multi Fiber Agreement) Phase Out: A Global Perspective', *Far East Journal of Psychology and Business*, 2(2), available at http://www.academia.edu/3413811/Changing_Structure_of_Indian_Textiles_Industry_after_MFA_Multi_Fiber_Agreement_Phase_out_A_Global_Perspective (last accessed on 25 February 2016).

Chowdhary, S.R. 1996. 'Industrial Restructuring, Unions and the State: Textile Mill Workers in Ahmedabad', *Review of Labour*, XXXI(8): L-7–L-13.

Confederation of Indian Textile Industry (CITI) 2008. *Handbook of Statistics on Textile Industry*, 30th edn. New Delhi: CITI.

———. 2012. 'News Clippings', News Report, 5 November, available at www.citiindia.com (last accessed on 10 September 2015).

———. various years. *Annual Report*. Mumbai: CITI.

Datta, R.C. 1996. 'Manangement, Production System and Labour: Case Study of a Textile Mill', *Economic and Political Weekly* (Review of Labour), XXXI(8): L2–L6.

Department of Chemicals and Petrochemicals. 1986. *Report of the Committee for Perspective Planning of Petrochemical Industry (1986–2000 A.D.): Main Report*, vol. 2. New Delhi: Ministry of Chemicals and Fertilizers, Government of India.

———. 1993. *Report of the Expert Group of Petrochemicals: Main Report*, vol. 2. New Delhi: Ministry of Chemicals and Fertilizers, Government of India.

———. 2001. *Data Fact Sheets (1990–91 to 2000–01)*. New Delhi: Ministry of Chemicals and Fertilizers, Government of India.

Development Commissioner for Handlooms. 1990. *Census of Handloom Weavers in India 1987–88*. Ministry of Textiles, GoI.

Dhar, Usha 1984. 'Domestic Resource Costs of Synthetic Fibres', working paper no. 15, Indian Council for Research on International Economic Relations, New Delhi.

Dikshit, P. 2002. *Dynamics of Indian Export Trade*. New Delhi: Deep & Deep Publications Pvt. Ltd.

Directorate General of Commercial Intelligence and Statistics (DGCIS). various years. *Statistics of the Foreign Trade of India by Countries*, vol. 2. Kolkata: Government of India.

———. various years. *Monthly Statistics of Foreign Trade of India*, vols 1 and 2. Kolkata: Government of India.

Directorate General of Commercial Intelligence and Statistics (DGCIS). various years. *Statistics of the Foreign Trade of India by Countries*, vol. 1. Kolkata: Government of India.

Duggal, R. 2007. 'Poverty and Health: Criticality of Public Financing', *Indian Journal of Medical Research*, October: 309–17, available at http://www. icmr.nic.in/ijmr/2007/october/1008.pdf (last accessed on 18 June 2009).

Economic and Political Weekly Research Foundation. 2002. *Annual Survey of Industries, 1973–74 to 1997–98: A Data Base on Industrial Sector in India*. Mumbai: EPW Research Foundation.

Goldar, B. 2005. 'Impact on India of Tariff and Quantitative Restrictions under WTO', working paper no. 172, Indian Council for Research on International Economic Relations, available at http://icrier.org/pdf/WP172.pdf (last accessed on 20 February 2010).

Goswami, O. 1985. 'Textile Industry: Analysis of Demand and Supply', *Economic and Political Weekly*, XX(38): 1603–14.

———. 1990. 'Sickness and Growth of India's Textile Industry: Analysis and Policy Options', *Economic and Political Weekly*, 25(44 and 45): 2429–40, 2496–506.

Government of India (GoI). 1990. *Report of the Committee to Review the Progress of Implementation of Textile Policy of June 1985*. New Delhi: GoI.

———. 2000. *All India Reports on Input Surveys*. New Delhi: Department of Agriculture, Cooperation and Farmers Welfare and Ministry of Agriculture and Farmers Welfare.

———. 2007. *All India Reports on Input Surveys*. New Delhi: Department of Agriculture, Cooperation and Farmers Welfare and Ministry of Agriculture and Farmers Welfare.

———. various years. *Economic Survey*. New Delhi: Ministry of Finance.

Himanshu. 2007. 'Recent Trends in Poverty and Inequality: Some Preliminary Trends', *Economic and Political Weekly*, 42(6): 497–505.

Himanshu and Kunal Sen. 2014. 'Measurement, Patterns and Determinants of Poverty', in *Persistence of Poverty in India*, pp. 67–98. New Delhi: Esha Beteille & Jonathan Parry, Social Science Press.

Indian Cotton Mill Federation (ICMF). 2002–03. *Indian Cotton Annual, No. 83*. Mumbai: ICMF.

———. various years. *Handbook of Statistics on Cotton Textile Industry*, various edns. New Delhi: ICMF.

INFAC. 1995. *Manmade Fibre Industry Report*, vol. 1. March. Mumbai: INFAC.

International Monetary Fund (IMF). various years. *International Financial Statistics*. Washington DC, US: IMF.

International Textile Manufacturers Federation (ITMF). 2009. *International Production Cost Comparison*. Switzerland: ITMF.

Jadhav, D.M. n.d. 'Industrial Policy since 1956', available at http://www. drnarendrajadhav.info/drnjadhav_web_files/Published%20papers/ Indian%20Industrial%20Policy%20Since%201956.pdf (last accessed on 16 January 2010).

Kannan, K.P. and G. Raveendran. 2009. 'Growth sans Employment: A Quarter Century of Jobless Growth in India's Organised Manufacturing', *Economic and Political Weekly*, XLIV(10): 80–91.

Kantilal, I. 1990. *The Apparel Industry in India*. Ahmedabad: National Information Centre for Textile and Allied Subjects.

Kapoor, R. 2013. 'Inequality Matters', *Economic and Political Weekly*, 48(2): 58–65.

Kar, M. 2015. *The Indian Textile and Clothing Industry: An Economic Analysis*. India: Springer.

Kar, S. and M. Kar. 2015. 'Multi-market Firms and Export Quota: Effects of the Withdrawal of the Multi-Fiber Arrangement', available at http://www. researchgate.net/publication/275887384 (last accessed on 15 February 2016).

Labour Bureau, Government of India. various years. *Annual Report on Consumer Price Index Numbers for Agricultural and Rural Labourers*. Shimla/Chandigarh: Labour Bureau, GoI.

————. various years. *Annual Report, Consumer Price Index Numbers for Industrial Workers*. Shimla: Labour Bureau, GoI.

Mehrotra, S., Ankita Gandhi, Partha Saha, and Bimal Kishore Sahoo. 2012. 'Joblessness and Informalization: Challenges to Inclusive Growth in India', Occasional Paper No. 9/2012, Institute of Applied Manpower Research, Planning Commission, GoI, available at http://iamrindia.gov. in/writereaddata/UploadFile/Joblessness.pdf (last accessed on 21 July 2016).

Ministry of Agriculture. various years. *Agriculture at a Glance*. New Delhi: Government of India.

Ministry of Human Resource Development (MHRD). 1995. *Budgetary Resources for Education (1951–52 to 1993–94)*. New Delhi: Department of Education, GoI.

Ministry of Labour and Employment. various years. *Consumer Price Index Numbers (for Industrial Workers)*. Shimla/Chandigarh: Labour Bureau.

————. various years. *Consumer Price Index Numbers for Agricultural and Rural Labourers: Annual Reports*. Shimla/Chandigarh: Labour Bureau.

Misra, S. 1993. *India's Textile Sector: A Policy Analysis*. Delhi: SAGE Publications.

Murty, G.V.S.N. and T.R. Sukumari. 1991. 'Demand for Textiles in India', *Economic and Political Weekly*, 26(21): M61–M67.

Murty, S. 1983. 'An Approach to Estimate Demand Models for Clothing in India', *Anvesak*, 13(1): 1–23.

Nalavade, S.G., S.K. Mali, S.M. Dalal, N. Padmanabhan, and D.R. Ananthaswamy. 1986. *Powerloom Weaving in Maharashtra: An In-depth Study*. Mumbai: Bombay Textile Research Association.

National Academy of Agricultural Sciences (NAAS). 2006. 'WTO and Indian Agriculture: Implications for Policy and R&D', Policy Paper No. 8, National Academy of Agricultural Sciences, New Delhi.

National Commission for Enterprises in the Unorganised Sector (NCEUS). 2007. 'Report on Conditions of Work and Promotion of Livelihoods in the Unorganised Sector', available at http://nceus.gov.in/Condition_of_workers_sep_2007.pdf (last accessed on 13 February 2009).

National Council of Applied Economic Research (NCAER). (2004). *Joint Census of Handlooms and Powerlooms, 1995–96*. New Delhi: NCAER.

———. 2010. *Handloom Census of India, 2009–10*. New Delhi: NCAER.

National Sample Survey Organisation (NSSO). 1987. *Tables with Notes on Survey of Unorganised Manufacture: Non-directory Enterprises and Own Account Enterprises*. NSS 33rd Round Report for 1978–79, Report No. 343. Ministry of Statistics and Programme Implementation, Government of India, New Delhi.

———. 1986. 'A Report on the Third Quinquennial Survey on Consumer Expenditure', NSS 38th Round Report for 1983, *Sarvekshana*, 9(4): S1–S102.

———. 1989. *Tables with Notes on Survey of Unorganised Manufacture: Non-directory Establishments and Own Account Enterprises*. NSS 40th Round Report for 1984–85, Report No. 363/1. Ministry of Statistics and Programme Implementation, GoI, New Delhi.

———. 1995. *Tables with Notes on Survey of Unorganised Manufacture: Non-directory Establishments and Own Account Enterprises*. NSS 45th Round Report for 1989–90, Report No. 396/1. Ministry of Statistics and Programme Implementation, GoI, New Delhi.

———. 1996. *Level and Pattern of Consumer Expenditure*. NSS 50th Round Report for 1993–94, Report No. 402. Ministry of Statistics and Programme Implementation, GoI, New Delhi.

———. 1998. *Unorganised Manufacturing Sector in India: It's Size, Employment and Some Key Estimates*. NSS 51st Round Report for 1994–95, Report No. 433. Ministry of Statistics and Programme Implementation, GoI, New Delhi.

———. 2001. *Energy Used by Indian Household*. NSS 55th Round Report for 1999–2000, Report No. 464. Ministry of Statistics and Programme Implementation, GoI, New Delhi.

National Sample Survey Organisation (NSSO) 2006. *Level and Pattern of Consumer Expenditure*. NSS 61st Round Report for 2004–05, Report No. 508. Ministry of Statistics and Programme Implementation, GoI, New Delhi.

————. 2007. *Nutritional Intake in India*. NSS 61st Round Report for 2004–05, Report No. 513. Ministry of Statistics and Programme Implementation, GoI, New Delhi.

————. 2011. *Key Indicators of Employment and Unemployment in India*. NSS 66th Round Report for 2009–10, Report No. NSS K1 (66/10). Ministry of Statistics and Programme Implementation, GoI, New Delhi.

National Science Foundation. 2006. 'Industry, Technology and the Global Marketplace', in *Science and Engineering Indicators*, Chapter 6, available at http://wayback.archive-it.org/5902/20160210224604/http://www.nsf.gov/statistics/seind06/c6/c6h.htm (last accessed on 25 December 2009).

Nalavade, S.G., S.K. Mali, S.M. Dalal, N. Padmanabhan, and D.R. Ananthaswamy. 1986. *Powerloom Weaving in Maharashtra: An In-depth Study*. Mumbai, India: Bombay Textile Research Association.

Oberoi, B. 2012. 'Structural Change, Technology and Employment in the Indian Textile Industry: 1980–2010', *Arthaniti*, 11(1–2): 25–46.

————. 2013. 'Determinants of Demand for the Indian Textile Industry', *Economic and Political Weekly*, XLVIII(3): 62–70.

————. 2014. 'Casualisation of Employment in the Indian Textile Industry', *Labour and Development*, 21(2): 121–42.

Office of Economic Advisor. various years. *Index Numbers of Wholesale Prices in India*. New Delhi: Department of Industrial Policy and Promotion, Ministry of Commerce and Industry, GoI.

Office of Textile Commissioner. various years. *Compendium of Textile Statistics*. Mumbai: GoI.

Pal, Parthapratim. 2005. 'Agricultural Subsidies and Negotiations, Strategies and Options', Paper No. 2, 'Hongkong Series of Papers' by the Centre for Trade and Development, Oxfam, New Delhi, November, available at http://www.esocialsciences.com/data/articles/Document125112009170.313244.pdf (last accessed on 10 February 2010).

Patnaik, U. 2006. 'Poverty and Neo-liberalism in India', available at http://www.networkideas.org/featart/jan2007/neo-liberalism.pdf (last accessed on 15 March 2009).

Pattanayak, S.S. and S.M. Thangavelu. 2005. 'Economic Reforms and Productivity Growth in Indian Manufacturing Industries: An Interaction of Technical Change and Scale Economies', working paper No. 0307,

Department of Economics, National University of Singapore, available at http://www.fas.nus.edu.sg/ecs/pub/wp/wp0307.pdf (last accessed on 15 April 2009).

Rajamanickam, R., D. Shanmuganandam, Indra Doraiswamy, and T.V. Ratnam. 2003. 'Looking Back to Look Ahead: Competitive Productivity and Wage Levels for Spinning Mills for 2005', SITRA research report, 47(14), Coimbatore.

Reserve Bank of India (RBI). various years. *Handbook of Statistics on Indian Economy*. Mumbai: GoI.

Sakthivel, A. 2004. 'Tirupur Knitwear Export Cluster, India', Paper presented at ITC Executive Forum on Competitiveness through Public–Private Partnership: Successes and Lessons Learned', available at http://www.intracen.org/wedf/ef2004/Montreux/background_papers/4-2%20-%20Clusters-Sakthivel.pdf (last accessed on 10 September 2008).

Shanbhag, V. and V. Padaki. 1985. *Issues in Modernisation of the Textile Industry*. Ahmedabad: Ahmedabad Textile Industry's Research Association.

Shanmuganandam, D. and J. Sreenivasan. 2008. 'Impact of Modernization on Profits, Productivity in Mills', available at http://www.indiantextile-journal.com/articles/FAdetails.asp?id=1430 (last accessed on 20 April 2010).

Shivakumar, S. 2007. 'Why Tirupur has Raced ahead of Ludhiana?', 20 November, available at http://www.merinews.com/article/why-tirupur-has-raced-ahead-of-ludhiana/127898.shtml (last accessed on 10 September 2008).

South India Textile Research Association (SITRA). 1982. *Cost Differential between Handlooms and Powerlooms*. Coimbatore: SITRA.

Shanmuganandam, D. and S. Mariappan. 2007. 'How to Achieve High Labour Productivity in Spinning', Case Studies, South India Textile Research Association, Coimbatore, available at http://www.fibre2fashion.com/industry-article/market-research-industry-reports/how-to-achieve-high-labour-productivity-in-spinning/how-to-achieve-high-labour-productivity-in-spinning1.asp (last accessed on 10 January 2009).

Textiles Committee. various years. *Consumer Purchase of Textiles, Part 2*. Mumbai: GoI.

————. various years. *National Household Surveys*. Mumbai: GoI.

Tewari, M. 2005. 'Post-MFA Adjustment in India's Textile and Apparel Industry: Emerging Issues and Trends', working paper no. 167, Indian Council for Research on International Economic Relations, New Delhi, available at https://core.ac.uk/download/files/153/6604723.pdf (last accessed on 2 July 2016).

The Stock Exchange Foundation. various years. *Bombay Stock Exchange Directory*. Mumbai: Stock Exchange Foundation.

Uchikawa, S. 1998. *Indian Textile Industry: State Policy, Liberalisation and Growth*. New Delhi: Manohar.

United Nations Conference on Trade and Development (UNCTAD). 2002. 'Trade and Development Report', UNCTAD/TDR/2002. New York and Geneva: UNCTAD, available at http://unctad.org/en/docs/tdr2002ch3a_en.pdf (last accessed on 2 July 2016).

US International Trade Commission. 2001. 'India's Textile and Apparel Industry: Growth Potential and Trade and Investment Opportunities', Staff Research Study 27, Office of Industries, US International Trade Commission, available at https://www.usitc.gov/publications/332/PUB3401.pdf (last accessed on 3 July 2016).

World Trade Organization (WTO). 2001. 'The Global Textile and Clothing Industry Post the Agreement on Textile and Clothing', Discussion Paper No. 5, available at http://www.wto.org/ english/res_e/booksp_e/discussion_papers5_e.pdf (last accessed on 18 September 2008).

———. (2014). *International Trade Statistics 2014*. Geneva, Switzerland: WTO, available at https://www.wto.org/english/res_e/statis_e/its2014_e/its2014_e.pdf (last accessed on 26 February 2016).

Index

About the Author

Bindu Oberoi is Associate Professor of Economics, Indraprastha College for Women, University of Delhi, India. She has also taught Economics at various colleges of the University of Delhi, including Delhi College of Arts and Commerce, Shivaji College, Sri Guru Gobind Singh College of Commerce, Dayal Singh College, and Miranda House. She has published articles on key domains of textiles and clothing industry in India in a number of peer-reviewed international journals. Her research interests include industrial economics, labour economics, and development economics.